Instructor's Resource Guide

THE PRACTICE OF
Econometrics
CLASSIC AND CONTEMPORARY

Ernst R. Berndt

Instructor's Resource Guide

THE PRACTICE OF
Econometrics
CLASSIC AND CONTEMPORARY

Ernst R. Berndt

*Massachusetts Institute of Technology and
the National Bureau of Economic Research*

Addison-Wesley Publishing Company
Reading, Massachusetts • Menlo Park, California • New York
Don Mills, Ontario • Wokingham, England • Amsterdam • Bonn
Sydney • Singapore • Tokyo • Madrid • San Juan • Milan • Paris

ISBN 0-201–17629–7

6 7 8 9 10-CRC-00

"Econometrics is something that should be done,

rather than talked about."

Trygve Haavelmo, "The Role of the
Econometrician in the Advancement
of Economic Theory," _Econometrica_,
26:3, July 1958, p. 351.

Acknowledgements

This Resource Guide was written in Paris during October 1990 while I was
a Visiting Professor at the École Nationale de la Statistique et de
l'Administration Économique (ENSAE), where I was provided office space and
computer support at their Centre de Recherche en Économie et Statistique
(CREST). I would like to thank Jacques Mairesse for inviting me, Christian
Gourieroux, Director of CREST, for his gracious hospitality, Michael Visser
for kindly sharing office space, and for enjoyable and stimulating
conversations with them as well as with Alain Bousquet, Mohamed El Babsiri,
Gauthier Lanot, Pierre Mohnen, Jean-Marc Robin and Jean-Michel Zakoian.

HOW TO TAKE ADVANTAGE OF THIS INSTRUCTOR'S RESOURCE GUIDE:

If you want information on --

- How do the chapters of this text match with those in your econometric theory textbook?—See Appendix I

- How might you choose chapters and topics most appropriate and interesting to undergraduate students, graduate MBA students or graduate economics students?—See "Notes on Course Planning"

- How can you best exploit the material in this text for a one-semester, a two-semester, or a one-, two-, or three-quarter course? —See "Notes on Course Planning"

- How many of the exercises should you assign in each chapter? —See "Notes on Course Planning"

- How can you obtain further information on the exercises in Chapters 1 through 11 of The Practice of Econometrics: Classic and Contemporary? —See Chapter Notes for Chapters 1 through 11 in this Resource Guide

- How can you get help on using statistical software for the exercises in The Practice of Econometrics: Classic and Contemporary?—See page viii

- What data sets might be available in addition to those provided on the floppy diskette accompanying The Practice of Econometrics: Classic and Contemporary?—See Chapter Notes for Chapters 2 through 11

ADDISON-WESLEY IS PLEASED TO OFFER "HANDS-ON" SUPPLEMENTARY MATERIALS

TO ASSIST YOU AND YOUR STUDENTS IN USING SEVERAL WIDELY KNOWN

STATISTICAL SOFTWARE PROGRAMS TO CARRY OUT THE EXERCISES IN

THE PRACTICE OF ECONOMETRICS: CLASSIC AND CONTEMPORARY

MicroTSP (for the IBM-PC and compatible computers):

Paul E. Greenberg, The Practice of Econometrics: A Computer Handbook Using MicroTSP, Reading, MA: Addison-Wesley Publishing Company, 1991 (52745)

PC-TSP and TSP (for many mainframe, IBM-PC and compatible and Apple Macintosh computers):

Bronwyn Hall, The Practice of Econometrics: A Computer Handbook Using PC-TSP, Reading, MA: Addison-Wesley Publishing Company, 1991 (54857)

SHAZAM (for many mainframe, IBM-PC and compatible and Apple Macintosh computers):

Kenneth J. White and Linda T.M. Bui, The Practice of Econometrics: A Computer Handbook Using SHAZAM, Reading, MA: Addison-Wesley Publishing Company (50048)

To obtain any of these supplementary materials, contact:

Addison-Wesley Publishing Company, Inc.
1 Jacob Way
Reading, MA 01867-9984
1-800-447-2226

TABLE OF CONTENTS

Instructor's Resource Guide

THE PRACTICE OF
Econometrics
CLASSIC AND CONTEMPORARY
Ernst R. Berndt

NOTES ON COURSE PLANNING WITH THIS TEXT

WHAT IS THE GOAL OF THIS TEXT?

The goal of this text is to engage students in learning how to carry out econometric research, using classic and contemporary data sets. Although I have tried to make the textbook discussions of the underlying theory, measurement concerns and econometric issues in each application chapter as readable and self-contained as possible, in my view the real value of this text lies in its encouraging students to engage in "hands-on" econometrics, i.e., in *doing the exercises*. So, however you use this text (and there are numerous different ways it can be used), by all means, have students get their hands dirty and have them do the exercises.

THE STRUCTURE OF THIS BOOK

The Practice of Econometrics: Classic and Contemporary consists of an introductory chapter, followed by ten applied topics of interest to economics and business students, emphasizing one set of tools per chapter. The order of the chapters has been designed to correspond with the sequence of topics typically taught in econometrics and forecasting courses, beginning with the bivariate regression model (Chapter 2), moving on to multiple regression and effects of omitted variables (Chapters 3 and 4), dummy variables and specification issues (Chapters 4 and 5), then to generalized least squares and distributed lags (Chapters 6 and 7), forecasting with generalized least squares and time series analysis (Chapter 7), causality and simultaneity (Chapter 8), systems of equations (Chapter 9), simultaneous equations (Chapter 10) and discrete dependent variable models (Chapter 11).

Each chapter begins with a discussion of the economic theory underlying the application, outlines issues in econometric implementation (including measurement issues), summarizes important empirical findings to date and then engages the student in a carefully designed set of seven to ten empirical exercises involving replication and extension of classic and contemporary empirical findings. Rather than presenting students with but one data base and one set of exercises per topic, in most chapters a number of data series are provided; students and instructors are invited to choose among them and experiment, thereby permitting greater individualization and self-learning.

Finally, each application chapter contains exercises corresponding with roughly two levels of difficulty. Most of the exercises focus on the use of one or two econometric procedures (as detailed in the previous paragraph), but the final one or two exercises often introduce procedures that might not yet be covered in the normal progression of an econometrics course. I have done this to permit instructors to return to a particular application topic several times during a course, thereby helping students to examine the sensitivity of results to alternative estimation procedures, and enabling them to appreciate the costs and benefits of employing more sophisticated tools.

HOW TO USE THIS TEXTBOOK IN YOUR ECONOMETRICS COURSE

The text is a long one, and as a supplement to a one-semester econometric theory course, it is clear that not all of the chapter materials can be utilized. Since tastes and interests of students and faculty vary, I have deliberately chosen application topics that are diverse. Instructors can therefore choose from the ten application chapters those that best match their particular interests and circumstances. Preliminary versions of this text have been used at a number of universities and colleges in the U.S. and abroad, and based on feedback from those experiences, I can offer a number of suggestions.

Employing this text as a supplement in a *one-semester* econometric theory course, most instructors have chosen between three and five chapters from The Practice of Econometrics: Classic and Contemporary. Here are some examples for one-semester courses, including possibilities that reflect differing dominant application interests of the instructor (one- or two-quarter courses can be down- or up-sized appropriately):

Undergraduate (general): Chapters 2 (CAPM), 5 (wage discrimination), 7 (electricity demand) and 10 (macroeconometric models)

Undergraduate (business): Chapters 2 (CAPM), 3 (learning curves), 4 (computer price indexes), 5 (wage discrimination) and 8 (advertising-sales)

Graduate economics (1st semester): Chapters 2 (CAPM), 4 (computer price indexes), 5 (wage discrimination) and parts of Chapter 6 (investment)

Graduate economics (2nd semester): Chapters 7 (electricity demand), parts of 8 (advertising-sales), 9 (interrelated factor demands), 10 (macroeconometric models) and 11 (labor supply)

Graduate MBA (one semester): Chapters 2 (CAPM), 3 (learning curves), 5 (wage discrimination), 7 (electricity demand) and 8 (advertising-sales)

Labor economics: Chapters 5 (wage discrimination), 10 (Phillips' curve and macroeconometric models) and 11 (labor supply)

Forecasting course: Chapters 3 (learning curves), 6 (investment expenditures) and 7 (electricity demand)

Microeconomics: Chapters 3 (learning curves), 4 (computer price indexes), 5 (wage discrimination) and 9 (interrelated factor demands)

Macroeconomics: Chapters 4 (computer price indexes), 6 (aggregate investment expenditures) and 10 (macroeconometric models)

Industrial organization: Chapters 3 (learning curves), 4 (computer price indexes) and 8 (advertising-sales)

Public policy: Chapters 5 (wage discrimination), 6 (taxes and aggregate investment), 7 (electricity demand) and 8 (advertising-sales)

It is becoming increasingly common, however, for universities and colleges to offer special courses in applied econometrics for students who have already completed one or more courses emphasizing econometric theory (e.g., a fourth-year undergraduate course, a master's thesis preparation course or a second- or third-year Ph.D. subject). In such cases, depending on students' backgrounds and instructor's interests, one can employ all the chapters in one of the above course outlines, expending greater attention on the detailed chapter material. It is worth noting that in this context two of the chapters provide particularly detailed discussions—Chapter 6 on comparing five alternative models of aggregate investment behavior, and Chapter 8 on various specification issues, estimation of duration levels and public policy debates—all involving advertising and sales. Indeed, one instructor has employed chapter 6 for an entire one-semester course in applied econometrics. Another simply asked that students choose a chapter to suit their tastes and write an empirical term paper on a topic addressed in that chapter.

Finally, for master's or Ph.D. students writing a thesis on a topic related to one of the chapters in The Practice of Econometrics, a number of instructors have involved their students in replicating some of the classic results in a particular chapter, and then have asked students to gather additional data, employing both classic and more contemporary estimation procedures. Possibilities for such additional data sets are discussed briefly in the Chapter Notes for each chapter in this Resource Guide.

In summary, the chapters in this text can be organized in a wide variety of ways to meet the needs of students and faculty in very diverse settings. There is no single best mix that I can suggest to you. But do the exercises!

How many of the exercises at the end of each chapter should students carry out? In a one-semester course where this text serves as a supplement, experience to date suggests much learning occurs by dividing the class into two or more groups, and having each group do up to four or so exercises. Student presentations of results can be very informative. Some instructors have encouraged students to choose from among the remaining unassigned exercises the topic for their term paper or thesis. Finally, in courses where this text is primary, it may be useful to have students do most of the exercises in each chapter. But in some chapters, several exercises employ roughly the same tools, and in this case division of exercises into groups of students may be preferable. For example, in Chapter 5, roughly similar procedures are used to assess whether union members earn premium wages (Exercise 5), and whether there is wage discrimination by race (Exercise 6), or by gender (Exercise 7). In this case, it probably does not make sense to have each student do all the exercises.

OTHER REMARKS ON COURSE PLANNING WITH THIS TEXT

My own experience in teaching "hands-on" econometrics has emphasized to me the importance of spending a fair bit of time early on in the course to get students comfortable with the computational facilities and software available at their particular university or college. Investing time at the beginning of the semester has typically saved many hours of student anxiety and "debugging" frustrations later on in the course (and office hours for the instructor).

Although appropriate practices may differ widely, I have found it useful to schedule one or two lab sessions for students within the first two weeks of the course, during which time I (or a teaching assistant) go through the basics of calling up a statistical software program, reading the data off the diskette, editing files, executing runs and so on. In this context, having students work through Chapter 1 has always proved to be useful. Note also that supplementary statistical software guides for widely used regression programs, such as MicroTSP, PC-TSP and SHAZAM, are available from Addison-Wesley Publishing Company; these software guides show how the exercises in The

Practice of Econometrics: Classic and Contemporary can be carried out using
these particular statistical software programs.

Finally, I have some uneasiness about the fact that most of the data
sets in this text are based on U.S. data (several Canadian and U.K. data sets
are included on the floppy diskette, but these are relatively few), for
econometrics is surely an internationally taught subject. To remedy this
deficiency, when teaching outside the U.S., I have tried to develop classic
and contemporary data sets for countries that are home to the students. I
would appreciate hearing from instructors abroad what data sets they have been
able to assimilate, what results or procedures were particularly instructive
for students and whether they would be willing to share these data sets with
me. In turn, I will pass this information on to people requesting it. You
can contact me at the MIT Sloan School of Management, 50 Memorial Drive—
E52-452, Cambridge, MA 02139 USA (FAX 617-258-6855).

WHAT IS IN THE REMAINDER OF THIS INSTRUCTOR'S RESOURCE GUIDE?

First, in the appendix that immediately follows these remarks, a list of
leading econometric theory textbooks is given, each of which has been
published in the 1980s or later. This is followed by a cross-reference match
or concordance of each of the "hands-on" exercises of the eleven chapters in
The Practice of Econometrics: Classic and Contemporary with chapters covering
the corresponding econometric theory issues in the leading econometric theory
textbooks. This appendix is entitled, "Matching the Exercises of The Practice
of Econometrics: Classic and Contemporary with Chapters in Leading Econometric
Theory Textbooks."

Second, in the remainder of this Resource Guide, chapter-specific
comments and suggestions are given, corresponding to each of the eleven
chapters in The Practice of Econometrics: Classic and Contemporary. More

specifically, for each chapter, the Chapter Notes begin with a list of econometric procedures employed in that chapter, comments are then provided on overall goals and issues of concern raised in the chapter, remarks are made on aspects of the various exercises, and finally, suggestions for additional data sources and exercises are presented.

Although the exercises in each chapter have been carefully designed, the practice of econometrics is diverse, and instructors may wish to follow up on some other types of exercises and data sets, rather than strictly following the set provided in the text. The remarks provided at the end of each chapter in the Chapter Notes are designed to assist you in thinking about such possible extensions and variations.

APPENDIX I: MATCHING THE EXERCISES OF

THE PRACTICE OF ECONOMETRICS: CLASSIC AND CONTEMPORARY

with

CHAPTERS IN LEADING ECONOMETRIC THEORY TEXTBOOKS

In this appendix we relate exercises from The Practice of Econometrics to specific chapters in over twenty leading econometric theory textbooks, all published in the 1980s or later. This information should help instructors in designing the most appropriate mix of theory and "hands-on" applications, given the econometric theory textbook that has been assigned to students. The next two pages of this appendix provide detailed references for twenty-three leading econometric theory textbooks, while the remaining pages present chapter-specific matches between exercises and the econometric theory textbook chapters. For each chapter of The Practice of Econometrics: Classic and Contemporary, the number of the exercise (or exercises) is presented first, followed by the appropriate chapter or chapters in the econometric theory textbook. For example, "3-ch. 4" indicates that Exercise 3 relates to material covered in Chapter 4 of that econometric theory textbook.

Two additional comments are worth noting. First, there are two Judge et al. textbooks—an advanced theory one we call "Big Daddy" Judge (see Judge et al. [1985]), and a more introductory version we name "Baby" Judge (Judge et al. [1988]). Second, the Intriligator et al. text is not yet published, but publication is expected by 1992. I have matched the exercises to that text using the preliminary table of contents provided me by its authors. It is possible, however, that the order of topics in the final version of that text will differ from the preliminary outline given me. Instructors using the Intriligator et al. text should therefore be aware of this possibility.

ECONOMETRIC THEORY TEXTBOOKS:

Amemiya, Takeshi [1985], <u>Advanced Econometrics</u>, Cambridge, MA: Harvard University Press.

Bacon, Robert [1988], <u>A First Course in Econometric Theory</u>, Oxford: Oxford University Press.

Chow, Gregory [1983], <u>Econometrics</u>, New York: McGraw-Hill Book Company.

Cramer, Jan S. [1986], <u>Econometric Applications of Maximum Likelihood Methods</u>, Cambridge: Cambridge University Press.

Doti, James L. and Esmael Adibi [1988], <u>Econometric Analysis: An Applications Approach</u>, Englewood Cliffs, NJ: Prentice Hall.

Fomby, Thomas B., R. Carter Hill and Stanley R. Johnson [1984], <u>Advanced Econometric Methods</u>, New York: Springer-Verlag.

Goldberger, Arthur S. [1991], <u>A Course in Econometrics</u>, Cambridge, MA: Harvard University Press.

Greene, William H. [1990], <u>Econometric Analysis</u>, New York: Macmillan Publishing Company.

Gujarati, Damodar N. [1988], <u>Basic Econometrics</u>, Second Edition, New York: McGraw-Hill Book Company.

Intriligator, Michael D., Ronald G. Bodkin and Cheng Hsiao [1992], <u>Econometric Models, Techniques and Applications</u>, Second Edition, Englewood Cliffs, NJ: Prentice Hall.

Johnson, Aaron C., Jr., Marvin B. Johnson and Rueben C. Buse [1987], <u>Econometrics: Basic and Applied</u>, New York: Macmillan Publishing Company.

Johnston, J. [1984], <u>Econometric Methods</u>, Third Edition, New York: McGraw-Hill Book Company.

Judge, George G., William E. Griffiths, R. Carter Hill, Helmut Lutkepohl and Tsoung-Chao Lee [1985], <u>The Theory and Practice of Econometrics</u>, Second Edition, New York: John Wiley and Sons. ("Big Daddy" Judge)

Judge, George G., R. Carter Hill, William E. Griffiths, Helmut Lutkepohl and Tsoung-Chao Lee [1988], <u>Introduction to the Theory and Practice of Econometrics</u>, Second Edition, New York: John Wiley and Sons. ("Baby" Judge)

Kelejian, Harry H. and Wallace E. Oates [1989], <u>Introduction to Econometrics: Principles and Applications</u>, Third Edition, New York: Harper & Row, Publishers.

Kennedy, Peter [1986], <u>A Guide to Econometrics</u>, Second Edition, Cambridge, MA: The MIT Press.

Kmenta, Jan [1986], <u>Elements of Econometrics</u>, Second Edition, New York: Macmillan Publishing Company.

Maddala, G.S. [1988], <u>Introduction to Econometrics</u>, New York: Macmillan Publishing Company.

Mirer, Thad W. [1988], <u>Economic Statistics and Econometrics</u>, Second Edition, New York: Macmillan Publishing Company.

Pindyck, Robert S. and Daniel L. Rubinfeld [1990], <u>Econometric Models & Economic Forecasts</u>, Third Edition, New York: McGraw-Hill Book Company.

Ramanathan, Ramu [1989], <u>Introductory Econometrics with Applications</u>, San Diego, CA: Harcourt Brace Jovanovich, Publishers.

Studenmund, A.H. and Henry J. Cassidy [1987], <u>Using Econometrics: A Practical Guide</u>, Boston: Little, Brown and Company.

Wallace, T. Dudley and J. Lew Silver [1988], <u>Econometrics: An Introduction</u>, Reading, MA: Addison-Wesley Publishing Company.

TEXTBOOK CROSS-REFERENCE WITH EXERCISES IN CHAPTER ONE OF BERNDT

Amemiya: 1-ch. 1

Bacon: 1-chs. 1,2

Chow: 1-ch. 2

Cramer: 1-ch. 1

Doti-Adibi: 1-chs. 2-4

Fomby et al.: 1-chs. 1,2

Goldberger: 1-chs. 10,11

Greene: 1-ch. 5

Gujarati: 1-chs. 1-3

Intriligator et al.: 1-chs. 1-4

Johnson et al.: 1-chs. 1,2,3,8

Johnston: 1-ch. 2

Judge (Big Daddy): 1-ch. 2

Judge (Baby): 1-ch. 5

Kelejian-Oates: 1-ch. 2

Kennedy: 1-chs. 2,3

Kmenta: 1-ch. 7

Maddala: 1-ch. 3

Mirer: 1-chs. 3,5

Pindyck-Rubinfeld: 1-chs. 1-3

Ramanathan: 1-chs. 2.6,3

Studenmund-Cassidy: 1-chs. 2-4

Wallace-Silver: 1-chs. 1,2

TEXTBOOK CROSS-REFERENCE WITH EXERCISES IN CHAPTER TWO OF BERNDT

Amemiya: 6,8-ch. 1.5.3; 10-chs. 5,6

Bacon: 1,2,3,4,5-chs. 2,3; 6-chs. 5,11.2; 7,8-chs. 2,3,5; 9-chs. 4,5; 10-chs. 7,11

Chow: 1,2,3,4,5,6,7,8,9-ch. 2; 10-ch. 3

Cramer: 1,2,3,5,7,8,9-chs. 1-3; 10-ch. 6

Doti-Adibi: 1,2,3,4,5,6-chs. 3,4; 7,8-ch. 6.2; 9-ch. 4; 10-chs. 5.2,5.3

Fomby et al.: 1,2,3,4,5,6,7,8,9-chs. 2,3; 10-chs. 8-10

Goldberger: 1-ch. 10; 2,3,4,5,6,7-chs. 10,11; 8,9-chs. 14-22; 10-chs. 26-28

Greene: 1,2,3,4,5-chs. 5-7; 6-ch. 7.3; 7,8-chs. 7.3,8.2; 9-chs. 6,7; 10-chs. 14,15

Gujarati: 1,2,3,4,5-chs. 1-6; 6,7,8-ch. 14; 9-chs. 7,8; 10-chs. 11,12

Intriligator et al.: 1,2,3,4,5-chs. 1-4; 6,7,8-chs. 3,6; 9-ch. 4; 10-chs. 5,6

Johnson et al.: 1,2,3,4,5-chs. 1-3,5,8; 6-ch. 6; 7,8-chs. 6,9; 9-chs. 3,4,13; 10-ch. 14

Johnston: 1,2,3,4,5-ch. 2; 6-ch. 6.2; 7,8-chs. 6.2,6.3; 9-chs. 3,5; 10-ch. 8

Judge (Big Daddy): 1,2,3,4,5-ch. 2; 6-ch. 12.1.2; 7,8-ch. 13.3,13.4; 9-ch. 2; 10-chs. 7,8,11

Judge (Baby): 1,2,3,4,5-chs. 5,6; 6-ch. 10.2; 7,8-ch. 10; 9-chs. 5,6; 10-chs. 8,9,22.2.1

Kelejian-Oates: 1-ch. 2; 2,3,4-chs. 2,3; 5-chs. 1-3; 6-chs. 2,3; 7,8-chs. 2,3,5.2; 9-ch. 4; 10-ch. 6.2,6.3

Kennedy: 1,2,3,4,5-chs. 2-4; 6-ch. 5.4; 7,8-chs. 5.4,13; 9-chs. 2-4; 10-ch. 7

Kmenta: 1,2,3,4,5-ch. 7; 6-ch. 10.2; 7,8-ch. 11.1; 9-ch. 10; 10-ch. 8

Maddala: 1,2,3,4,5-ch. 2; 6-ch. 4.11; 7,8-chs. 4.11,8; 9-ch. 4; 10-chs. 5,6

Mirer: 1,2,3,4,5-chs. 5,6,12,13; 6-ch. 15.1; 7,8-chs. 7.3,15.1; 9-ch. 7; 10-chs. 14,19.1

Pindyck-Rubinfeld: 1,2,3,4,5-chs. 1-3; 6,7,8,9-chs. 4,5; 10-ch. 6

Ramanathan: 1,2,3,4,5-ch. 3; 6-ch. 6.5; 7,8-ch. 6.1; 9-ch. 4; 10-chs. 8,11

Studenmund-Cassidy: 1,2,3,4,5-chs. 2-5; 6-ch. 5; 7,8-ch. 3; 9-chs. 2-5; 10-chs. 9,10

Wallace-Silver: 1,2,3,4,5-chs. 2-4; 6,7,8-ch. 5; 9-chs. 2-4; 10-chs. 6.2,7.1

TEXTBOOK CROSS-REFERENCE WITH EXERCISES IN CHAPTER THREE OF BERNDT

Amemiya: 1,2,3,4,5,6,9,10-ch. 1; 7,8-chs. 5,6

Bacon: 1-ch. 2; 2,3,4,5,6-chs. 2-5; 7,8-chs. 7,8; 9-chs. 5,11.2; 10-ch. 4

Chow: 1,2,3,4,5,6,9-ch. 2; 7,8-chs. 2,3; 10-ch. 2.9

Cramer: 1,2,3,4,5,6,9-chs. 2,3,6; 7,8-chs. 7,9

Doti-Adibi: 1-chs. 3,4; 2,3,4,5,6,9-ch. 4; 7,8-chs. 4,5.2; 10-ch. 4.5

Fomby et al.: 1,2,3,4,5,6,9-chs. 2-4; 7,8-chs. 8,10; 9-ch. 23.3

Goldberger: 1-chs. 10,11; 2,3,4,5,6,9,10-chs. 14-22; 7,8-chs. 26-28

Greene: 1-ch. 5; 2,3,4,5,6,9-chs. 6,7; 7,8-chs. 13,15; 10-ch. 6.8

Gujarati: 1-chs. 2-5; 2,3,4,5,6-chs. 7,8; 7,8-ch. 12; 9-ch. 14; 10-ch. 9.9

Intriligator et al.: 1,2,3,4,5,6,9-chs. 4,6,8; 7,8-ch. 5; 10-ch. 15

Johnson et al.: 1-chs. 1-3; 2,3,4,5,6,9-chs. 4-10; 7,8-ch. 14; 10-ch. 18

Johnston: 1-ch. 2; 2,3,4,5,6,9-chs. 3,5,6; 7,8-ch. 8; 10-ch. 5.4

Judge (Big Daddy): 2,3,4,5,6,9-chs. 2,5; 7,8-ch. 8; 10-ch. 4.5

Judge (Baby): 1,2,3,4,5,6,9-chs. 3,5; 7,8-chs. 8,9; 10-ch. 5

Kelejian-Oates: 1-chs. 2,3; 2,3,4,5,6,9-ch. 4; 7,8-ch. 6.2; 10-ch. 3.5

Kennedy: 1,2,3,4,5,6,9-chs. 3,4; 7,8-ch. 7; 10-ch. 15

Kmenta: 1,2,3,4,5,6,9-chs. 7,10; 7,8-chs. 8,12; 10-ch. 7.4

Maddala: 1-ch. 3; 2,3,4,5,6,9-ch. 4; 7,8-chs. 6,12; 10-ch. 4.7

Mirer: 1-chs. 5,6; 2,3,4,5,6-chs. 7,10-13,15.1; 7,8-chs. 13,14; 9-ch. 15.1;
    10-ch. 13.2

Pindyck-Rubinfeld: 1-ch. 2; 2,3,4,5,6,9-chs. 4,5; 7,8-ch. 6; 10-ch. 8

Ramanathan: 1-ch. 3; 2,3,4,5,6,9-ch. 4; 7,8-ch. 8; 10-ch. 10

Studenmund-Cassidy: 1,2,3,4,5,6-chs. 2-5; 7,8-ch. 9; 9-chs. 5-7; 10-ch. 13

Wallace-Silver: 1-ch. 2; 2,3,4,5,6,9-chs. 2-4; 7,8-ch. 7; 10-ch. 4.2

TEXTBOOK CROSS-REFERENCE WITH EXERCISES IN CHAPTER FOUR OF BERNDT

Amemiya: 1,2,4,6-ch. 2; 3,5-ch. 6; 7-ch. 8.1.2

Bacon: 1,2-chs. 2-4; 3,4,5,6-chs. 4-7

Chow: 1,2,4,6-ch. 2; 3,5-chs. 2,3

Cramer: 1,2,3,4-chs. 2,3,6; 5,6-chs. 6,7; 7-ch. 8

Doti-Adibi: 1,2,4,6-chs. 3,4,6.2; 3,5-chs. 5.3,6.2

Fomby et al.: 1,2,6-chs. 2,3; 3,4,5-chs. 3,4,8,9; 8-ch. 18

Goldberger: 1,2,4,6-chs. 14-22; 3,5-chs. 27,28; 7-ch. 29

Greene: 1,2,4,6-chs. 6-8; 3,5-chs. 13,14; 7-ch. 11.7

Gujarati: 1,2,4,6-chs. 7,8,14; 3,5-chs. 11,14

Intriligator et al.: 1,2,3,4,5,6-chs. 4,6

Johnson et al.: 1-chs. 1-5,8; 2,4,6-chs. 4-9; 3,5-ch. 14; 7-ch. 11

Johnston: 2,4,6-chs. 4,5,6; 3,5-chs. 5,6,8; 7-ch. 3.3

Judge (Big Daddy): 2,4,6-chs. 2,5; 3,5-chs. 2,5,11; 7-chs. 7.7,20.5

Judge (Baby): 1,2-ch. 5; 3,4,5-chs. 5,8-10; 6-ch. 10; 7-ch. 12.5

Kelejian-Oates: 1,2,4,6-chs. 3,4,5.2; 3,5-chs. 4,5.2,6.3

Kennedy: 1,2,4,6-chs. 4,5,13; 3,5-chs. 7,13; 7-ch. 5.3

Kmenta: 1,2,4,6-chs. 7.4,10; 3,5-chs. 8,10,12; 7-ch. 11.3

Maddala: 1,2,4-ch. 4; 3,5,6-chs. 4,5,8; 7-ch. 5.6

Mirer: 1,2,4,6-chs. 5,7,10-13,15.1; 3,5-chs. 7,14,15.1

Pindyck-Rubinfeld: 1,2,4,6-chs. 4,5; 3,5-chs. 5,6

Ramanathan: 1,2-ch. 4; 3,5-chs. 4,6,11; 4,6-chs. 4,6; 7-ch. 4.6

Studenmund-Cassidy: 1,2,4,6-chs. 2-7; 3,5-chs. 3,10

Wallace-Silver: 1-chs. 2,3; 2,4,6-chs. 3-5; 3,5-chs. 3-5,6.2

TEXTBOOK CROSS-REFERENCE WITH EXERCISES IN CHAPTER FIVE OF BERNDT

Amemiya: 2,3,4,5,6,7-ch. 2; 8-ch. 6

Bacon: 2,3,4,5,6,7-chs. 4,5,8,11; 8-ch. 7

Chow: 2,3,4,5,6,7-ch. 2; 8-chs. 2,3

Cramer: 2,3,4,5,6,7-chs. 4,6; 8-ch. 7

Doti-Adibi: 1-ch. 3; 2,3,4,5,6,7-chs. 4,6.2; 8-chs. 5.3,6.2

Fomby et al.: 2,3,4,5,6,7-chs. 2,3; 8-chs. 8,9

Goldberger: 1-chs. 1-10; 2,3,4,5,6,7-chs. 14-22; 8-chs. 27,28

Greene: 2,3,4,5,6,7-chs. 6-8; 8-chs. 13,14

Gujarati: 2,3,4,5,6,7-chs. 7-9,14; 8-chs. 11,14

Intriligator et al.: 2,3,4,5,6,7-chs. 4-6; 8-ch. 6

Johnson et al.: 1-chs. 7,8; 2,3,4,5,6,7-chs. 4-6,9; 8-ch. 14

Johnston: 2,3,4,5,6,7-chs. 5,6; 8-ch. 8

Judge (Big Daddy): 2,3,4,5,6,7-chs. 2,5; 8-ch. 11

Judge (Baby): 1-ch. 2; 2,3,4,5,6,7-chs. 3,5,10; 8-chs. 8-10

Kelejian-Oates: 1-ch. 1; 2,3,4,5,6-chs. 4,5; 7-chs. 5,6

Kennedy: 1-ch. 5; 2,3,4,5,6,7-chs. 4,5,13; 8-chs. 7,13

Kmenta: 1,2,3,4,5,6,7-ch. 10; 8-chs. 8,10,12

Maddala: 1-ch. 2; 2,3,4,5,6,7-chs. 4,8; 8-ch. 5

Mirer: 1-chs. 2-4; 2,3,4,5,6,7-chs. 7,10-13,15; 8-ch. 14

Pindyck-Rubinfeld: 1-ch. 2; 2,3,4,5,6,7-chs. 4,5; 8-chs. 5,6

Ramanathan: 2,3,4,5,6,7-chs. 4,6,7.3; 8-ch. 10

Studenmund-Cassidy: 2,3,4,5,6,7-chs. 2-7; 8-ch. 10

Wallace-Silver: 2,3,4,5,6,7-chs. 2-5; 8-chs. 5,6

TEXTBOOK CROSS-REFERENCE WITH EXERCISES IN CHAPTER SIX OF BERNDT

Amemiya: 2-ch. 6.3.7; 3-ch. 1; 4,5,6,9-ch. 5.6.3; 7-ch. 5.3; 10-chs. 5,6

Bacon: 2-chs. 7-9; 3-chs. 4,5; 4,5,6,8,9-chs. 7,8,10; 10-chs. 4,5,7-10,11

Chow: 2,4,5,6,9-chs. 3,7; 3-ch. 2; 7-ch. 6; 8-chs. 4-6; 10-chs. 2-7

Cramer: 2-chs. 6,9; 3-chs. 2,3; 4,5,6,7,9-chs. 6,9; 8-chs. 7.5,9; 10-chs. 6,7,9

Doti-Adibi: 1-chs. 3,4; 2,4,5,6,9-chs. 5.2,6.2; 3-chs. 4,5.2; 8-ch. 6; 10-chs. 4-6

Fomby et al.: 2-ch. 10; 3-chs. 2,3; 4,5,6,7,9-chs. 10,11,17; 8-chs. 19-21; 10-chs. 2,3,10,11,17,19-21

Goldberger: 2-ch. 28; 3-chs. 14,16; 4,5,6,7,9-chs. 24,26,28; 8-chs. 31-34; 10-chs. 14,16,24,26,28

Greene: 2-ch. 15.7; 3-chs. 6,7; 4,5,6,7,9-ch. 18; 8-ch. 19.4.4e; 10-chs. 5,15,18

Gujarati: 1-chs. 1,10; 2,4,5,6,9-ch. 16; 3-chs. 7,8; 8-ch. 16.9; 10-chs. 12,16

Intriligator et al.: 1-ch. 3; 2,4,5,6,9-ch. 6; 3-chs. 4,5; 7-chs. 6,14; 8-ch. 10; 10-chs. 4-6,10,14

Johnson et al.: 2-ch. 14; 3-chs. 4-6; 4,5,6,9-ch. 14; 7-ch. 18; 10-chs. 4-7, 14,18

Johnston: 2-ch. 8.5; 3-chs. 5,6; 4,5,6,7,9,10-chs. 8.5,9; 8-chs. 8.5,11

Judge (Big Daddy): 2-ch. 8.4; 3-chs. 2,5; 4,5,6,9-chs. 9,10; 7-ch. 7; 8-chs. 8,15; 10-chs. 2,5,8,9,15

Judge (Baby): 2-ch. 9.5; 3-chs. 5,6; 4,5,6,9-chs. 17,21; 7-chs. 16-18; 8-ch. 15; 10-chs. 5,6,15-18,21

Kelejian-Oates: 2-ch. 6.2; 3-ch. 4; 4,5,6,9-chs. 5,6.2; 8-chs. 7,8; 10-chs. 4-8

Kennedy: 2-ch. 8; 3-chs. 3,4; 4,5,6,9-chs. 8,11; 7-ch. 15; 8-chs. 8,9; 10-chs. 3,4,8,9,11,15

Kmenta: 2-ch. 8; 3-ch. 10; 4,5,6,9-chs. 8,10,11; 8-ch. 13; 10-chs. 8,10,11,13

Maddala: 2-ch. 6.7; 3-ch. 4; 4,5,6,9-chs. 6,7,10; 8-ch. 9; 10-chs. 4,6,7,9,10

Mirer: 2-chs. 14,16; 3-ch. 13; 4,5,6,7,9-chs. 14-16; 8-chs. 16,17; 10-chs. 13-17

Pindyck-Rubinfeld: 2-chs. 6,9; 3-chs. 4,5; 4,5,6,9-chs. 6,9; 7-chs. 15-18; 8-chs. 6,11; 10-chs. 4-6,9,11,15-18

Ramanathan: 1-chs. 1,5,14; 2-chs. 8,9.2; 3-chs. 4,8; 4,5,6,9-chs. 5,7.A,9; 7-ch. 10.7; 8-ch. 13.4; 10-ch. 10

Studenmund-Cassidy: 2,4,5,6,9-ch. 9; 3-chs. 4-6; 7,10-ch. 13; 8-chs. 9,12

Wallace-Silver: 2-ch. 7.2; 3-chs. 3,4; 4,5,6,9-ch. 7.3; 8-ch. 8.5; 10-chs. 7,8

TEXTBOOK CROSS-REFERENCE WITH EXERCISES IN CHAPTER SEVEN OF BERNDT

Amemiya: 3,5-ch. 6; 4-ch. 1; 6,8-ch. 5

Bacon: 3-ch. 7; 4-ch. 8.1; 5,6-ch. 10

Chow: 3-ch. 3; 4-ch. 2; 5,6-chs. 3,6,7; 7,8-ch. 6

Cramer: 3-chs. 6,7; 4-ch. 2; 5-ch. 6; 6-chs. 6,9; 8-ch. 9

Doti-Adibi: 1,2-ch. 3; 3-chs. 4,5.3; 4,5-ch. 4; 6-chs. 5.2,6.2; 7-ch. 4.5

Fomby et al.: 3-ch. 9; 4-ch. 18.2; 5,6-chs. 11,17; 7-ch. 10; 8-chs. 10,17

Goldberger: 3-ch. 28; 4-chs. 14-17; 5,6-chs. 26-28

Greene: 3-ch. 14; 4-ch. 8.4.2; 5-ch. 15; 6-chs. 15,18; 7-ch. 6.8

Gujarati: 1,2-ch. 2; 3-ch. 11; 4-ch. 13.3; 5-ch. 12; 6-ch. 16; 7-chs. 7,8

Intriligator et al.: 3-ch. 5; 4-ch. 4; 5,6-ch. 6; 7-ch. 14; 8-chs. 13,14

Johnson et al.: 3-ch. 14; 4-ch. 13; 5,6-ch. 14; 7,8-chs. 14,15,18

Johnston: 3-ch. 8.4; 4-chs. 5,6; 5-ch. 8.5; 6,7,8-ch. 9

Judge (Big Daddy): 3-ch. 11; 4-ch. 2; 5-ch. 8; 6-ch. 10; 7-ch. 7; 8-chs. 7,8

Judge (Baby): 3-ch. 9.3; 4-chs. 5,6; 5,6-ch. 17; 7-ch. 16; 8-chs. 16,17

Kelejian-Oates: 3-ch. 6.3; 4-ch. 6.4; 5-chs. 5,6.2; 7-ch. 3.5

Kennedy: 3-ch. 7; 4-ch. 5; 6-ch. 8; 7-ch. 15; 8-chs. 8-10,15

Kmenta: 3-ch. 8.2; 4-ch. 10; 5,6-ch. 11; 7-ch. 12.1

Maddala: 3-ch. 5; 4-ch. 12; 5,6-chs. 6,7,10; 8-ch. 10

Mirer: 3-ch. 14; 4-ch. 13; 5,6-chs. 14,16; 7-ch. 13; 8-ch. 16

Pindyck-Rubinfeld: 3-ch. 6; 4-chs. 4,5; 5,6-chs. 6,9; 7-chs. 8,14; 8-chs. 14-19

Ramanathan: 1,2-chs. 1,14; 3-chs. 4,11; 4-chs. 4.7,4.A.3; 5-ch. 8; 6-ch. 9; 7,8-ch. 10

Studenmund-Cassidy: 3-ch. 10; 4-chs. 3-5; 5,6-ch. 9; 7,8-ch. 13

Wallace-Silver: 3-ch. 6.2; 4-ch. 3; 5,6-ch. 7; 7-ch. 4.2

TEXTBOOK CROSS-REFERENCE WITH EXERCISES IN CHAPTER EIGHT OF BERNDT

Amemiya: 1-chs. 7,8.3; 2-ch. 1; 3-ch. 6; 4-ch. 6.1.5; 6-ch. 6.3.7; 8-ch. 6

Bacon: 1-chs. 8,9; 2,4-ch. 4; 3-ch. 7; 6-ch. 9; 8-ch. 7

Chow: 1-chs. 4,5; 2,4-ch. 2; 3,8-ch. 3; 5-ch. 6.9; 6-ch. 5; 7-ch. 7

Cramer: 1,6-ch. 7; 2-chs. 2,3; 3-ch. 9; 4-ch. 7.3; 7-chs. 6.5,6.6; 8-ch. 7

Doti-Adibi: 1,6-ch. 6.3; 2,4-ch. 4; 3-chs. 4,5.2

Fomby et al.: 1-chs. 18,21; 2,4-ch. 3; 3-chs. 3,10; 6-chs. 19-21; 7-Appendix A; 8-ch. 15

Goldberger: 1,6-chs. 31-34; 2-chs. 14-17; 3-chs. 26-28; 4-ch. 30; 7-ch. 29; 8-ch. 27

Greene: 1-ch. 19; 2-chs. 6,7; 3-ch. 15; 4-ch. 17.3; 6-ch. 19.4.4e; 7-ch. 11; 8-ch. 16

Gujarati: 1-chs. 17-19; 2,4-chs. 7,8; 3-chs. 12,13; 5-ch. 16.14; 6-chs. 16-19; 7-chs. 7,8

Intriligator et al.: 1-chs. 9,10,12; 2,4-chs. 4,5; 3-ch. 6; 6-ch. 6; 7-chs. 10,11,13; 8-ch. 5

Johnson et al.: 2,4-chs. 4-6; 3-chs. 13-14; 8-ch. 9

Johnston: 1,6-ch. 11; 2-chs. 5,6; 3-chs. 8,9; 4-chs. 5,6,8.6; 5-ch. 9; 8-ch. 10.3

Judge (Big Daddy): 1-ch. 15; 2,4-chs. 2,5; 3-chs. 6,8; 5-ch. 16.2; 6-chs. 15,16; 7-ch. 6; 8-ch. 13

Judge (Baby): 1-chs. 14,15; 2,4-chs. 5,6; 3-ch. 9; 5-ch. 18.5; 6-ch. 15; 7-ch. 12; 8-ch. 11

Kelejian-Oates: 1-ch. 7; 2,4-ch. 4; 3-chs. 5.1,6.2; 6-chs. 6.2,7,8; 7-ch. 8; 8-ch. 6.3

Kennedy: 1-ch. 9; 2,3,4-chs. 3,4,8; 6-chs. 8,9; 8-ch. 7

Kmenta: 1-ch. 13; 2,4-ch. 10; 3-chs. 11,12; 5-ch. 13.1; 6-ch. 13; 7-ch. 11.3; 8-ch. 12.2

Maddala: 1-chs. 9,12; 2,4-ch. 4; 3-chs. 5,10,12; 6-ch. 9; 8-ch. 5

Mirer: 1-ch. 17; 2,4-ch. 13; 3-chs. 14-16; 6-chs. 16,17; 8-ch. 14

Pindyck-Rubinfeld: 1-chs. 7,11; 2,4-chs. 4,5; 3-ch. 6; 5-ch. 9; 6-ch. 11; 7,8-ch. 9

Ramanathan: 1-ch. 13; 2-chs. 4-6; 3-chs. 7-9; 4-ch. 4; 5-ch. 10; 6-ch. 13; 7-chs. 4,6; 8-ch. 11

Studenmund-Cassidy: 1-ch. 12; 2,4-chs. 4-6; 3-ch. 9; 6-chs. 9,12; 7-ch. 7; 8-ch. 12.7

Wallace-Silver: 1-ch. 8; 2,4-chs. 4,5; 3-ch. 7; 5-ch. 7.5; 6-chs. 7,8; 8-ch. 6

TEXTBOOK CROSS-REFERENCE WITH EXERCISES IN CHAPTER NINE OF BERNDT

Amemiya: 2-ch. 1; 3,4,5,6,7,8,9-chs. 6.4,7.4

Bacon: 2-ch. 2; 3,4,7-ch. 7.3

Chow: 2-ch. 1; 3,4,5,7,8,9-ch. 5

Cramer: 2-ch.1; 3,4,5,6,7,9-ch. 7

Doti-Adibi: 2-ch. 4

Fomby et al.: 2-ch. 2; 3,4-ch. 8

Goldberger: 2-ch. 10; 3,4,5,6,7,9-ch. 30

Greene: 2-ch. 5; 3,4,5,6,7,8,9-ch. 17

Gujarati: 2-ch. 2

Intriligator et al.: 2-ch. 4; 3,4,5,7,9-ch. 8

Johnson et al.: 2-ch. 3

Johnston: 2-ch. 2; 3,4,5,6,7,9-ch. 8.6

Judge (Big Daddy): 2-chs. 2,5; 3,4,5,6,7,8,9-ch. 12

Judge (Baby): 2-ch. 5; 3,4,5,6,7,9-chs. 11,15; 8-ch. 12.4

Kelejian-Oates: 2-ch. 2

Kennedy: 2-ch. 4; 3,4,5,9-ch. 9.4

Kmenta: 2-ch. 7; 3,4,5,7,8,9-ch. 12.3

Maddala: 2-ch. 11.4

Mirer: 2-chs. 5,6

Pindyck-Rubinfeld: 2-ch. 3; 3,4,5,7,9-Appendix 11.4

Ramanathan: 2-ch. 3

Studenmund-Cassidy: 2-ch. 2; 3,4,5,9-ch. 12.7

Wallace-Silver: 2-ch. 3; 3,4,5,9-ch. 8.1

TEXTBOOK CROSS-REFERENCE WITH EXERCISES IN CHAPTER TEN OF BERNDT

Amemiya: 1,2,3,4,5,6,7,8,9-ch. 7; 10-chs. 6,8

Bacon: 1,2,3,4-chs. 8,9; 5-chs. 9,10; 6,7-ch. 9

Chow: 1,2,6,7,8,9-ch. 5; 3-chs. 5,11; 10-chs. 7,11

Cramer: 1,6,8,9-ch. 7; 10-chs. 6,7,9

Doti-Adibi: 1,2,3,5,6,9-ch. 6.3

Fomby et al.: 1,2-ch. 21; 3-chs. 21,25.6; 4-ch. 18.3; 5-ch. 11; 6,7,8,9-chs. 19-23; 10-chs. 10,25.6

Goldberger: 1,2,3,6,7,8,9-chs. 32-34

Greene: 1,2,3,6,7,8,9-ch. 19; 4-ch. 9.5.6; 5-chs. 15,19; 10-chs. 17-19

Gujarati: 1,2,3,6-ch. 19

Intriligator et al.: 1,2,3,4,6,7,8,9-chs. 9,10

Johnson et al.: Simultaneous equations not covered in this text.

Johnston: 1,2,3,6,7,8,9-ch. 11

Judge (Big Daddy): 1,2,3,4,5,6,7,8,9-ch. 15; 10-ch. 16

Judge (Baby): 1,2,3,6,7,8,9-chs. 14,15; 4-ch. 20.4; 5-chs. 9.5.3,15; 10-chs. 12,16

Kelejian-Oates: 1,2,3,5,6-ch. 7

Kennedy: 1,2,3,4,6,7,8,9-ch. 9

Kmenta: 1,2,3,4,6,7,8,9-ch. 13; 5-chs. 8,13; 10-chs. 8.3,13

Maddala: 1,2,4-ch. 9; 3-chs. 9,10; 5-chs. 6,9,10; 6,7,8,9-ch. 9; 10-ch. 10

Mirer: 1,2,3,6-ch. 17

Pindyck-Rubinfeld: 1,2,3,6,7,8,9-ch. 11; 4-ch. 7.4; 5-ch. 11.6; 10-chs. 11,19

Ramanathan: 1,2,3,5,6-ch. 13

Studenmund-Cassidy: 1,2,3,6,7,9-ch. 12

Wallace-Silver: 1,2,3,6,7,8,9-ch. 8

TEXTBOOK CROSS-REFERENCE WITH EXERCISES IN CHAPTER ELEVEN OF BERNDT

Amemiya: 2,5-ch. 1; 3,4,6,7,8-ch. 9

Bacon: 2,5-chs. 4,5

Chow: 2,5-ch. 2; 3,4,6,7,8-chs. 7,8

Cramer: 2,5-ch. 1; 3-ch. 10; 4,6,7,8-ch. 10

Doti-Adibi: 2,5-ch. 4

Fomby et al.: 2-chs. 3,4; 3,6,8-ch. 25

Goldberger: 2,5-ch. 14; 3,4-ch. 29

Greene: 2,5-ch. 6; 3-ch. 20; 4,6,7,8-ch. 21

Gujarati: 2,5-ch. 7; 3-ch. 15

Intriligator et al.: 2,5-ch. 4; 3,5,6,7-ch. 5

Johnson et al.: 2,5-ch. 4

Johnston: 2,5-ch. 5; 3,4-ch. 10.5

Judge (Big Daddy): 2,5-ch. 2; 3,4,6,7,8-ch. 18

Judge (Baby): 2,5-chs. 5,6; 3,4,6,7,8-ch. 19

Kelejian-Oates: 2,5-ch. 4

Kennedy: 2,5-chs. 3,4; 3,4,6,7-ch. 14

Kmenta: 2,5-ch. 10; 3,4,6,7-chs. 11.5,11.6,11.8

Maddala: 2,5-ch. 4; 3-chs. 8.7-8.9; 4-ch. 8.11

Mirer: 2,5-ch. 7

Pindyck-Rubinfeld: 2,5-chs. 4,5; 3,4,6,7-ch. 10

Ramanathan: 2,5-ch. 4; 3,4,6,7-ch. 12

Studenmund-Cassidy: 2,5-chs. 4,5

Wallace-Silver: 2,5-ch. 3

INSTRUCTOR'S NOTES FOR CHAPTER ONE:
COMPUTERS AND THE PRACTICE OF ECONOMETRICS

ECONOMETRIC AND COMPUTATIONAL PROCEDURES EMPLOYED IN THE EXERCISE OF CHAPTER ONE:

- Call up a statistical software program for computational use

- Enter data directly from keyboard

- Print data to screen and on to a "hard copy" printer

- Compute and print means and standard deviations of two variables

- Compute and print a sample correlation coefficient

- Generate log-transformations of the variables

- Plot two log-transformed variables

- Enter the same data from the data diskette and verify that the data are identical to that entered directly from the keyboard

- Run a bivariate regression, compute and plot residuals

- Comment on whether results are consistent with a priori expectations

GOALS FOR CHAPTER ONE:

To involve students in practicing basic computer skills to ensure they are ready and able to perform the empirical exercises found at the end of each remaining chapter in this textbook.

GENERAL COMMENTS TO THE INSTRUCTOR:

Having students become familiar and comfortable with their statistical computing environment is critical if they are to become actively involved in "hands-on" econometrics. This process of learning to use computers, word processors and statistical software programs is often frustrating and time-consuming—and for some students anxieties can become intense if other class members have wide-ranging familiarity with computers. Helping students become comfortable with computational facilities is an investment well worth making, however.

What the optimal situation will be in terms of your own contact time with students in a lab versus that of a teaching assistant during this initiation process will of course vary, depending on numerous circumstances. Some instructors have told me they scheduled two one-hour labs for students early in the semester, one in which a teaching assistant introduced students to the lab and the editor (word processing) software, and the other in which the instructor introduced students to the statistical software package. Other instructors have covered all this material in one lab session, while some have assigned everything to a TA. I think it is essential, however, that all students be required to carry out the single exercise at the end of Chapter 1, or its equivalent using another data base; the procedures covered in this exercise are absolutely critical for subsequent "hands-on" involvement.

Regardless of how you carry this out, my own experience has been that becoming comfortable with the statistical computational environment is typically a very frustrating yet critical step for students in this type of a course. It's worth planning it well. In this context, three other comments are worth noting.

First, if your university or college has computer labs with staff people assigned to them, those people may be able to help you in obtaining learning materials and documentation.

Second, if you are uncertain as to what statistical software to employ, you might find it useful to examine the two appendices to Chapter 1 in the main text, The Practice of Econometrics: Classic and Contemporary. The first provides an overview of statistics and econometrics software for mainframes and personal computers, and the second lists specific vendors for mainframes, IBM-PC and compatibles and Apple Macintosh computers. The first appendix also provides references for reviews of various statistical software programs.

Third, if you are using as your statistical software MicroTSP, PC-TSP, TSP or SHAZAM, you might want to have your students work through the supplementary computer handbook for these programs; more details are given at the beginning of this Resource Guide.

NOTES ON THE EXERCISE IN CHAPTER ONE:

1. There are clear time trends in the data, for while the price of color TV's falls from $777 in 1964 to $360 in 1979, the cumulative production increases from 3.104 to 113.170 million units over the same time period. This trend could reflect in part the effects of learning on production costs.

2. The mean and standard deviation of the PRICE variable are 562.50000 and 152.07323, respectively, while those for CUMPRD are 50.59756 and 35.76020.

3. The sample covariance between CUMPRD and PRICE is -5261.23060, while the sample correlation coefficient between them is -0.96746.

4. The least squares coefficient estimate, standard error and t-statistic for the constant term in a regression of log(PRICE) on log(CUMPRD) are -7.1380, 0.092375 and 77.272, respectively, while those for the slope coefficient are -0.23711, 0.025036 and -9.4706. The equation R^2 is 0.864984. The negative and statistically significant estimated slope coefficient is consistent with the learning curve hypothesis.

5. The residuals display a very notable trend. In particular, the first two residuals are negative, the next seven are positive, and the final seven are negative. This autocorrelated pattern to the residuals shows up in a rather low Durbin-Watson test statistic, 0.4623. Finally, towards the end of the sample the negative residuals are becoming increasingly larger in absolute value, suggesting that the least squares fitted value is over-predicting log(PRICE) by an increasingly large amount in the late 1970s. This pattern of residuals might suggest a problem in the equation specification. In particular, the issue of whether economies of scale also affect production

costs, and therefore whether current production is an inappropriately omitted variable in this bivariate regression model, is taken up in detail in Chapter 3 of the textbook.

INSTRUCTOR'S NOTES FOR CHAPTER TWO:

<u>THE CAPITAL ASSET PRICING MODEL:
AN APPLICATION OF BIVARIATE REGRESSION ANALYSIS</u>

ECONOMETRIC PROCEDURES EMPLOYED IN THE EXERCISES OF CHAPTER TWO:

- Generate transformed variables

- Compute a least squares coefficient estimate by brute force as the
correlation coefficient times the ratio of standard deviations

- Run a bivariate regression using computer software, compute
confidence intervals, interpret coefficient estimates, t-statistics
and R^2

- Do a reciprocal regression of X on Y and compare results

- Compute means, standard deviations and correlations

More-advanced procedures:

- Test for parameter equality using the Chow test procedure

- Do an event study using dummy variables, and interpret the dummy
variable coefficients

- Compare a simple with a multiple regression

- Test for homoskedasticity, the absence of AR(1) or MA(1) processes
in the disturbances and normality of the disturbances

GOALS FOR CHAPTER TWO:

To help students gain an empirical "hands-on" experience and
understanding of the capital asset pricing model (CAPM) using bivariate
least squares regression techniques. In the more advanced procedures,
students undertake more sophisticated analyses of the data, and test
traditional assumptions.

GENERAL COMMENTS TO THE INSTRUCTOR:

Subsequent to the writing of the text, in October of 1990 it was
announced that Harry Markowitz (whose work on diversification is featured in

Chapter 2), William Sharpe (one of the original developers of the CAPM) and Merton Miller had been awarded the 1990 Nobel Prize in Economics. Students might be interested to know that in this chapter they can learn about some of the most fundamental ideas in finance—ideas that won the Nobel Prize for their originators.

To carry out the exercises, it will be necessary for all students to input data from the diskette into their statistical software program. Make sure students know how to format their data files, so that files can properly be imported into the statistical software program.

Exercises 1 through 5 use rather simple estimation and computational procedures, while Exercises 6 through 10 employ slightly more advanced procedures. See the above list for details.

COMMENTS ON SPECIFIC EXERCISES:

Exercise 1: Getting Started with the Data

TASKS: Plot data, construct firm-specific and market risk premia, speculate on value of β, calculate variances and covariances, standard deviations and correlations and then compute β by brute force.

COMMENTS: This is a rather straightforward exercise, but it does require a fair amount of data importing and data manipulation. Students can select their own company. As a check on the data and software, note that over the 120 month period, the sample mean of the monthly risk-free rate of return is 0.00684, while that for the market risk premium is 0.00715. As an example of one company for the final 36-month time period, consider Mobil. Its β is computed, rearranging (2.18), as $\beta = \rho * s_{MOBIL}/s_{MARKET} = 0.65586*0.07116/ 0.06389 = 0.73049$.

Exercise 2: Least Squares Estimates of β

TASKS: Do OLS on data from selected firms. Look at $\hat{\beta}$ and residuals. Test H_0: $\alpha = 0$ against H_1: $\alpha \neq 0$, and interpret results. Construct 95% confidence interval for β. Test H_0: $\beta = 1$ against H_1: $\beta \neq 1$. Using the measured R^2, compute the proportion of risk that is systematic, and that which is diversifiable.

COMMENTS: One of the lessons students should learn from this exercise is that in the CAPM context, R^2 has a clear interpretation and should be estimated, not maximized.

Although it will not be feasible to provide comparable detail for other exercises in this and subsequent chapters, at this point it may be useful to present a full set of estimation results on OLS estimates of α, β and R^2 for each of the seventeen companies, over the the entire 1/78-12/87 sample time period, and then for the 1/78-12/82 and 1/83-12/87 sub-sample time periods. This is done in Table 2.1 below. Absolute values of t-statistics are in parentheses.

Some other comments on Exercise 2. For many companies, residuals are rather large in October 1987. For all companies in all time periods except for CONED in 1/78-12/87 and 1/83-12/87, one cannot reject the null hypothesis that $\alpha=0$ at the 95% significance level. The R^2 values vary considerably, from 0.0200 for CONED in 1/83-12/87 to 0.5536 for MOTOR in the same time period; roughly speaking, for a typical company the R^2 is about 0.3, implying that about 30% of the typical company's risk is non-diversifiable. Also, estimates of β do not increase monotonically with R^2; for example, in the 1/78-12/82 data sample, Tandy has the largest β at 1.0500, but its R^2 value of 0.3191 is less than the R^2 of WEYER at 0.4346, whose estimated β is smaller at 0.8207.

Finally, it is of interest to note that in this particular sample of companies chosen, a rather small number have β's larger than one, although the proportion of such companies is larger in the 1/83-12/87 sub-sample.

Table 2.1

OLS ESTIMATES OF α AND β IN CAPM MODEL, VARYING TIME PERIODS

Company	Jan 1978-Dec 1987			Jan 1978-Dec 1982			Jan 1983-Dec 1987		
	α	β	R^2	α	β	R^2	α	β	R^2
MOBIL	.0042 (0.721)	0.7147 (8.348)	.3713	.0008 (0.086)	0.6798 (5.848)	.3709	.0079 (1.019)	0.7815 (5.974)	.3810
TEXACO	.0007 (0.115)	0.6132 (6.746)	.2783	-.0035 (0.404)	0.6433 (5.741)	.3624	.0047 (0.515)	0.5724 (3.708)	.1917
IBM	-.0005 (0.106)	0.4568 (6.763)	.2793	-.0002 (0.036)	0.3390 (3.818)	.2008	-.0000 (0.004)	0.6545 (6.356)	.4106
DEC	.0068 (0.921)	0.8474 (7.825)	.3416	.0003 (0.031)	0.7068 (6.303)	.4065	.0142 (1.193)	1.0993 (5.464)	.3399
DATGEN	-.0067 (0.686)	1.0308 (7.218)	.3063	-.0150 (1.043)	1.0056 (5.390)	.3337	.0016 (0.119)	1.0923 (4.783)	.2829
CONED	.0110 (2.398)	0.0932 (1.395)	.0162	.0082 (1.214)	0.1405 (1.597)	.0421	.0135 (2.152)	0.0200 (0.189)	.0006
PSNH	-.0126 (1.259)	0.2135 (1.467)	.0179	-.0016 (0.275)	0.2180 (2.862)	.1238	-.0235 (1.230)	0.1805 (0.560)	.0054
WEYER	-.0031 (0.520)	0.8207 (9.524)	.4346	-.0047 (0.520)	0.7079 (6.056)	.3874	-.0008 (0.106)	1.0141 (7.882)	.5172
BOISE	.0031 (0.461)	0.9359 (9.438)	.4302	-.0013 (0.117)	0.8846 (6.309)	.4070	.0078 (0.926)	1.0323 (7.249)	.4753
MOTOR	.0053 (0.730)	0.8482 (8.092)	.3569	.0060 (0.596)	0.5560 (4.272)	.2394	.0063 (0.672)	1.3381 (8.482)	.5536
TANDY	.0107 (1.099)	1.0500 (7.437)	.3191	.0311 (1.997)	1.0308 (5.092)	.3089	-.0095 (0.847)	1.0350 (5.442)	.3380
DELTA	.0013 (0.163)	0.4897 (4.061)	.1226	.0076 (0.621)	0.3921 (2.460)	.0945	-.0043 (0.383)	0.6395 (3.377)	.1643
PANAM	-.0086 (0.762)	0.7345 (4.486)	.1457	-.0137 (0.894)	0.7467 (3.761)	.1960	-.0036 (0.215)	0.7258 (2.568)	.1021
CONTIL	-.0132 (1.007)	0.7311 (3.839)	.1110	-.0075 (0.670)	0.3886 (2.660)	.1088	-.0017 (0.722)	1.2944 (3.314)	.1592
CITCRP	.0002 (0.040)	0.6670 (7.438)	.3192	.0006 (0.065)	0.4466 (3.746)	.1948	.0012 (0.161)	1.0370 (8.126)	.5324
GERBER	.0051 (0.720)	0.6256 (6.084)	.2388	-.0007 (0.069)	0.4632 (3.748)	.1949	.0118 (1.159)	0.9122 (5.328)	.3286
GENMIL	.0078 (1.358)	0.2702 (3.227)	.0811	.0042 (0.541)	0.0987 (0.969)	.0159	.0124 (1.549)	0.5670 (4.204)	.2336

Exercise 3: Why Gold Is Special

TASKS: Estimate β for GOLD, and interpret negative estimate. Compute 95% confidence interval for β, and then reestimate using more recent data. Interpret change to positive estimate of β.

COMMENTS: The first point to note here is that the data sample time period has changed from that used in the previous exercises of this chapter. In this exercise the data begin in January 1976, and thus the market and risk-free variables need to come from a different data file; these variables are called MARK76 and RKFR76, respectively.

Using the 48-month sample beginning in January 1976, the OLS estimate of β is -0.2348, having a standard error of 0.14364 and an R^2 of 0.0549; the 95% confidence region for β therefore spans from about -0.52 to about +0.05. If one instead estimates using the later time period from January 1980 through December 1985, one obtains an estimate of β equal to 0.4058, a standard error of 0.14488 and an R^2 of 0.1008; this estimate is significantly different from zero at the 95% confidence level.

Investors are very much attracted to assets whose β's are negative, for such assets are valuable in the diversification process. One possible reason β changed from negative to positive is that investors may have begun to understand this attribute of GOLD, and therefore they may have increased demand for it when the market was down, and decreased demand for it when the market was up. The shifting demand and supply curves may have thereby changed the price enough to alter the correlation between the GOLD and MARK76 risk premiums.

Exercise 4: Consequences of Running the Regression Backwards

TASKS: Explore consequences of running regression backwards, using DELTA Airlines data for 1/83-12/87. Do OLS regression of Y on X, then of X on Y.

Obtain same R^2 since in the bivariate regression case this R^2 is the square of the sample correlation between X and Y.

COMMENTS: Results from a reciprocal regression in which the MARKET risk premium variable is regressed on a constant and the DELTA risk premium are that the estimate of γ is 0.25695 and the R^2 is 0.164329; if one instead runs the usual CAPM regression over the 1/83-12/87 time period, one obtains an estimate of β equal to 0.63953, and the identical R^2 value of 0.164329. Note that the t-statistics corresponding to the null hypothesis that the slope coefficient is equal to zero are identical in the reciprocal and traditional regressions—t = 3.3772.

Since the estimate of γ is an implicit estimate of $1/\beta$, the implied estimate of β from the reciprocal regression is $1/.25695 = 3.89181$. Note that this makes sense, for by equation (2.23), $R^2 = b_y/b_x$ here implies 0.164329 = 0.63953/3.89181 (with small rounding error).

Which estimate of β one prefers (see part (e) of Exercise 4) depends in part on the source of the disturbance term. In the absence of measurement error, for example, it would in most cases appear more likely that the market risk premium was exogenous and uncorrelated with the disturbance term ϵ, than that the DELTA risk premium was exogenous and uncorrelated with v. If such an exogeneity argument is valid, then the direct regression estimate b_y is preferable.

Exercise 5: Using the CAPM to Construct Portfolios

TASKS: Choose four companys' returns and construct alternative portfolios consisting of these companys' assets weighted in different ways. Compute correlation coefficients, means and standard deviations, and compare the means and standard deviations of the portfolio to those of the constituent firms. Estimate by OLS a CAPM equation for the portfolios, then for the constituent firms, and compare results, including the R^2 and β values.

COMMENTS: This exercise is of particular value to students with strong interests in finance, for it illustrates the benefits of diversification. The results students obtain will of course vary with the particular companies chosen for the portfolios.

If one takes food products as a safe industry (GERBER and GENMIL) and electronics as a risky industry (TANDY and DATGEN) over the 1/83-12/87 time period, for example, and if Portfolio I is 50% GERBER and 50% TANDY, Portfolio II is 50% GERBER and 50% GENMIL while Portfolio III is 50% TANDY and 50% DATGEN, then simple correlations between returns of the two assets in each portfolio are 0.29798, 0.39224 and 0.36799 in Portfolios I, II and III, respectively. Since returns in Portfolio I had the lowest correlation, diversification would appear to be most promising for this portfolio in terms of reducing risk. However, the means and standard deviations of returns for the three portfolios are, respectively, 0.00413 and 0.08110 (I), 0.01437 and 0.06916 (II), -0.00066 and 0.09472 (III), while the means and standard deviations of the individual company's returns are 0.01459 and 0.09495 (GERBER), 0.01414 and 0.07000 (GENMIL), -0.00633 and 0.10623 (TANDY), and 0.00501 and 0.12255 (DATGEN). In this particular example, therefore, Portfolio II would have been most desirable, for with it not only was the standard deviation lower than that for any other portfolio (and for any one of the four companies), but its return was also highest among the portfolios.

The R^2 from the Portfolio I CAPM equation is 0.513107, while that for its component companies is 0.328627 (GERBER) and 0.338018 (TANDY). Notice that the proportion of diversifiable risk for the portfolio is about 48.7% for Portfolio I, considerably less than that for GERBER (67%) or TANDY (66%), due to the effects of diversification.

Exercise 6: Assessing the Stability of β over Time and among Companies

TASKS: Assuming i.i.d. errors, use the Chow test procedure to test for stability of β over time, and for equality among companies, using data from selected companies and industries. Note that for this Chow test, the degrees of freedom in the numerator is that corresponding to the unconstrained regression (the total number of observations in the two estimations minus the total number of parameters estimated), while the degrees of freedom in the numerator of the F-test statistic is the difference in the degrees of freedom in the unconstrained and constrained regressions.

COMMENTS: The results obtained in this exercise depend of course on the companies and industries chosen for estimation. As an example, consider companies in the airlines (DELTA and PANAM) and oil (MOBIL and TEXACO) industries. The sum of squared residuals based on various OLS regressions involving these four companies are summarized in Table 2.2 below, and form the basis of various Chow F-test statistics.

Table 2.2

SUMS OF SQUARED RESIDUALS FROM VARIOUS REGRESSIONS

	1/78-12/82	1/83-12/87	1/78-12/87
DELTA	0.512818	0.436960	0.96103
PANAM	0.795681	0.973270	1.77196
MOBIL	0.272812	0.208488	0.48445
TEXACO	0.253425	0.290334	0.54622
DELTA & PANAM			2.75378
MOBIL & TEXACO			1.03464
ALL 4 COMBINED			3.79493

For part (a) of Exercise 6 in the airlines industry, for Delta the Chow test statistic for parameter equality is computed as $\{[0.961031 - (0.512818 + 0.436960)]/[0.512818 + 0.436960]\}*[(120-4)/2] = 0.687$ with 2 and 116 degrees of freedom, which is less than the F-critical value at any reasonable level of significance. Similar calculations can be done for the other four airlines, yielding test statistics of 0.099 (PANAM), 0.380 (MOBIL) and 0.263; each of these test statistics suggests that at usual significance levels, the null hypothesis of parameter equality over time would not be rejected.

Concerning part (b) of Exercise 6, and using the entries in Table 2.1, students might notice that there is some ambiguity on precisely what the alternative hypothesis is here. They will have to state it explicitly, and then carry out the appropriate calculation. The Chow test statistic for parameter equality between DELTA and PANAM over the entire 1/78-12/87 time period when the alternative hypothesis is that the DELTA and PANAM coefficients are not equal over the same entire time period is computed as $\{[2.75378 - (0.961031 + 1.77196)]/[0.961031 + 1.77196]\}*[(240-4)/2] = 0.898$, while the corresponding calculation for the Chow test involving MOBIL and TEXACO yields a test statistic of 0.454; at usual significance levels with 2 and 236 degrees of freedom, the null hypothesis is not rejected in both cases.

Finally, again there is ambiguity in part (c) of Exercise 6 concerning the formulation of the alternative hypothesis. Let the null hypothesis be that of parameter equality between the DELTA & PANAM and the MOBIL & TEXACO pooled regressions over the entire 1/78-12/87 time period, while the alternative hypothesis is that over this same entire time period, the parameters from the pooled DELTA & PANAM regression are not equal to those from the pooled MOBIL & TEXACO regression. In this case the Chow test statistic is computed as $\{[3.79493 - (2.75378 + 1.03464)]/[2.75378 + 1.03464]\}$

*[(480-4)/2], which turns out to be 0.411, less than the F-table critical value with 2 and 476 degrees of freedom at any reasonable significance level.

It is worth noting that other Chow tests could be computed, corresponding with different alternative hypotheses. However, in this sample and for these firms and industries, apparently the precision with which parameters are estimated is sufficiently small that the null hypothesis of parameter equality and/or stability (for most any alternative hypothesis) is typically not rejected.

Exercise 7:   Three Mile Island, and the Conoco Takeover—Event Studies

TASKS: Generate requisite variables over the time period beginning January 1976 (not January 1978), compute and print out sample means. Compare fitted value for one observation based on OLS estimate with that observation deleted to OLS estimate of dummy variable coefficient on variable that is equal to one for only that observation. Interpret dummy variable coefficients, and relate to various residuals from a related regression.

COMMENTS: This is a rather useful exercise for the interpretation of dummy variables and their relationships to residuals from related regressions. It is also useful in that event studies are increasingly commonplace within the applied finance literature.

(a) To ensure the data have been properly generated, check for sample means. The mean risk premiums for the 120 months from 1/76 to 12/85 for GPU, DUPONT, DOW and the overall market are 0.00091, 0.00389, -0.00092 and 0.00968, respectively, while that for CONOCO from 1/76 thru 9/81 is 0.01193.

(b) Based on the OLS regression with 4/79 deleted, the predicted value for that month is 0.00768, while the actual value is -0.33841, implying a residual error equal to -0.34609. This is a very large residual, occurring just after the Three Mile Island nuclear power accident to GPU, the parent holding company of Three Mile Island.

(c) When the TMIDUM variable is added in a regression using all observations from 1/76 thru 12/85, i.e., when the GPU premium is regressed on a constant term, the market risk premium and the TMIDUM dummy variable, the coefficient on the dummy variable is exactly equal to the residual computed in (b) above, i.e., it equals -0.34609 and has a t-statistic of -4.0881, indicating that Three Mile Island was a statistically significant event. Moreover, the estimated value of β is identical in the two regressions (0.44806).

(d) The average residuals computed in this portion of Exercise 7 should equal -0.0252375 (DUPONT), -0.0199175 (DOW) and +0.135085 (CONOCO). Note that the companies fighting each other for the takeover (DUPONT and DOW) have negative average residuals, while the takeover target (CONOCO) has a positive residual.

(e) OLS estimates of the FIGHT dummy variable (defined to be one during June, July, August and September 1981, else zero) are not quite the same as these 4-period average residuals, although they are very close: -0.025952 (DUPONT), -0.020193 (DOW) and +0.14506 (CONOCO). Estimates of the β's also vary a bit in the comparable regressions. Note that the coefficient estimate on the CONOCO FIGHT dummy variable is statistically significant (t = 3.6561), while those for DUPONT and DOW are not (t = -0.96013 and -0.64379).

Exercise 8: Is January Different?

TASKS: Consider alternative ways of formulating and implementing an hypothesis. Run several regressions with a dummy variable included, and interpret results. The goal here is to build interpretive skills in operationalizing hypothesis testing.

COMMENTS: The hypothesis that January returns are slightly higher, other things equal, has received considerable press in recent years.   Perhaps because of this market participants have altered their behavior, and this may have reduced considerably the somewhat unusual behavior of asset returns in January.   As a result, it appears that January may not be as different as it used to be.

(a) In the context of this portion of the exercise, it is of interest to note that if one defines a dummy variable for January as JDUM and then runs an OLS regression of the market return (not market risk premium) on a constant and JDUM, the dummy variable coefficient is positive (0.019209) but insignificant (t = 0.84986); a similar regression with the RKFREE variable as dependent variable has a dummy variable coefficient much smaller (0.0003266) and insignificant as well (t = 0.45070).

(b) Obviously, this result makes testing the January-is-different hypothesis most difficult in the CAPM framework.   Incidentally, if one runs a regression similar to those in (a) above but with the market risk premium as the dependent variable, the coefficient on the JDUM dummy variable is positive (0.018882) but insignificant (t = 0.83223).

(c) Results will depend of course on the companies chosen.   For IBM, DEC and DATGEN, the JDUM estimated coefficients (t-statistics) are: 0.017327 (0.88802), 0.081873 (2.5578), and 0.041145 (0.97656).   Hence, while for all three companies the January return is slightly higher, only for DEC is it statistically different.

(d) Note that with the Chow test here, one is testing for equality of both intercept and slope coefficient over the January and non-January samples. In this case the Chow test statistics turn out to be 0.2019 (IBM), 3.2674 (DEC) and 0.2179 (DATGEN) with 2 and 116 degrees of freedom.   At usual significance levels, therefore, only for DEC is the null hypothesis of parameter equality rejected.

(e) Results are again consistent with those from (c) and (d). In particular, the coefficients (t-statistics) on the dummy variable DUMJ in an expanded CAPM equation for IBM, DEC and DATGEN are 0.0084243 (0.50147), 0.065929 (2.5101), and 0.021480 (0.60508), respectively.

(f) Something strange is happening at DEC in January.

Exercise 9: Comparing the Capital Asset and Arbitrage Pricing Models

TASKS: Compare bivariate and multivariate regression estimates, and "test" the CAPM as a special case of the APM. Calculate "surprise" variables as deviations from sample means. Test the null hypothesis that coefficients on the surprise variables are simultaneously equal to zero.

COMMENTS: A typical result here is that you'll not be able to reject the null hypothesis that coefficients on the "surprise" variables are simultaneously equal to zero.

(a) Sample means for RINF, ROIL and GIND are 0.0092218, 0.0045479 and 0.0021570, respectively, while sample means for the corresponding "surprise" variables are by definition equal to zero.

(b) Two companies whose returns might be affected by economywide events are PANAM and BOISE. For PANAM, the coefficients on the surprise variables are all negative, but each is statistically insignificant using t-statistic criteria; the joint F-test with 3 and 115 degrees of freedom is 0.1520. For BOISE, results are very similar—each coefficient on the surprise variable is negative but statistically insignificant, and the F-test statistic is 0.5156. Hence in these two instances, CAPM is not rejected as a special case of the APM.

NOTE: It is not clear that OLS is the proper way in which to test CAPM as a special case of the APM. See the references provided in the text for additional discussion (especially the Huang-Litzenberger textbook), including the use of factor analysis and ARCH (autoregressive conditional heteroskedasticity) models.

Exercise 10: What About Assumptions Concerning Disturbances? Did We Mess Up?

TASKS: Test underlying stochastic assumptions—homoskedasticity, the absence of AR(1) or MA(1) disturbances and normality of the disturbances.

COMMENTS: The four parts of this exercise are independent, and they need not all be done, nor are they sequential. It is perfectly possible to do only any subset of the four parts of this exercise. Results will vary of course with the company chosen for analysis.

(a) For IBM, if one takes the residuals from the CAPM equation based on the 1/78-12/87 time period, squares them, and then runs a regression of these squared residuals on a constant term and the market risk premium squared, the R^2 is 0.00019647; in this case, T = 120, so T*R^2 equals 0.0236—a chi-square variable certainly less than the critical value at usual significance levels. For Tandy, the corresponding chi-square test statistic is 0.0409. In these cases, therefore, the null hypothesis of homoskedasticity is not rejected.

(b) On the basis of Durbin-Watson statistics, over the entire 1/78-12/87 time period for each of the seventeen companies, the Durbin-Watson is quite high—the lowest is 1.8221 (CITCRP). However, in sub-samples, there's a bit more ambiguity -- in the 1/78-12/82 sub-sample, the Durbin-Watson is as low as 1.56664 (IBM), and for 1/83-12/87 it is 1.5790 (CITCRP). In each of these cases, however, based on iterative Cochrane-Orcutt procedures, the null hypothesis of AR(0) against the alternative of AR(1) is not rejected.

(c) An easy way to test for MA(1) disturbances is to employ the Breusch-

Godfrey test procedure. Run the CAPM equation for a company, and compute residuals for observations 1 through T, where T is the sample size; then for observations 2 through T, run an OLS regression of the residual on a constant, the market risk premium and the lagged residual. Compute T times the R^2 from this regression, and compare this to a chi-square critical value with 1 degree of freedom. Incidentally, an interesting feature of this test is that the alternative hypothesis can be either an AR(1) or an MA(1) specification. See your econometric theory textbook for further details.

(d) References for testing for normality are given in the text. It is worth noting that there's a substantial literature, some of it quite sophisticated, on testing for normality of returns. For discussion, see the Huang-Litzenberger text reference in Further Readings at the end of Chapter Two in the textbook, as well as the references cited therein.

FINAL COMMENTS:

Many universities subscribe to stock return data tapes from the Center for Research in Securities Prices at the University of Chicago. To obtain updated data, contact them. Other private sector firms also provide comparable data; see, for example, COMPUSTAT. In countries other than the U.S., often the research divisions of central banks have access to appropriate returns data. You may wish to contact them to obtain such data.

INSTRUCTOR'S NOTES FOR CHAPTER THREE:

<u>COSTS, LEARNING CURVES AND SCALE ECONOMIES:</u>
<u>FROM SIMPLE TO MULTIPLE REGRESSION</u>

ECONOMETRIC PROCEDURES EMPLOYED IN THE EXERCISES OF CHAPTER THREE:

- Run bivariate regression, test hypotheses

- Perform multiple regression, test simple and joint hypotheses
   and compute confidence intervals

- Verify algebra of omitted variable bias in multiple regression

- Compare R^2 from simple and multiple regressions

- Compute and plot residuals

- Do a variety of constrained and unconstrained OLS regressions,
   and choose preferred specifications

- Compute returns to scale based on OLS parameter estimates

More-advanced procedures:

- Test for AR(0) when alternative hypothesis is AR(1)

- Estimate by GLS using Hildreth-Lu or Cochrane-Orcutt procedures

- Implement Chow test procedure, and choose a preferred specification

- Compute and interpret forecast and forecast error variance based
   on OLS estimation of bivariate regression model

GOALS FOR CHAPTER THREE:

To engage students in estimating effects on costs of learning curves
and returns to scale, using bivariate and multiple regression
procedures. Also, to assess the effects of inappropriately omitting a
variable, and to test single and joint hypotheses, using the t- and F-
statistic procedures, respectively.

GENERAL COMMENTS TO THE INSTRUCTOR:

In this chapter I integrate the economic theory of cost and production with the learning curve literature. This provides, I believe, a nice introduction to using economic theory to help in specifying the form of the econometric model. Exercises 1 through 5 employ rather simple estimation and computational procedures, while Exercises 6 through 10 utilize slightly more advanced tools. See the above list for details.

Several other comments. Students will not be able to replicate the classic Nerlove results, for as Nerlove has noted in informal discussions, an early version of his data was published (and is used here), but the data actually used in the final regressions apparently have been lost. Also, in the updated electric utility data file called UPDATE, some of the data are not employed in the exercises; in particular, data on the cost shares SK, SL and SF are provided but not used. These data might form the basis of additional exercises in Chapter 9 on interrelated factor demands.

NOTES ON THE EXERCISES IN CHAPTER THREE:

It is again worth emphasizing that before students can do any of the exercises, the data files on their floppy diskette must be properly edited so that data can be read in by their statistical software program.

Exercise 1: Estimating Parameters of a Learning Curve

TASKS: Logarithmically transform data, plot two series, do a bivariate regression, interpret coefficients and test hypotheses.

COMMENTS: Students can choose from the POLY and TIO2 data files. If TIO2 is used, they must first deflate the UCOSTT data by dividing UCOSTT by DEFL.

(a) The plot of unit cost against cumulative production is particularly striking with the TIO2 data, although the negative relationship is also clear based on the POLY data. With both data sets, the shape of the plot suggests that a logarithmic transformation might yield a linear relationship between the two variables.

   (b) With the TIO2 data, the OLS estimate of the constant term is 1.4139 (t = 5.144), and the slope estimate is -0.38570 (t = -10.710). The R^2 is 0.8912, but the Durbin-Watson test statistic is only 0.6634. With the POLY data, the OLS estimate of the constant term is 1.0040 (t = 8.5547), and that for the slope coefficient is -0.27167 (t = -18.657). The R^2 is higher for POLY at 0.9694, but the Durbin-Watson is still low at 0.8409. In each case, the null hypothesis that the learning curve elasticity is zero is rejected, using typical significance levels. Using equation (3.9) in the text, one can compute the slope of the learning curve as 76.5% for TIO2 and 82.8% for POLY. These results are in line with findings reported in the literature and summarized in Table 3.1 in the text.

Exercise 2: Testing the Simple Learning Curve Specification

   TASKS: Logarithmically transform data, run a multiple regression, compare results with that from a bivariate regression and verify the omitted variable bias, relate R^2 in the simple and multiple regressions and explain inference based on t-statistics and F-statistics.

   COMMENTS: As in Exercise 1, students have a choice of using the POLY or TIO2 data sets. If the TIO2 data are employed, the UCOSTT data must be deflated, dividing UCOSTT by DEFL.

   (a) The OLS regression results are as follows (t-stats in parentheses):

For TIO2, LNUC = 1.4374 - 0.3023*LNCP - 0.1306*LNY R^2 = 0.8966
                (5.14)   (2.794)   (0.819)   DW = 0.6097

   while for the simple regression equation based on TIO2 data

        LNUC = 1.4139 - 0.38570*LNCP R^2 = 0.8912
               (5.144)   (10.71)   DW = 0.6634.

   For TIO2, the auxiliary regression equation has the form

$$LNY = 0.17987 + 0.63878*LNCP \qquad R^2 = 0.8866$$
$$\quad (0.386) \quad (10.46) \qquad\qquad DW = 1.0613.$$

For POLY, $LNUC = 1.0081 - 0.22129*LNCP - 0.0570*LNY \quad R^2 = 0.9732$
$$\qquad\quad (8.760) \quad (5.010) \qquad\qquad (1.205) \qquad DW = 0.9851.$$

The simple learning curve regression for POLY is

$$LNUC = 1.0040 - 0.27167*LNCP \qquad R^2 = 0.9694$$
$$\qquad (8.555) \quad (18.657) \qquad\qquad DW = 0.8409$$

and the POLY auxiliary regression equation is

$$LNY = 0.07162 + 0.88383*LNCP \qquad R^2 = 0.8956$$
$$\qquad (0.098) \quad (9.716) \qquad\qquad DW = 2.4418.$$

Note that estimates of returns to scale and the learning curve elasticity in the multiple regression can be computed using equation (3.35) in the text. Returns to scale estimates turn out to be 1.1502 for TIO2 and 1.0604 for POLY, while the learning curve elasticity estimates are -0.3477 and -0.2347, respectively. Based on the t-statistics from these multiple regressions, in each of the two equations the null hypothesis of constant returns to scale cannot be rejected.

(b) The omitted variable bias follows the algebra presented in equation (3.38) of the text, where $a_1 - b_1 = d_1 b_2$. Using numbers given in (a) above, for TIO2,

$$-0.3857 - (-0.3023) = -0.0834 = 0.6388*-0.1306$$

while for POLY,

$$-0.27167 - (-0.22129) = -0.05038 = 0.88383*-0.0570.$$

In these cases, the bias is relatively small because the OLS estimate of b_2 is not very large. As expected, however, d_1 is positive in both cases.

(c) As shown above in part (a), the R^2 from the multiple regression is always larger than that from the simple regression, for the simple regression corresponds to a model with a zero constraint imposed, and the error sum of squares from an unconstrained regression is always $\leq$ to that from a constrained regression.

(d) To do this F-statistic using the change in the error sums of squared version of the test, students will need to do a constrained regression in which LNUC is regressed on only a constant term. For TIO2, the F-statistic corresponding to the null hypothesis that both slope coefficients are zero is 56.3396 with 2 and 13 degrees of freedom, while for POLY it is 121.2819 with 2 and 10 degrees of freedom; in both cases, the null is decisively rejected. The pattern of test results corresponds to that in case (ii) discussed in Section 3.5.3 of the text—which is a rather common outcome.

Exercise 3: R^2 in Simple and Multiple Regressions—A Surprise

TASKS: Compare the R^2 in a multiple regression to those from two simple regressions—and find a somewhat surprising outcome.

COMMENTS: Students who do this exercise will tend not to forget it, for the example is rather striking.

(a) The simple correlations are relatively innocuous—0.00250 (Y,X1), 0.43407 (Y,X2) and -0.89978 (X1,X2).

(b) In time series applications, frequently the R^2 from simple regressions is above 0.9—hence it is often the case that the sum of R^2's from K simple regressions is less than the R^2 in a multiple regression with K regressors. As we shall now see, however, this is not always the case.

(c,d) In the first simple regression, we have (with t-statistics in parentheses)

$$Y = 11.989 + 0.0037476*X1 \qquad R^2 = 0.0000062401$$
$$(9.463) \quad (0.009007)$$

indicating that Y is almost orthogonal to X1. In the second simple regression

$$Y = 10.632 + 0.19546*X2 \qquad R^2 = 0.188416$$
$$(13.111) \quad (1.7373)$$

the R^2 is a bit higher, but still not that high. Note that in both simple regressions, by the t-statistic criterion neither coefficient is statistically significant. The sum of the R^2 from these two regressions is 0.1884222401.

Incidentally, if one runs an auxiliary regression of X2 on X1, one obtains

$$X2 = 15.995 - 2.9978*X1 \qquad R^2 = 0.809598$$
$$\quad (13.028) \ (-7.4348)$$

which is also uninspiring. However, the multiple regression turns out to be

$$Y = -4.5154 + 3.0970*X1 + 1.0319*X2, \quad R^2 = 0.999847$$
$$\quad (-73.851) \ (252.31) \qquad (280.08)$$

whose R^2 is much larger than the sum of the two bivariate R^2's. Notice also the large magnitude of the t-statistics.

For a discussion, see the Harold Watts article referenced in the text, as well as the piece by David Hamilton, from which this data set is taken.

Exercise 4: Replicating Nerlove's Classic Results on Scale Economies

TASKS: Generate log-transformed variables, do a multiple regression, compute confidence intervals and estimates of returns to scale, interpret plausibility of parameter estimates and compute and plot residuals.

COMMENTS: You will find it is not possible to replicate Nerlove's results exactly. But the same qualitative findings emerge.

(a) Notice that observations are not quite monotonic in KWH—observations whose values for the ORDER variable are 119-120, 324-325 and 408-409 contain instances where KWH declines with increases in ORDER. These might be typos from the original data used by Nerlove.

(b) The estimated OLS equation you obtain should look like this:

$$LNCP3 = -4.6908 + 0.72069*LNKWH + 0.59291*LNP13 - 0.00738*LNP23 \quad R^2 = 0.9316$$
$$\quad (-5.301) \quad (41.334) \qquad\quad (2.898) \qquad\quad (-0.039)$$

where t-statistics are in parentheses. Note that this estimate of β_y is close to that of Nerlove, as is the R^2, but estimates of β_1 and β_2 differ by a larger amount.

(c) With a 95% critical t-value of 1.96, the 95% confidence interval for β_y is 0.72069 plus or minus 1.96*.017436, which turns out to be P[0.686515 $\leq$ $\beta_y \leq$ 0.754865] = 0.95.   Hence the null hypothesis that β_y = 1 is rejected, implying that constant returns to scale is also rejected.   The implied estimate of returns to scale, r = $1/b_y$, is here equal to 1/0.72069 = 1.3876, which implies that returns to scale are increasing, and scale economies are positive.

(d) The implied estimate of α_2, based on equation (3.22) is b_2*b_y, which in this case is equal to -0.00738*0.72069 = -0.00532.   Because of the nonlinearities, it is not immediately clear whether this estimate of α_2 is statistically significant, although it would not be surprising if it were not (if one employs a nonlinear regression, the estimated asymptotic t-statistic for α_2 turns out to be -0.0387).   The fact that the estimate of α_2 is negative, however, is unattractive, for if the marginal product of capital is positive, this coefficient should also be positive.

(e) Roughly speaking, the residuals seem to follow a U-shape pattern when plotted against LNKWH.   However, since LNKWH is a regressor, the first order conditions for obtaining the least squares estimates ensure that the sample correlation of residuals with LNKWH over the entire sample is zero.

Exercise 5: Assessing Alternative Returns to Scale Specifications

TASKS: Partition sample into five sub-groups, and estimate by OLS a multiple regression for each sub-group.   Notice pattern of returns to scale estimate with level of KWH production.   Then estimate a variety of other, related specifications, and compare returns to scale results.

COMMENTS: Again, you will find students will be unable to replicate Nerlove's reported results exactly, although the qualitative findings are essentially unchanged.

(a) The results you obtain should look something like this (absolute values of t-statistics are in parentheses):

Parameter Estimated:	β_y	β_1	β_2	R^2
Sub-sample I	0.40029 (4.740)	0.61517 (0.843)	-0.08136 (0.115)	0.5134
Sub-sample II	0.65815 (5.659)	0.09380 (0.342)	0.37794 (1.367)	0.6328
Sub-sample III	0.93828 (4.740)	0.40226 (2.017)	0.25001 (1.337)	0.5732
Sub-sample IV	0.91204 (8.485)	0.59686 (2.704)	-0.09335 (0.569)	0.8726
Sub-sample V	1.0444 (16.072)	0.60259 (3.054)	-0.28944 (1.655)	0.9210

Estimates of β_y are quite close to those reported by Nerlove (see the Exercise in the text for his results), but in Sub-sample IV the estimates of β_1 and β_2 differ considerably from those reported by him.

(b) The five implied returns to scale estimates are (in the same order as above): 2.4982, 1.5194, 1.0658, 1.0964 and 0.9575, which tend to fall with size, although not quite perfectly so. Obviously, one wants a specification where the degree of returns to scale is not constrained to be the same value over the entire sample.

(c) When this model is estimated, the five intercept terms (in the same order as above, and with absolute values of t-statistics in parentheses) turn out to be -4.1798 (5.952), -5.0524 (4.491), -6.630 (2.964), -6.729 (3.024) and -8.083 (5.857); the five estimates of β_y are 0.397 (9.214), 0.648 (4.402), 0.885 (2.976), 0.909 (3.321) and 1.063 (8.091); the common estimates of β_1 and β_2 are 0.4256 (2.608) and 0.1037 (0.681), while the equation R^2 is 0.9602.

(d) The implied returns to scale estimates based on the β_y estimates reported in (c) above are 2.5197, 1.5428, 1.1302, 1.1004 and 0.9410. In this case, returns to scale fall monotonically with LNKWH across the sub-groups.

(e) The sum of squared residuals from the constrained regression in (c) is 12.5773, while those for the five regressions in (a) are 8.88522, 1.46905, 0.980163, 0.363593 and 0.564404; these five sum to 12.26243. Assuming homoskedasticity across sub-samples (in this case this appears to be a dubious assumption, especially for Sub-sample I compared to the others), the F-statistic with 8 and 125 degrees of freedom is 0.3912, which is less than the corresponding critical value at typical significance levels. Hence the null hypothesis associated with (c) as a special case of (a) is not rejected.

(f) The equation estimated using Nerlove's reported data should look something like this (with absolute values of t-statistics in parentheses):

$$LNCP3 = -3.7646 + .1526*LNY + .0505*(LNY)^2 + .4806*LNP13 + .0742*LNP23$$
$$\quad\quad (5.365) \quad (2.466) \quad\quad (9.418) \quad\quad\quad (2.984) \quad\quad\quad (0.494)$$

with an R^2 of 0.9581. Note that this estimate of β_{yy} is quite different from that reported by Nerlove—here it is roughly only half the size of Nerlove's estimate.

To test the null hypothesis of constant returns to scale, i.e., to test $\beta_y = 1$ and $\beta_{yy} = 0$, it is useful first to define a new dependent variable as LNNEW ≡ LNCP3 - LNY, and then run a regression of LNNEW on a constant, LNP13 and LNP23; this corresponds to the constrained run in which constant returns to scale is imposed, i.e., $\beta_y = 1$ and $\beta_{yy} = 0$. Then do an unconstrained run with LNNEW regressed on a constant term, LNY, $(LNY)^2$, LNP13 and LNP23—note that this places no restrictions on returns to scale, although the estimate on the LNY variable should now be interpreted as $\beta_y - 1$, due to the redefining of the dependent variable. The sum of squared residuals from this unconstrained regression is 283.856, while that from the constrained regression is 622.471; the corresponding F-statistic with 2 and 140 degrees of freedom is 83.5038, which is much larger than the critical value at any reasonable level of significance. Hence the null hypothesis of constant returns to scale is decisively rejected.

Finally, returns to scale at the median output level firms in each of the five sub-samples are estimated to equal 1.87782, 1.34982, 1.16161, 1.07381 and 0.97243.

Exercise 6: Comparing RTS Estimates from 1955 with Updated 1970 Data

TASKS: Generate logarithmic transformation of variables, compare sample means of KWH in 1955 and 1970, estimate by OLS a multiple regression equation, compute confidence intervals and implied returns to scale estimates and compare these 1970 results with those from 1955 reported by Nerlove.

COMMENTS: This is a useful exercise for demonstrating the changes in electricity generation that occurred from 1955 to 1970. Also, as noted earlier, the SK, SL and SF cost share data in the UPDATE file are not used in any of the exercises in this chapter. Instructors might want to use this data for additional exercises in Chapter 9 on interrelated factor demand models.

(a) The sample mean of the KWH variable for the 1970 data is 8999.73, while that from 1955 is much smaller at 2133.1; in 1955 the range of smallest to largest was from 2.0 to 16719, while in 1970 it varied from 8.0 to 53918. It seems reasonable to conclude therefore that electric utility companies in 1970 were on balance generating much larger levels of KWH than in 1955.

(b) Using the 1970 data, estimates of β_0, β_y, β_1 and β_2 (absolute values of t-statistics in parentheses) turn out to be -6.8851 (11.720), 0.8214 (61.003), 0.0987 (0.737) and 0.0214 (0.169). A 95% confidence interval for β_y is from 0.7950 to 0.8478. Given the small standard error for β_y (0.013465), the null hypothesis of constant returns to scale ($\beta_y = 1$) is decisively rejected; 1.00 does not fall in this 95% confidence interval. The estimated value of β_y at 0.82141 implies an estimate of returns to scale equal to 1.2174, which is somewhat smaller than the 1.3876 estimate for the 1955 data, as reported in Exercise 4, part (b). Since generation levels are larger, this smaller estimate of returns to scale is entirely plausible.

(c) Estimates of β_0, β_y, β_{yy}, β_1 and β_2 with the 1970 data are (absolute values of t-statistics in parentheses) -7.7675 (14.135), 0.8953 (47.838), 0.0426 (5.133), 0.0370 (0.309) and 0.0337 (0.299), respectively. The null hypothesis that $\beta_{yy} = 0$ (that returns to scale does not depend on the level of output) is decisively rejected, given the 5.133 t-statistic. So too is the null hypothesis of constant returns to scale.

(d) The results you obtain with the UPDATE 1970 data should look something like this (absolute values of t-statistics are in parentheses):

Parameter Estimated:	β_y	β_1	β_2	R^2
Sub-sample I	0.66951 (14.63)	0.26328 (0.594)	-0.08843 (0.203)	0.9307
Sub-sample II	0.81290 (5.830)	-0.52252 (2.090)	0.37561 (1.549)	0.7126
Sub-sample III	1.1882 (10.76)	0.12152 (0.893)	-0.19026 (1.377)	0.8803
Sub-sample IV	0.91204 (8.485)	0.59686 (2.704)	-0.09335 (0.569)	0.8726
Sub-sample V	0.86948 (5.652)	-0.03555 (0.276)	0.09781 (0.811)	0.6997

The returns to scale estimates implied by the five β_y estimates are 1.4936, 1.2302, 0.8416, 1.0964 and 1.1501. At smaller levels of output, returns to scale in 1970 are smaller than in 1955, but the reverse holds at larger levels of output.

(e) This conclusion may be supported by the data, but to conclude with that result it would be useful to weight the estimated returns to scale of each firm by the relative KWH output it produced, and thereby obtain an output-weighted estimate of returns to scale. If this were much closer to one in 1970 than in 1955, then the conclusion would hold.

Exercise 7: Autocorrelation in the Learning Curve Model

TASKS: Estimate bivariate and multivariate versions of the learning curve model, and test for autocorrelation using the Durbin-Watson test statistic. Then estimate the same models by GLS, and compare results.

COMMENTS: Students can choose either the TIO2 or POLY data; if the TIO2 data are employed, they must first be deflated (see the beginning of Exercises 1 and 2 in this chapter for details).

(a) The OLS parameter estimates for the POLY and TIO2 models are reported above, for Exercise 1(a) and 2(b). The results reported there also include Durbin-Watson test statistics, indicating that the null hypothesis that $\rho = 0$ is rejected at typical significance levels.

(b) With the POLY data and the generalized learning curve model, the iterative Cochrane-Orcutt procedure yields an estimate of ρ equal to 0.7003, with an asymptotic standard error of 0.206; although the sample size is rather small (T = 13), the ratio of ρ to its estimated asymptotic standard error is still quite large (3.398), suggesting that first order autocorrelation is likely to be present. With this GLS procedure, the estimates of β_1 and β_2 are -0.2960 and -0.0385 (t-values are 5.906 and 1.224), suggesting a slightly larger learning curve elasticity (in absolute value) and slightly smaller returns to scale with GLS, as compared to the OLS results.

With the TIO2 data and the generalized learning curve model, the iterative Cochrane-Orcutt estimate of ρ is 0.6727, the asymptotic standard error is 0.1911 and their ratio is 3.5208, again implying that first order autocorrelation may be present, although the small sample size of 16 warrants that caution be used in applying large sample distribution theory results. With this GLS procedure, the estimates of β_1 and β_2 are -0.4776 and -0.1320 (t-values are 4.493 and 1.211), suggesting a considerably larger learning curve elasticity (in absolute value) and almost identical returns to scale with GLS, as compared to the OLS results.

The only surprise here is that in both cases, when one allows for first order autocorrelation, the estimate of the learning curve elasticity increases in absolute value.

Exercise 8: Misspecification in the Nerlove Returns to Scale Model

TASKS: Estimate a multiple regression model by OLS using cross-sectional data, and then use the Durbin-Watson test statistic as a diagnostic for equation misspecification.

COMMENTS: Here you use the Durbin-Watson test statistic in a somewhat unorthodox way, particularly since the data is cross-sectional. Since the data are ordered by firm size, autocorrelation in the residuals provides a diagnostic on whether residuals are systematically related to firm size. But in this case, the "fix" for a significant Durbin-Watson test statistic is not to do GLS, but rather to work on the specification of the underlying model. In general, one should not rely on the Durbin-Watson to uncover misspecification in cross-sectional data, but its use here is instructive to students in becoming familiar with the interpretation of common test procedures in somewhat unconventional circumstances.

(a) The equation estimated is that whose results are reported above in Exercise 4(b). The Durbin-Watson test statistic is 1.1054, which suggests a possible problem with autocorrelation, although at some plausible significance levels the inference is inconclusive. Incidentally, if one retrieves the residuals from this regression and then runs a regression of the residuals on a constant term and $(LNKWH)^2$, the slope coefficient estimate is positive (0.00236) but not that significant (t = 1.625).

(b) Fix the model, not the disturbances!

Exercise 9: Testing for Parameter Equality in the 1955 and 1970 RTS Models

TASKS: Use the Chow test procedure to test for parameter equality among groups within the 1955 and 1970 samples, and between them.

COMMENTS: This is a good exercise for students to appreciate the value of the Chow test procedure. For parts (a) and (b), parameter estimates were reported earlier (see results of Exercises 5 and 6 above). To conserve on space, I will simply report the Chow test final results, and not the detailed calculations.

(a) The sum of the sum of squared residuals from the five separate 1955 equations is 12.26243, while that from the pooled constrained equation is 21.6403; the resulting F-statistic with 16 and 125 degrees of freedom is 5.9747, which is greater than the critical value at typical significance levels. Hence the null hypothesis of parameter equality here is rejected.

(b) The sum of the sum of squared residuals from the five separate 1970 equations is 2.619393, while that from the pooled constrained equation is 3.72331; the resulting F-statistic with 16 and 79 degrees of freedom is 2.0809, larger than the critical value at typical significance levels (specifically, at any significance level less than 98.266%). Hence the null hypothesis of parameter equality here is rejected again, although not as decisively as with the 1955 data.

(c) The constrained run with the 1955 and 1970 pooled data yields a sum of squared residuals equal to 29.7035; the sum of the five SSR in 1955 was noted in (a) above to be 12.26243, while in (b) that for the five 1970 regressions was 2.619393, yielding a grand sum over the ten sub-samples of 14.881823. The F-statistic with 36 and 204 degrees of freedom is 5.6438; hence the null hypothesis is decisively rejected. When the alternative hypothesis is changed to parameter equality among companies within the 1955 and within the 1970 samples, the unconstrained sum of squared residuals is

21.6403 + 3.72331 = 25.36361 (see parts (a) and (b) above). Now the Chow test statistic becomes 10.0953, which is larger than the critical F-statistic with 4 and 236 degrees of freedom at typical significance levels. Again, the null hypothesis of parameter equality is decisively rejected.

(d) For the generalized Cobb-Douglas model with varying returns to scale, the sum of squared residuals for the 1955 data is 13.2475, for the 1970 data it is 3.72331 and for the pooled 1955 and 1970 data it is 29.3542; the Chow test statistic with 5 and 234 degrees of freedom is 34.1494, suggesting decisive rejection of the null hypothesis.

(e) The cost and price data are in 1955 dollars in the 1955 data set, and in 1970 dollars in the 1970 data set. As a result, one would expect intercept terms to differ in the two data sets, although elasticity (slope coefficient) estimates are directly comparable. Hence one would in fact want to do a slightly amended Chow test for parameter equality over time, either by deflating the data to a common year, or by testing for equality of only the slope coefficients. It would not be surprising, however, for the null hypothesis of parameter equality between 1955 and 1970 still to be rejected.

Exercise 10: Forecasting Unit Cost After Further Learning Occurs

TASKS: Estimate a bivariate learning curve model by OLS, construct an out-of-sample forecast for unit cost, as well as an estimated forecast error variance. Comment on factors affecting the size of the forecast confidence interval.

COMMENTS: This exercise will help emphasize to the student the rather enormous adverse impact of small sample size on the forecast error variance. As a practical matter, it calls into question the usefulness of a learning curve regression equation in forecasting unit costs precisely, when the estimated equation is based on a rather small sample.

(a) OLS estimates of the POLY and TIO2 bivariate learning curve equation are given in Exercise 1(b) above.

(b) For POLY, the cumulative production at which unit cost is to be forecasted is 50,000, while for TIO2 it is 6976; natural logarithms of these values are 10.81978 and 8.85023. Hence forecasted LNUC is -1.9354 for POLY and -1.9996 for TIO2. If one simply exponentiates these forecasted LNUC (and strictly speaking, this is not quite appropriate), the forecasted unit costs are 0.14437 and 0.13538.

(c) In the sample, the variance of $\ln n_t$ was 2.0791 for POLY and 0.12816 for TIO2; multiplying these by 12 and 15, respectively, yields the value of the summation term in the denominator of the equation in Exercise 10; these values are 24.9492 and 1.9224, respectively. Since the sample mean of $\ln n_t$ is 7.9400 for POLY and 7.6249 for TIO2, the entire term in the square brackets in the equation of Exercise 10 is 1.40932 for POLY and 1.70406 for TIO2. Given estimates of the standard error of the regression, 0.07273 for POLY and 0.04993 for TIO2, squaring these and multiplying by the term in square brackets yields a forecasted error variance for POLY equal to 0.00745, and a standard error of the forecast equal to 0.0863; for TIO2, the forecasted error variance is 0.004248, and the standard error of the forecast is 0.0652.

Finally, to compute 95% confidence intervals, use t-critical values of 2.20 for POLY and 2.14 for TIO2. Hence for POLY, the 95% confidence interval for forecasted LNUC is -1.9354 plus or minus 2.20*0.0863, or between -2.1253 and -1.74554, while for TIO2 it is -1.9996 plus or minus 2.14*0.04993, or between -2.1064 and -1.8928; when exponentiated, these confidence intervals become 0.1193 and 0.1746 for POLY, and 0.1217 and 0.1506 for TIO2. Especially for POLY, this confidence interval for the forecast is very large.

(d) It is clear from the equation in Exercise 10 that the forecast error variance declines with increases in T, and when T is rather small, this forecast error can be reduced considerably by adding observations.   Also, the further away is the value of x_T from that of the sample mean, other things equal, the greater the forecast error variance.

FINAL COMMENTS:

It is often quite easy to obtain data on prices and cumulative production, but data on unit costs are more difficult to come by.   Some studies simply use average labor costs as a proxy for average total cost.   For data from some other studies, see the papers cited in Chapter 3 by Gallant [1968], by Womer and Patterson [1983] and by Womer [1984].

INSTRUCTOR'S NOTES FOR CHAPTER FOUR:

THE MEASUREMENT OF QUALITY CHANGE: CONSTRUCTING AN HEDONIC
PRICE INDEX FOR COMPUTERS USING MULTIPLE REGRESSION METHODS

ECONOMETRIC PROCEDURES EMPLOYED IN THE EXERCISES OF CHAPTER FOUR:

- Perform OLS multiple regression, and compute means, variances and
  covariances of data

- Compute R^2 and other measures of goodness of fit

- Run a regression of actual Y on fitted Y and a constant term, and
  interpret results

- Generate log-transformations of the variables, construct dummy
  variables and then compute quality-adjusted price indexes

- Allow for heteroskedasticity by doing weighted least squares

- Interpret coefficients on time dummy variables by replacing them
  with a single continuous time variable

- Do traditional and modified Chow tests for parameter equality over
  subsets of coefficients

- Compute a chained price index based on adjacent-year regressions
More-advanced procedures:

- Test for homoskedasticity

- Use Box-Cox and Box-Tidwell procedures to choose a functional form

GOALS FOR CHAPTER FOUR:

To help students gain an understanding of how price indexes are
constructed and interpreted, how quality and price are related, and how
multiple regression analysis can be used to account for the effects of
quality change on price. Attention is focused on the interpretation of
estimated coefficients in a multiple regression, including the dummy
variable parameters.

GENERAL COMMENTS TO THE INSTRUCTOR:

This chapter is somewhat different from the preceding ones in that the role of economic theory is very limited, and more "data analysis" is employed. However, students will find the tasks of replicating classic findings and interpreting the results to be challenging and most interesting.

Exercises 1 through 6 employ procedures typically taught in the multiple regression portion of an econometrics course (although generalized least squares issues are encountered in Exercises 3(e) and 5(d)), but Exercise 7 utilizes the Box-Cox estimation method and therefore requires familiarity with more advanced material.

COMMENTS ON SPECIFIC EXERCISES:

Exercise 1: Examining Waugh's 1927 Data

TASKS: An OLS multiple regression is performed, and the underlying summary statistics of the data are compared to those originally reported by Waugh in his pioneering 1929 Ph.D. dissertation.

COMMENTS: The purpose of this exercise is to involve students in an important process of the scientific method, namely, an attempt to replicate others' empirical findings (here, only partially successful).

(a) The fitted equation you obtain here should look something like the following (absolute values of t-statistics in parentheses):

PRICE = 40.761 + 0.13760*GREEN - 1.3573*NOSTALKS - 0.34528*DISPERSE
      (7.651)   (19.382)   (8.999)   (2.663)

having an R^2 of 0.726799. Note that the coefficient on DISPERSE is quite different from that reported by Waugh, reproduced in equation (4.3).

(b) The sample means you compute should be the same as those reported by Waugh.

(c) The variance-covariance matrix you compute will look something like

	PRICE	GREEN	NOSTALKS	DISPERSE
PRICE	868.740	3448.185	-93.385	-87.430
GREEN		24439.384	-17.092	-180.057
NOSTALKS			60.731	24.924
DISPERSE				83.487

(I've rounded off), which is quite different from that presented in Exercise 1. Note that there's no ordinal relationship between these and Waugh—some are larger than Waugh's, others are smaller.

(d) For the GREEN attribute, results obtained here suggest that an extra inch of GREEN raises the price by 0.13760*2.782 cents, or 38.3 cents, whereas Waugh reported 38.5; for NOSTALKS, while Waugh reported a partial effect of 4.6 cents (he should have reported 4.3 cents, since 1.53394*2.782 = 4.2674), here the effect is smaller at 3.8 cents (1.3573*2.782 = 3.7760). These results are therefore not qualitatively different from those reported by him.

(e) Not clear.

Exercise 2: Exploring Relationships Among R^2, Coefficients of Determination and Correlation Coefficients

TASKS: Compute a correlation matrix among the variables, run several bivariate regressions and their reciprocals, observe and interpret what happens to R^2 when you add a regressor, compute and interpret coefficients of determination and then run a regression of actual Y on a constant and fitted Y, comparing the R^2 and interpreting the zero and unit coefficients.

COMMENTS: The goal of this exercise is to gain an understanding of relationships among the various coefficients of determination, R^2 and correlation coefficients, as well as to comprehend better the implications of the extent of correlation among regressors.

(a) Note that GREEN and PRICE are most highly correlated, while GREEN and NOSTALKS are almost orthogonal.

(b) The three R^2 values are 0.560017, 0.165293 and 0.105394. The square roots of these R^2 values are equal to the corresponding sample correlation coefficients in the table, since in the bivariate regression model R^2 also happens to equal the square of the simple correlation coefficient. The R^2's from the reciprocal regressions are identical, since they in fact again are nothing other than the square of the simple correlation coefficient between X and Y.

(c) Since an omitted variable effectively has a coefficient constrained to zero, when a variable is added to a regression equation the sum of squared residuals cannot increase, but will usually decrease. The almost orthogonal relationship between GREEN and NOSTALKS does not tell us much about how large a change in R^2 will be when NOSTALKS is added as a regressor, for in this case that will depend more on the relationship between NOSTALKS and PRICE, which is modest; in fact, the R^2 increases to 0.714040. Similarly, there's very little intuition on relative changes in R^2 in the other two regressions. Incidentally, in the Goldberger [1968] book, there's a very useful presentation of R^2's in simple and multiple regressions, and how to interpret them.

(d) On this issue, Exercise 3 in Chapter 3 is really very dramatic.

(e) Using equation (4.3), you should obtain a value of 0.44597 for the coefficient of determination for GREEN. Regarding the last issue, the number should have been the R^2 value of 0.726799 (see Exercise 1 above), not the 0.57524 value given by Waugh.

(f) The R^2 is the same, and except for rounding error, the intercept is zero and the slope coefficient is one. This simply follows from the algebra of least squares and correlation coefficients. You might want to have students demonstrate this analytically.

Exercise 3: Alternative Price Indexes for Computers Based on Chow's Data

TASKS: Construct transformed and dummy variables, compute and comment on correlation matrices, check for colinearity, do multiple regressions, compute a price index series by taking anti-logarithms of estimated dummy variable coefficients, specify and estimate a more general specification and test the implicit hypothesis, estimate a model by weighted least squares assuming specific form of heteroskedasticity and compare estimated coefficients and standard errors with OLS estimates.

COMMENTS: The goals of this exercise are to construct a price index for computers using hedonic regression techniques, to replicate Chow's results and then to assess the stability of the price index to several changes in specification.

(a) The highest simple correlation between regressors in the entire 137 observation sample is 0.87557—that between LNMULT and LNACCESS (0.86269 in 1954-59 and 0.77393 in 1960-65), but these values are not particularly worrisome. Correlation patterns in the two sub-periods are roughly similar, although correlation coefficients generally appear to be lower in absolute value in the 1960-65 sub-sample. While some colinearity is present, it is not so high as to worry about computational accuracy or inability to obtain clear statistical inference.

(b) You should be able to replicate these results, as reported in Tables 4.1 and 4.2 in the text.

(c) Since LNMEM = LN(BINARY*DIGITS*WORDS), LNMEM = LNLENGTH + LNWORDS when LNLENGTH ≡ LN(BINARY*DIGITS). OLS estimates of the coefficients on LNLENGTH and LNWORDS are 0.33681 and 0.23000, having standard errors of 0.05935 and 0.06596, respectively. The F-statistic (using the relative change in the sum of squared residuals procedure) with 1 and 72 degrees of freedom is $[(10.7732 - 10.6709)/10.6709]*72 = 0.690$, which is less than the 0.05

critical value at most any reasonable significance level. Hence the null hypothesis is not rejected, lending support to Chow's specification.

(d) The 1954-65 price index series resulting from this regression is 1.000, 0.9469, 0.8087, 0.7524, 0.6213, 0.4995, 0.3205, 0.2900, 0.1975, 0.1768, 0.1316 and 0.0997. The two indexes compare rather favorably; from 1954 to 1965, Triplett's best practice price index declines by a factor of about 11 (1139 to 100), while the index here declines by about a factor of ten (1.000 to 0.0997).

(e) With this type of heteroskedasticity, results are altered. In particular, the GLS estimate on LNMULT changes sign, and the rate of quality-adjusted price decline is considerably smaller, for with GLS the coefficient on DUM65 is -0.7365, whereas with OLS it was -1.163. Interestingly, not all standard error estimates increase with the use of GLS—see, for example, the standard errors on LNMULT and DUM65 which are smaller under GLS.

Exercise 4: Price Indexes for Disk Drives—A Closer Look at the IBM Study

TASKS: Estimate by OLS an hedonic regression equation with time dummy variables, replicate old and compare with revised results, test homogeneity hypothesis and compare specifications with discrete dummy and continuous time variables.

COMMENTS: The purpose of this exercise is to replicate, interpret and extend selected results reported by Cole et al. in the IBM study of price indexes for hard disk drives.

(a) You should be able to replicate the results reported at the beginning of Exercise 4 in the text, except for s, which should be 0.22495, not 0.51.

(b) With the revised data, results are not affected much. In particular, the dummy variable coefficients change little, the coefficient on

LNSPEED changes from 0.41 to 0.39 (t = 3.1), while that on LNCAP remains at 0.46 (t = 5.8). The R^2 falls slightly to 0.834 from 0.844, and the new standard error of the regression is 0.22980.

(c) A standard deviation for the estimated sum of the two coefficients is 0.0743, while the point estimate of their sum is 0.84967; if one multiplies the standard deviation by 1.96 (roughly corresponding with a 95% t-value with 76 degrees of freedom), the 95% confidence interval barely excludes 1.000—it goes from 0.7040 to 0.9953. Hence at the 95% significance level the null hypothesis of linear homogeneity in attributes is barely rejected. It is worth noting, incidentally, that in her preferred regression runs, Dulberger had variables in addition to LNSPEED and LNCAP as regressors, and it was from these augmented regression runs that she reported nonrejection of the null hypothesis of linear homogeneity.

(d) This alternative estimated equation has the form (with absolute values of t-statistics in parentheses)

$$LNPRICE = 9.781 + 0.434*LNSPEED + 0.443*LNCAP - 0.105*TIME$$
$$\quad\;\; (15.30) \quad (3.988) \qquad\quad (6.746) \qquad\quad (8.424)$$

with an R^2 of 0.824 and an estimated standard error of the regression equal to 0.2199. This parsimonious specification is also supported by the results of the hypothesis test; the F-statistic with 11 and 76 degrees of freedom is 0.372, which is insignificant at most any reasonable level of significance. The null hypothesis of constant price decline is consistent with the data. On average, therefore, adjusted for quality change, prices for hard disk drives declined at about 10.5% per year over the 1972-84 time period.

Exercise 5: Assessing the Stability of the Hedonic Price Equation for First and Second Generation Computers

TASKS: Assess parameter equality over subsets of the Chow data, using a variant of the Chow test procedure, based on a number of multiple regressions.

COMMENTS: The issue of special interest here is whether the characteristics of first (1954-59) and second (1960-65) generation computers were priced identically in the marketplace. While <u>a priori</u> it would appear that stable pricing was unlikely to be the case, the small sample sizes used in estimation might yield rather imprecisely estimated parameters. For the most part, this is what happens with this data.

(a) The sums of squared residuals for the 1960 through 1965 regressions are 1.15465, 0.927399, 1.68995, 0.873766, 1.36874 and 3.02185, respectively, while that for the 1960-65 pooled regression with differing intercepts by year is 10.7732. The F-statistic is therefore computed as $[(10.7732 - 9.0364)/9.0364]*(58/15) = 0.743$, which is similar to the 0.74 value reported by Chow.

(b) The sums of squared residuals for the 1954 through 1959 regressions are 0.291086, 0.293471, 1.02209, 0.968198, 0.328629 and 0.147483, respectively, while that for the 1954-59 pooled regression with differing intercepts by year is 4.27982. The F-statistic is therefore computed as $[(4.27982-3.050857)/3.050857]*(31/15) = 0.833$, which is less than the F-critical value at usual significance levels. Again, the null hypothesis of parameter equality within this generation of computers is not rejected. Incidentally, you'll not be able to replicate any of Chow's 1955 through 1958 results, and will only be successful for 1959; why this is so is not clear, but see the discussion in the text accompanying Exercise 5.

(c) As noted in parts (a) and (b) above, the sums of squared residuals from the partially pooled 1954-59 and 1960-65 regressions are 4.27982 and 10.7732; that from a similarly partially pooled model (equal slopes, but different intercepts) for the overall 1954-65 time period is 16.4664. The F-statistic with 3 and 119 degrees of freedom is therefore computed as $[(16.4662-15.0530)/15.0530]*(119/3) = 3.72$, which is larger than the critical value at usual significance levels. The somewhat interesting result here, therefore, is that the pricing of characteristics in second generation computer models differed from that in first generation computers.

From (a) and (b) above, the grand sum of sums of squared residuals from the twelve separate year-by-year regressions is 3.050857 + 9.0364 = 12.087257. Comparing this with the 1954-65 partially pooled sum of squared residuals in (c), we have an F-statistic computed as $[(16.4664-12.087257)/12.087257]*(89/33) = 0.977$, which is less than the F-critical value at most any reasonable level of significance. The null hypothesis of parameter equality here is therefore not rejected.

Note that the inference changes from "reject" to "not reject," depending on the alternative hypothesis. When within-generation parameter equality is imposed (which is not rejected statistically), parameters from the two generations are computed with sufficient precision to reject the null of parameter equality between generations; but when within-generation parameter equality is not imposed, the parameters are not estimated as precisely, and therefore the confidence regions are larger. On balance, the appropriate conclusion would be that between the two generations, parameters changed.

(d) The Bartlett u-statistic (for a discussion see, for example, the "Big Daddy" Judge et al. textbook, pp. 447-449, referenced in Appendix I in this Instructor's Resource Guide) for homoskedasticity within the 1954-59 regressions is 37.38, while that for the within 1960-65 regressions is 82.08; hence 2 ln u, a χ^2 random variable with 5 degrees of freedom here, is 7.24 for 1954-59 and 8.82 for 1960-65. Since the 0.10 critical value is 9.24, the null hypothesis of homoskedasticity is not rejected. (Note that these calculations are based on the sums of squared residuals reported in parts (a) and (b) above, not those reported by Chow and reproduced in Table 4.1 in the text.) To test for homoskedasticity between the two generations, the Bartlett u-statistic becomes 1520.90, and 2 ln u is 14.65, which is greater than the χ^2

critical value with 1 degree of freedom at most any significance level. The implication here is that the rejection result reported in (c) above may be called into question, for under the null hypothesis homoskedasticity between generations was assumed, an assumption that is rejected here. Incidentally, see the "Big Daddy" Judge et al. text (or most other textbooks) for appropriate Chow test procedures in the presence of heteroskedasticity.

Exercise 6: Using Time-Varying Hedonic Price Equations to Construct Chained Price Indexes for Computers

TASKS: Estimate a series of eleven adjacent year regression equations, compute implicit price indexes and compare with the index based on a pooled regression that constrained slope coefficients to equality across all twelve years.

COMMENTS: Since the dummy variable specification in the series of twelve adjacent year regression equations refers to a continually shifting base year, a proper comparison of the two procedures involves comparing changes in the entirely pooled regression dummy variable coefficients to levels of dummy variable coefficients in the adjacent-year regressions.

(a) Changes (all with negative sign omitted) between the dummy variable coefficients in the pooled regression [levels of dummy variable coefficients in the adjacent year regressions] are, for 1954-55 through 1964-65: 0.054609 [0.06746], 0.15768 [0.13119], 0.07220 [0.12640], 0.19148 [0.34000], 0.21809 [0.20202], 0.44394 [0.50356], 0.1000 [0.04143], 0.3838 [0.28575], 0.1108 [0.1296], 0.2956 [0.31577] and 0.2776 [0.21824]. Especially for 1957-58 and 1960-61, the two procedures yield rather different results on percent changes in quality-adjusted prices between adjacent years.

(b) The adjacent-year regression yields the following price index for computers, quality-adjusted, for 1954-65: 1.0000, 0.9348, 0.7225, 0.5142,

0.4202, 0.2539, 0.2436, 0.1831, 0.1608, 0.1173 and 0.0943. Comparing these with those given above in Exercise 3(d), we see that the 1965 indexes are remarkably similar, 0.0997 for the pooled and 0.0943 for the adjacent-year regression model, although some year-to-year variations are more substantial. Which index is preferable is not clear on <u>a priori</u> grounds—see the text references for further discussion.

Exercise 7: <u>Exploring Alternative Functional Forms for the Hedonic Price Equation Using Box-Cox Procedures</u>

TASKS: Estimate parameters of hedonic price equations using Box-Cox or Box-Tidwell estimation procedures, and on the basis of the empirical findings, choose a preferred functional form specification.

COMMENTS: Doing this exercise thoroughly can take quite some time. Detailed results of such estimations have been written up in two MIT Alfred P. Sloan School of Management Working Papers. These are: Ernst R. Berndt, Mark H. Showalter and Jeffrey M. Wooldridge, "A Theoretical and Empirical Investigation of the Box-Cox Model and a Nonlinear Least Squares Alternative," July 1990; and by the same authors, "On the Sensitivity of Hedonic Price Indexes for Computers to the Choice of Functional Form," November 1990.

Based on Box-Cox and Box-Tidwell (quasi) maximum likelihood estimation procedures, the authors report that the restrictions associated with the log-log specification originally employed by Chow are not rejected, but support for the COLE et al. log-log specification is not as clear-cut. However, there are a number of serious scaling and other problems with the Box-Cox and Box-Tidwell estimation procedures; see the above papers for further discussion.

FINAL COMMENTS:

Other data sets that could be employed in alternative or additional exercises include data for cucumbers and tomatoes provided in Frederick Waugh's [1929] Ph.D. dissertation, and data on used trucks in Robert E. Hall

[1971]. On a more practical and close-to-home level, in many communities in the U.S. and Canada housing values are assessed by tax assessors using hedonic equations (some consulting firms now specialize in doing such analyses). The underlying real estate housing transactions price data, along with data on housing characteristics and attributes, may be available in your community, and your students might find that type of data to be particularly interesting.

Finally, the index number procedures used here based on hedonic regressions are very simple, particularly when compared to what in fact is done in some government statistical agencies and by other researchers. For a discussion and empirical implementation of how hedonic methods can be used to predict prices of goods prior to being on the market or after exiting it (such data are often needed in doing chained Divisia indexes), see Ernst R. Berndt and Zvi Griliches, "Price Indexes for Microcomputers: An Exploratory Study," Cambridge, MA: National Bureau of Economic Research Working Paper No. 3378, June 1990, as well as the references cited therein.

INSTRUCTOR'S NOTES FOR CHAPTER FIVE:

ANALYZING DETERMINANTS OF WAGES AND MEASURING WAGE DISCRIMINATION:
DUMMY VARIABLES IN REGRESSION MODELS

ECONOMETRIC PROCEDURES EMPLOYED IN THE EXERCISES OF CHAPTER FIVE:

- Generate log-transformed variables and dummy variables

- Compute arithmetic and geometric means, standard deviations

- Print data to screen and on to a "hard copy" printer

- Sort data by various characteristics and examine selected statistics
  for sub-groups

- Compare normal with log-normal distribution

- Perform OLS multiple regression with dummy variables, compute
  confidence intervals and comment on R^2

- Compare and verify empirically the numerical relationships that hold
  among alternative dummy variable specifications

- Construct, estimate and interpret models with dummy interaction
  variables

- Do several multiple regressions over subsets of data, and test for
  parameter equality among subsets using the Chow test procedure

- Use Blinder-Oaxaca procedure to measure and interpret wage
  discrimination by race, and by gender

More-advanced procedures:

- Calculate White's heteroskedasticity-consistent standard errors,
  test for homoskedasticity using White's augmented $T*R^2$ approach
  and do a weighted least squares regression

GOALS FOR CHAPTER FIVE:

To acquaint students with the human capital model—a widely accepted
framework for thinking about wage differentials, to provide a selective

survey of principal empirical findings on determinants of wages, and to involve students in computing and interpreting measures of wage discrimination by race and by gender.

GENERAL COMMENTS TO THE INSTRUCTOR:

This chapter addresses a number of controversial issues, generally concerned with analyzing determinants of wages and measures of wage discrimination. From my own experience, and from what I have learned from other instructors who have used this chapter, I know that students find the material in this chapter to be very engaging, provocative and instructive. It surely covers relevant material!

The last three exercises in this chapter use similar techniques to assess whether union members earn premium wages (#5) and to construct measures of wage discrimination by race (#6) and by gender (#7). I recommend that any student do only one of these three, for the tools are repetitious. A practice I have found to be quite useful is to divide the class into several groups, and using the data on the data diskette, have each group work on one of these three exercises as a team. In one case, I divided a class into four groups, assigned one group to present evidence in support of the argument that wage discrimination by race is large and increasing, another to present evidence for the counter view, and the last two groups to take opposite viewpoints on wage discrimination by gender. Each group made a class presentation, and was open to questions from the "other side." While certainly not feasible in all classroom settings, that experience was very instructive and valuable to students in that MBA class.

Exercises 1 through 7 use material typically taught up to and including the standard multiple regression model (with a bit of emphasis on dummy variables), but Exercise 8 requires knowledge of generalized least squares estimation.

As is noted in the text, it is highly recommended that all students work through Exercise 1, "A Review of Essential Facts—Inspecting the Data," using both the CPS78 and CPS85 data sets.

COMMENTS ON SPECIFIC EXERCISES IN CHAPTER FIVE:

Exercise 1: A Review of Essential Facts—Inspecting the Data

TASKS: Compute and compare arithmetic means, geometric means and standard deviations for the entire sample, and for data sorted into various sub-groups. As an option, students can compare the normal and log-normal statistical distributions to the distribution of wage rates.

COMMENTS: The purpose of this exercise is to help students become familiar with features of the data in CPS78 and CPS85, and to gain empirical experience in sorting data sets into relevant sub-groups.

(a) For CPS78, the arithmetic mean and standard deviation of LNWAGE are 1.68100 and 0.49016, respectively; the geometric mean is 5.3709, implying a 2000-hour annual income of $10,741.80. The mean of LNWAGE exponentiated is 6.06277, which is larger than the geometric mean, reflecting in part the presence of a fat upper tail in the distribution of wages. The mean and standard deviation of ED are 12.536 and 2.772, while those for EX are 18.718 and 13.347, respectively.

(b) The sample mean of NONWH is 0.10364, based on 57 individuals. The proportion and number of HISP individuals is 0.06545 and 36, while for FE it is 0.37636 and 207, respectively.

(c) The mean and standard deviation of ED for males is 12.399 and 3.052 years, while for females it is 12.763 and 2.220; the geometric mean wage rate for males is $6.128, and for females it is $4.316. The mean and standard deviation of ED for whites are 12.814 and 2.494, for NONWH 11.719 and 3.437 and for HISP 10.306 and 3.655, respectively. The mean and standard deviation of LNWAGE for whites are 1.71383 and 0.49143, for NONWH 1.51340 and 0.50053 and for HISP 1.52965 and 0.37126; the implied geometric means for wages are $5.55, $4.54 and $4.62, respectively. The variation of LNWAGE is largest for NONWH, as measured by the standard deviation.

(d) For CPS85, the overall mean and standard deviation of LNWAGE is 2.05918 and 0.52773, corresponding to a geometric mean wage rate of $7.84, or $4.75 in constant $1978, implying an annual wage income of $9500 constant $1978; the mean and standard deviation of exp(LNWAGE) is $9.02395 and $5.13887. For ED, the mean and standard deviation is 13.01873 and 2.61534 years, while for EX it is 17.82210 and 12.37971.

The number and proportion of white individuals in CPS85 is 440 and 82.40%, for NONWH it is 67 and 12.55%, for HISP it is 27 and 5.06% and for FE it is 245 and 45.88%. The mean and standard deviation of ED for males is 13.014 and 2.77, for FE 13.024 and 2.43, for whites 13.168 and 2.48, for NONWH 12.642 and 2.60 and for HISP 11.519 and 4.05; for LNWAGE, the numbers are 2.165 and 0.534 for males, 1.934 and 0.492 for FE, 2.088 and 0.528 for whites, 1.966 and 0.497 for NONWH and 1.819 and 0.530 for HISP. Amongst the races, as measured by the standard deviation, HISP have the greatest variation in LNWAGE, and among the genders, males display more variation. The implicit geometric mean wage rates are in current and 1978 constant $, respectively, $8.72 and $5.29 for males, $6.92 and $4.19 for FE, $8.07 and $4.89 for whites, $7.14 and $4.33 for NONWH and $6.16 and $3.74 for HISP. In terms of real wage changes between 1978 and 1985, all three races suffered mean real wage losses, as did both genders, although the percentage drop was smallest for females.

For the entire sample, as well as for both genders and all three racial groupings, mean years of education increased from 1978 to 1985. That overall mean real wages fell is not necessarily inconsistent with the human capital model, since a more detailed and disaggregated approach would be required to establish that. Moreover, other factors should also be taken into account (e.g., cyclical macroeconomic impacts).

(e) For LNWAGE in CPS78, the number of observations in each interval is 9, 80, 194, 193, 63 and 11, corresponding to proportions of 1.64%, 14.55%, 35.27%, 35.09%, 11.45% and 2.00%, respectively. For WAGE in CPS78, the comparable numbers are 0, 45, 278, 164, 45 and 18, corresponding to proportions of 0%, 8.18%, 35.27%, 29.82%, 8.18% and 3.27%. The LNWAGE more closely approximates the normal, for which the proportions in the six intervals are 2.28%, 13.59%, 34.13%, 34.13%, 13.59% and 2.28%. If, for example, one takes the differences between actual and normal-predicted percentages, squares the difference, and then sums over the six intervals, for LNWAGE the statistic is 8.2104 while for exp(LNWAGE) it is more than ten times larger at 84.5904.

For LNWAGE in CPS85, the number of individuals by group is 3, 93, 174, 180, 72 and 12 (corresponding to percentages of 0.56%, 17.4%, 32.58%, 33.71%, 13.48% and 2.25%), while the distribution of exp(LNWAGE) is more skewed with a fatter upper tail, numbering 0, 51, 272, 142, 37 and 32, and having proportions by group equal to 0%, 9.55%, 50.94%, 26.59%, 6.93% and 5.99%. Again, LNWAGE appears to follow the normal distribution much more closely than does exp(LNWAGE); the sum of squared deviation statistic (see previous paragraph) is 20.0663 for LNWAGE, and 419.0674 for exp(LNWAGE).

Exercise 2: Confirming Relationships Among Alternative Dummy Variable Specifications: Earnings and Returns To Schooling

TASKS: Estimate parameters in a stylized human capital model, verify empirically and then comment on the numerical relationships among parameter estimates in alternative but equivalent dummy variable specifications.

COMMENTS: The goal of this exercise is to help students interpret coefficients in a variety of dummy variable specifications (including a singular one which they can't implement empirically).

(a) For CPS78, the estimated equation has the form LNWAGE = 1.0304 + 0.0519*ED, with t-statistics of 11.115 and 7.187, and an R^2 of 0.086. For CPS85, the equation is LNWAGE = 1.0599 + 0.0768*ED, t-values are 9.866 and 9.488 and the R^2 is 0.145. The implied rate of return to schooling is 5.19% in 1978, and a higher 7.68% in 1985.

(b) For CPS78, the equation with the UNION dummy variable added is (absolute value of t-statistics are in parentheses)

$$\text{LNWAGE} = 0.8592 + 0.3051*\text{UNION} + 0.0581*\text{ED} \qquad R^2 = 0.167$$
$$\quad\;\;(9.38)\quad\;\;(7.30)\qquad\quad\;(8.36)$$

while for CPS85 it is

$$\text{LNWAGE} = 0.9926 + 0.2983*\text{UNION} + 0.0778*\text{ED} \qquad R^2 = 0.192.$$
$$\quad\;\;(9.43)\quad\;\;(5.57)\qquad\quad\;(9.88)$$

Hence the effect of union membership, holding education fixed, is positive and significant in both samples; the effect of adding UNION on R^2 is particularly large in CPS78, and in both cases it slightly increases returns to schooling. The slightly higher coefficient on ED when UNION is added can be interpreted as indicating that regardless of the level of ED, union workers earned higher wages, and by failing to take this differential into account, one depressed the estimated returns to schooling.

(c) For CPS78, the equation with both the NONU and UNION dummy variables included but with no constant term (absolute values of t-statistics in parentheses) looks like

$$\text{LNWAGE} = 0.8592*\text{NONU} + 1.1643*\text{UNION} + 0.0581*\text{ED} \qquad R^2 = 0.167$$
$$\quad\;\;(9.38)\qquad\qquad(12.87)\qquad\qquad(8.36)$$

while for CPS85 it is

$$\text{LNWAGE} = 0.9926*\text{NONU} + 1.2909*\text{UNION} + 0.0778*\text{ED} \qquad R^2 = 0.192.$$
$$\quad\;\;(9.43)\qquad\qquad(11.48)\qquad\qquad(9.88)$$

The estimate of α_0 is the level of LNWAGE for nonunion members with no schooling, while the estimate of α_1 is that for union members with no schooling. The estimate of α_0 should be the same as that of α, and the estimate of α' should equal the difference between α_1 and α_0; the estimated slope coefficient should be unchanged, as should the R^2. These analytical relationships are borne out by the numbers given above.

(d) Since the unit vector of the constant term is equal to the sum of NONU + UNION, the rank of the X matrix is 3, not 4, it is singular, and therefore the computer should not be able to invert X'X. Computer programs vary in how they report being unable to invert X'X; some try to compute the generalized inverse.

(e) When LNWAGE is regressed on a constant term, a NONU dummy variable and ED, the OLS results for CPS78 are

$$\text{LNWAGE} = 1.1643 - 0.3051*\text{NONU} + 0.0581*\text{ED} \qquad R^2 = 0.167$$
$$\phantom{\text{LNWAGE} = }(12.87) \quad (7.30) \qquad\quad (8.36)£$$

while for CPS85 they are

$$\text{LNWAGE} = 1.2909 - 0.2983*\text{NONU} + 0.0778*\text{ED} \qquad R^2 = 0.192.$$
$$\phantom{\text{LNWAGE} = }(11.48) \quad (5.57) \qquad\quad (9.88)$$

These numerical results are consistent with analytical relationships.

Exercise 3: Dummy Interaction Variables: The Earnings of Single and Married Males and Females

TASKS: Construct, implement and interpret OLS multiple regression results when the equation specification includes dummy interaction variables as regressors.

COMMENTS: The empirical issue of interest here is whether the statistical earnings functions of married females differ from those of married or single males, or from single females. According to the human capital framework, such differences might occur to the extent married females differ from single females, and from married or single males, in their frequency of leaving the labor force temporarily to rear children.

(a) For CPS78, the OLS estimated equation (t-values in parentheses) is

$$\text{LNWAGE} = 0.3939 + 0.0726*\text{ED} + 0.0296*\text{EX} - 0.0003*\text{EXSQ} \qquad R^2 = 0.2402$$
$$(3.78) \quad (10.15) \qquad (5.72) \qquad (3.00)$$

while for CPS85 it has the form

$$\text{LNWAGE} = 0.5203 + 0.0898*\text{ED} + 0.0349*\text{EX} - 0.0005*\text{EXSQ} \qquad R^2 = 0.2382.$$
$$(4.21) \quad (10.79) \qquad (6.18) \qquad (4.31)$$

These estimates are plausible, in that returns to schooling are in the range reported in the literature, and the coefficients on EX and EXSQ are positive and negative, respectively, as predicted by human capital theory.

(b) Adding the FE gender dummy variable in CPS78 yields an equation like

$$\text{LNWAGE} = 0.5261 - 0.3352*\text{FE} + 0.0742*\text{ED} + 0.0281*\text{EX} - 0.0003*\text{EXSQ} \quad R^2 = 0.3485$$
$$(5.40) \quad (9.52) \qquad (11.18) \qquad (5.86) \qquad (3.20)$$

while for CPS85 it has the form

$$\text{LNWAGE} = 0.6007 - 0.2570*\text{FE} + 0.0913*\text{ED} + 0.0360*\text{EX} - 0.0005*\text{EXSQ} \quad R^2 = 0.2968.$$
$$(5.03) \quad (6.64) \qquad (11.40) \qquad (6.63) \qquad (4.52)$$

The null hypothesis that, other things equal, gender has no impact on LNWAGE is decisively rejected in both samples. Note that the point estimate of the gender effect is smaller in absolute value in CPS85 than in CPS78, but returns to schooling are higher.

(c) When in addition to the regressors in (b) above, one includes the MAR dummy variable, one obtains for CPS78

$$\text{LNWAGE} = 0.5126 - 0.3281*\text{FE} + 0.0336*\text{MAR} + 0.0742*\text{ED} + 0.0270*\text{EX} - 0.0003*\text{EXSQ}$$
$$(5.19) \quad (9.08) \qquad (0.86) \qquad (11.19) \qquad (5.41) \qquad (2.96)$$

with an R^2 of 0.3494. For CPS85, the equation is

$$\text{LNWAGE} = 0.5902 - 0.2564*\text{FE} + 0.0508*\text{MAR} + 0.0911*\text{ED} + 0.0341*\text{EX} - 0.0005*\text{EXSQ}$$
$$(4.93) \quad (6.63) \qquad (1.18) \qquad (11.38) \qquad (6.00) \qquad (4.15)$$

with an R^2 of 0.2986. Note that in each sample, the coefficient on MARR is insignificantly different from zero at usual significance levels, although it is a bit larger in 1985 than in 1978.

(d) You should have no problem showing that CHECK = 0, i.e., that INFMAR = MARRFE. Since the effect of MARR on LNWAGE now depends on FE, the dummy variable INFMAR is an interaction one, not a linear one.

(e) The OLS model for CPS78 with the linear and interaction variables included is a very nice one, having the form

$$LNWAGE = 0.4724 - 0.2322*FE + 0.1079*MARR - 0.1586*INFMAR + 0.0739*ED$$
$$\quad\quad (4.71) \quad\quad (4.01) \quad\quad\quad (2.06) \quad\quad\quad\quad (2.11) \quad\quad\quad\quad (11.16)$$

$$\quad + 0.0265*EX - 0.0003*EXSQ,$$
$$\quad\quad (5.33) \quad\quad\quad (2.99)$$

with an R^2 of 0.3547. For CPS85, the negative effect experienced by married as compared to single females is about the same. Specifically,

$$LNWAGE = 0.5618 - 0.1277*FE + 0.1427*MARR - 0.1946*INFMAR + 0.0893*ED$$
$$\quad\quad (4.69) \quad (1.92) \quad\quad\quad (2.47) \quad\quad\quad\quad (2.38) \quad\quad\quad\quad (11.15)$$

$$\quad + 0.0337*EX - 0.0005*EXSQ$$
$$\quad\quad (5.96) \quad\quad\quad (4.20)$$

since (0.1079 - 0.1586 = -0.0507) from CPS78 is about the same as (0.1427 - 0.1946 = -0.0519) from CPS85. The CPS85 equation has an R^2 of 0.3061. The null hypothesis that the effect of marital status on LNWAGE, holding other things constant, does not depend on gender is decisively rejected in both samples.

Exercise 4: Examining Experience-Earnings Profiles

TASKS: Based on OLS estimates of the human capital model with experience included in linear and squared form, compute the years of experience at which LNWAGE is maximized for individuals with varying education levels; graph the implied age-earnings profile, and compare its shape to that predicted by human capital theory.

COMMENTS: The goal of this exercise is to give students "hands-on" experience in estimating and graphing the age-earnings profile, and to assess whether its shape is consistent with the predictions of human capital theory.

(a) The "base model" statistical earnings function for CPS78 is (with absolute values of t-statistics in parentheses)

$$LNWAGE = 0.4882 - 0.3060*FE + 0.2071*UNION - 0.1573*NONWH - 0.0272*HISP$$
$$\quad\;\;(4.96)\quad\;\;(8.89)\qquad\;(5.62)\qquad\qquad(2.86)\qquad\qquad(0.39)$$

$$+ 0.0746*ED + 0.0262*EX - 0.0003*EXSQ \qquad R^2 = 0.3924$$
$$\quad(11.22)\qquad\;(5.55)\qquad\;\;(3.03)$$

while that based on CPS85 data turns out to be

$$LNWAGE = 0.6247 - 0.2318*FE + 0.2116*UNION - 0.1252*NONWH - 0.0807*HISP$$
$$\quad\;\;(5.19)\quad\;\;(6.00)\qquad\;(4.19)\qquad\qquad(2.17)\qquad\qquad(0.92)$$

$$+ 0.0888*ED + 0.0345*EX - 0.0005*EXSQ \qquad R^2 = 0.3243.$$
$$\quad(11.16)\qquad\;(6.41)\qquad\;\;(4.46)$$

Estimates of β_2 and β_3 are consistent with human capital theory. For CPS78, the number of years of experience at which LNWAGE is maximized is 42.495, and this is the same for individuals with 8, 12 or 16 years of schooling; however, the *age* at which LNWAGE is maximized is 56.495, 60.495 and 64.495 for individuals with these three levels of schooling. For CPS85, the number of years of EXP at which LNWAGE is maximized is 32.702, and the implied age at which LNWAGE is maximized is 46.702 for individuals with 8 years' schooling, 50.702 with 12 years', and 54.702 with 16 years' schooling.

(b) To conserve on space, the graph is not presented here. In CPS78, LNWAGE is maximized at rather high ages, so make sure students extend the range of the age variable to around 70 or so. In CPS85, LNWAGE is maximized at age 52, where exp(LNWAGE) = $9.55.

(c) The OLS estimates of the equation in (a) with the EDEX interaction variable added as a regressor are, for CPS78,

$$LNWAGE = 0.3759 - 0.3043*FE + 0.2074*UNION - 0.1644*NONWH - 0.0320*HISP$$
$$\quad\;\;(2.20)\quad\;\;(8.81)\qquad\;(5.63)\qquad\qquad(2.95)\qquad\qquad(0.46)$$

$$+ 0.0824*ED + 0.0329*EX - 0.0004*EXSQ - 0.0004*EDEX \quad R^2 = 0.3932$$
$$\quad(7.00)\qquad\;\;(3.44)\qquad\;\;(3.01)\qquad\qquad(0.80)$$

and for CPS85,

$$LNWAGE = 0.3380 - 0.2294*FE + 0.2098*UNION - 0.1273*NONWH - 0.0884*HISP$$
$$\quad\;\;(1.62)\quad\;\;(5.95)\qquad\;(4.16)\qquad\qquad(2.21)\qquad\qquad(1.01)$$

$$+ 0.1087*ED + 0.0512*EX - 0.0006*EXSQ - 0.0010*EDEX \quad R^2 = 0.3279.$$
$$(7.62) \qquad (4.52) \qquad (4.73) \qquad (1.68)$$

Note that both estimates of the EDEX interaction variable are negative, that each is statistically insignificant, and that the age-earnings profile of the more educated is slightly steeper.

The years' experience for which LNWAGE is maximized depends on ED; for CPS78, EX^* is 41.743 years for 8 years' education, 39.608 for 12 years' and 37.474 for 16 years'; the corresponding ages at which LNWAGE is maximized are closer together—56.743, 57.608 and 59.474, respectively. For CPS85, the EX^* are 34.112, 30.958 and 27.804 for 8, 12 and 16 years of schooling, respectively, while the corresponding ages are very, very close—48.112, 48.958 and 49.804 years.

(d) For CPS78 and the 103 married women, the wage equation is estimated rather imprecisely (absolute values of t-statistics in parentheses):

$$LNWAGE = 0.3232 + 0.2606*UNION - 0.0120*NONWH - 0.0324*HISP$$
$$(0.70) \qquad (2.41) \qquad (0.10) \qquad (0.10)$$

$$+ 0.0666*ED + 0.0219*EX - 0.0002*EXSQ - 0.00002*EDEX \quad R^2 = 0.2435$$
$$(2.01) \qquad (0.82) \qquad (0.79) \qquad (0.01)$$

while for the 104 single women in CPS78, the corresponding equation is

$$LNWAGE = -0.2286 + 0.2438*UNION - 0.0307*NONWH + 0.0425*HISP$$
$$(0.43) \qquad (2.70) \qquad (0.23) \qquad (0.32)$$

$$+ 0.1224*ED + 0.0337*EX + 0.00006*EXSQ - 0.0025*EDEX \quad R^2 = 0.2505.$$
$$(3.16) \qquad (1.11) \qquad (0.21) \qquad (1.37)$$

The years' experience at which LNWAGE is maximized for married women in CPS78 is 45.965 (8 years' schooling), 45.774 (12 years') and 45.583 (16 years'); the implied ages at which LNWAGE is maximized are 59.965, 63.774 and 67.583, for 8, 12 and 16 years of schooling, respectively. Note that since the coefficient on EXSQ is positive for single women in CPS78, the results on EX^* are rather meaningless, i.e., -106.30 for 8 years' schooling, -26.228 for 12 years, and 53.844 for 16 years. In this case the sample size apparently is simply not large enough to obtain plausible and reliable estimates.

For the 83 married women in CPS85, the wage equation is again estimated imprecisely:

$$\text{LNWAGE} = \underset{(0.91)}{0.5446} + \underset{(0.41)}{0.0700}*\text{UNION} - \underset{(0.38)}{0.0761}*\text{NONWH} - \underset{(0.93)}{0.2692}*\text{HISP}$$

$$+ \underset{(2.22)}{0.0935}*\text{ED} + \underset{(0.27)}{0.0076}*\text{EX} - \underset{(0.66)}{0.0002}*\text{EXSQ} + \underset{(0.39)}{0.0006}*\text{EDEX} \quad R^2 = 0.2701.$$

The years' experience at which LNWAGE is maximized for married women in CPS85 is 29.925 (8 years' schooling), 35.776 (12 years') and 41.627 (16 years'); the implied ages at which LNWAGE is maximized are 43.925, 53.776 and 63.627, for 8, 12 and 16 years of schooling, respectively.

Finally, for the 162 single women in CPS85, the wage equation is estimated considerably more precisely:

$$\text{LNWAGE} = \underset{(0.22)}{-0.0949} + \underset{(2.40)}{0.2341}*\text{UNION} - \underset{(0.36)}{0.0333}*\text{NONWH} - \underset{(1.32)}{0.1710}*\text{HISP}$$

$$+ \underset{(4.05)}{0.1234}*\text{ED} + \underset{(2.16)}{0.0505}*\text{EX} - \underset{(2.67)}{0.0006}*\text{EXSQ} - \underset{(0.70)}{0.0010}*\text{EDEX} \quad R^2 = 0.3451.$$

The years' experience at which LNWAGE is maximized for single women in CPS85 is 33.017 (8 years' schooling), 30.076 (12 years') and 27.136 (16 years'); the implied ages at which LNWAGE is maximized are 47.017, 48.076 and 49.136, for 8, 12 and 16 years of schooling, respectively. For this 1985 data sample, therefore, the shape of the age-earnings profile for single women looks more similar to that for the entire population than it does to that for married women.

Exercise 5: Do Union Workers Earn Premium Wages?

TASKS: Calculate sample means of variables for data sorted according to union status, estimate by OLS the parameters in sorted and pooled regressions, do a Chow test for parameter equality, and then implement the Bloch-Kuskin [1978] procedure for estimating union-nonunion wage differentials.

COMMENTS: This is the first of three exercises utilizing a common procedure for decomposing wage differentials—this one examines union-nonunion wage differences, while the other two examine wage discrimination by race (Exercise 6) and by gender (Exercise 7). It is worth noting that whether or not unions cause wages to rise is a rather different issue, one not considered here.

(a) OLS estimation results for this equation are, for CPS78 (t-statistics in parentheses),

$$\begin{aligned}
\text{LNWAGE} = \quad & 0.4874 + 0.2074*\text{UNION} - 0.1573*\text{NONWH} - 0.0271*\text{HISP} \\
& (5.01) \quad (5.66) \qquad\qquad (2.88) \qquad\qquad (0.39)
\end{aligned}$$

$$\begin{aligned}
& + 0.0746*\text{ED} + 0.0262*\text{EX} - 0.0003*\text{EXSQ} \qquad R^2 = 0.3924 \\
& \quad (11.23) \qquad (5.56) \qquad\quad (3.04)
\end{aligned}$$

with a sum of squared residuals equal to 80.1380; and, for CPS85,

$$\begin{aligned}
\text{LNWAGE} = \quad & 0.6239 + 0.2172*\text{UNION} - 0.1252*\text{NONWH} - 0.0808*\text{HISP} \\
& (5.22) \quad (4.26) \qquad\qquad (2.17) \qquad\qquad (0.92)
\end{aligned}$$

$$\begin{aligned}
& + 0.0888*\text{ED} + 0.0345*\text{EX} - 0.0005*\text{EXSQ} \qquad R^2 = 0.3243 \\
& \quad (11.17) \qquad (6.42) \qquad\quad (4.47)
\end{aligned}$$

with a sum of squared residuals equal to 100.308. Holding other factors fixed, this indicates that in 1978 union workers earned about 23.0% higher wages, while in 1985 the premium was about 24.3%. These results are reasonably consistent with those in the literature, although they are a bit on the high side. Note that the model assumes all slope coefficients are the same for union and nonunion workers.

(b) For UNION = 1 (UNION = 0), sample means in CPS78 are 1.8631 (1.6009) for LNWAGE, 0.28571 (0.41623) for FE, 0.13095 (0.09162) for NONWH, 0.04167 (0.07592) for HISP, 12.024 (12.762) for ED, 22.548 (17.034) for EX and 683.56 (459.84) for EXSQ. For CPS85, these values are 2.2935 (2.0078) for LNWAGE, 0.29167 (0.49543) for FE, 0.18750 (0.11187) for NONWH, 0.05208 (0.05023) for

HISP, 12.885 (13.048) for ED, 20.938 (17.139) for EX and 595.27 (443.27) for EXSQ. Mean union-nonunion differences in LNWAGE are 0.26224 in CPS78 and 0.28562 in CPS85, in ED they are -0.738 and -0.163 in 1978 and 1985, and in EX they are 5.513 (1978) and 3.798 (1985). The proportion of NONWH is larger for UNION = 1, but by 1985 there is little difference in HISP by union membership.

(c) Based on the CPS78 data, the UNION equation is (with estimated t-statistics in parentheses)

$$LNWAGE = 1.0759 - 0.2239*FE - 0.2325*NONWH + 0.0742*HISP + 0.0400*ED$$
$$\quad\quad (5.37) \quad\quad (3.27) \quad\quad\quad (2.53) \quad\quad\quad\quad (0.47) \quad\quad\quad (2.89)$$

$$+ 0.0314*EX - 0.0005*EXSQ \quad\quad R^2 = 0.2019$$
$$\quad (3.17) \quad\quad\quad (2.24) \quad\quad\quad\quad\quad SSR = 24.8423$$

while that estimated for nonunion individuals is

$$LNWAGE = 0.3606 - 0.3258*FE - 0.1096*NONWH - 0.0444*HISP + 0.0852*ED$$
$$\quad\quad (3.23) \quad\quad (8.19) \quad\quad\quad (1.59) \quad\quad\quad\quad (0.58) \quad\quad\quad (11.28)$$

$$+ 0.0255*EX - 0.0003*EXSQ \quad\quad R^2 = 0.4229$$
$$\quad (4.73) \quad\quad\quad (2.39) \quad\quad\quad\quad\quad SSR = 53.5239.$$

With the CPS85 data, the UNION equation is estimated to be

$$LNWAGE = 1.1785 - 0.2149*FE - 0.0659*NONWH + 0.1748*HISP + 0.0516*ED$$
$$\quad\quad (4.48) \quad\quad (2.58) \quad\quad\quad (0.68) \quad\quad\quad\quad (0.96) \quad\quad\quad (3.11)$$

$$+ 0.0561*EX - 0.0011*EXSQ \quad\quad R^2 = 0.3122$$
$$\quad (4.47) \quad\quad\quad (4.25) \quad\quad\quad\quad\quad SSR = 11.7283$$

while that estimated for nonunion individuals is

$$LNWAGE = 0.5475 - 0.2259*FE - 0.1403*NONWH - 0.1086*HISP + 0.0958*ED$$
$$\quad\quad (4.07) \quad\quad (5.23) \quad\quad\quad (2.05) \quad\quad\quad\quad (1.09) \quad\quad\quad (10.70)$$

$$+ 0.0312*EX - 0.0004*EXSQ \quad\quad R^2 = 0.3044$$
$$\quad (5.20) \quad\quad\quad (3.22) \quad\quad\quad\quad\quad SSR = 86.9273.$$

There is no clear pattern on the gender and race variables over both samples, but the nonunion rate of return to schooling is about twice as large as that for union members; absolute values of the union EX and EXSQ coefficients are larger than those for nonunion individuals. The evidence on relative flatness is not clear-cut, but union earnings peak earlier (at age 53 in CPS78, 44 in

CPS85) than do those for nonunion individuals (63 years in CPS78, 55 in CPS85).

(d) For CPS78, the sum of the SSR for the two separate regressions is 78.3662, while that for the pooled regression is 84.8095; the Chow test statistic with 7,536 degrees of freedom is 6.2957, which is larger than the F-critical value at any reasonable significance level. Hence the null hypothesis that parameters are identical in the union and nonunion regression equations in CPS78 is decisively rejected. For CPS85, the sum of the separate SSR is 98.6556, while that for the pooled regression is 103.658. The Chow test statistic with 7,520 degrees of freedom turns out to be 3.7667, which is again larger than any reasonable F-critical value; the null hypothesis is again rejected.

(e,f) For CPS78, the difference in mean LNWAGE is 0.26224, while the difference in log-endowments weighting by the union parameters is 0.05983, and by the nonunion parameters it is 0.05323. When the difference in LNWAGE minus the difference in log-endowments is exponentiated, these two log-differences are 22.43% and 23.25%; the estimated differential in (a) for CPS78 was 23.0%. The various estimates are therefore remarkably similar. For CPS85, the difference in mean LNWAGE is 0.28562, while the difference in log-endowments weighting by the union parameters is 0.07564, and by the nonunion parameters it is 0.07275. When subtracted from the mean LNWAGE differences and then exponentiated, these differences become 23.37% and 23.72%, just slightly less than the simple regression estimate of 24.0% from part (a). Since there's so little difference, the question of choice among them is not a binding one.

(g) In all three methods, there's a slight—very slight—increase in union wage premia from 1978 to 1985. But the difference is very small, and undoubtedly it is statistically insignificant. Assuming that the covariance between the dummy variable coefficient estimates from part (a) in the CPS78 and CPS85 regressions is zero, the difference in estimated parameters is 0.2074 - 0.2172 = -0.0098, and the standard error is 0.0628, implying a t-statistic of the null hypothesis of parameter equality equal to 0.156, certainly less than the critical value at any reasonable significance level. This suggests that the null hypothesis of constant wage premia for union members in the 1978 and 1985 samples is not rejected.

Exercise 6: Measuring and Interpreting Wage Discrimination by Race

TASKS: Estimate parameters of a stylized human capital equation by OLS, and sort data by race. Using dummy variable procedures, Chow tests and the Blinder-Oaxaca procedure, obtain and compare alternatiave measures of wage discrimination by race.

COMMENTS: The data by race is for nonwhites and non-Hispanics (NONWH), Hispanic (HISP) and OTHER (primarily, whites). It is useful to remind students that in the Blinder-Oaxaca procedure, any effect not properly captured by the measured endowment variables (e.g., variations in the quality of schooling experienced by peoples of different races) is attributed to wage discrimination.

(a) Results for this OLS model are given in Exercise 4(a) of this chapter. The test of the null hypothesis that racial status does not matter ($\alpha_H = \alpha_N = 0$) is rejected in both data sets; for CPS78, the constrained and unconstrained SSR are 81.3488 and 80.1376, respectively, and the F-statistic with 2,542 d.f. is 4.10, while for CPS85 the corresponding SSR are 101.306 and 100.308, yielding an F-statistic with 2,526 d.f. equal to 2.62. The null hypothesis that $\alpha_H = \alpha_N$ yields a constrained SSR for CPS78 of 80.5008 and a t-statistic of 1.567, while for CPS85 the constrained SSR is 100.345 and the t-statistic is 0.44. Hence in both samples this null hypothesis is not rejected at usual significance levels.

(b) For CPS78, there are 57 NONWH = 1 individuals, 36 HISP = 1, and 457 OTHER; in CPS85, these three numbers are 67, 27 and 440. Sample means for the various variables in the two samples are tabled below:

	NONWH78	HISP78	OTHER78	NONWH85	HISP85	OTHER85
LNWAGE	1.51340	1.52965	1.71383	1.96633	1.81852	2.08809
FE	0.49123	0.33333	0.36543	0.41791	0.48148	0.46364
UNION	0.38596	0.19444	0.30416	0.26866	0.18519	0.16591
ED	11.71930	10.30556	12.81400	12.64179	11.51852	13.16818
EX	22.15789	21.05556	18.10503	18.79104	17.00000	17.72500
EXSQ	654.92982	616.55556	505.40481	500.22388	497.22222	464.45227

(c) The separate OLS equations estimated for CPS78 are as follows:

Variable	NONWH = 1 Estimate	t-Stat	HISP = 1 Estimate	t-Stat	OTHER = 1 Estimate	t-Stat
C	0.75539	1.9426	0.68212	2.9118	0.45571	4.1027
F	-0.59321E-01	0.4111	-0.23495	2.2675	-0.33826	9.1377
UNION	0.20459	1.4710	0.41700	3.3948	0.19733	4.9483
ED	0.54265E-01	2.1185	0.55034E-01	3.5880	0.76623E-01	10.1920
EX	0.34228E-02	0.1729	0.20820E-01	1.4817	0.28080E-01	5.4115
EXSQ	-0.54992E-05	0.0148	-0.26075E-03	0.9454	-0.33345E-03	2.9128
R^2	0.1492		0.4894		0.4204	
SSR	11.9364		2.46310		63.8304	

while for CPS85 they turn out to be

Variable	NONWH = 1 Estimate	t-Stat	HISP = 1 Estimate	t-Stat	OTHER = 1 Estimate	t-Stat
C	0.42712	1.3355	0.67632	1.6998	0.58772	4.2741
F	-0.14499	1.2751	-0.41932	-2.0779	-0.23414	5.4797
UNION	0.28164	2.2581	0.28467	1.1506	0.18819	3.2669
ED	0.82492E-01	3.8319	0.82442E-01	3.0438	0.92624E-01	10.088
EX	0.45812E-01	2.9231	0.31686E-01	1.3645	0.34338E-01	5.6058
EXSQ	-0.75879E-03	1.9981	-0.39599E-03	0.9084	-0.53959E-03	4.0090
R^2	0.3831		0.4046		0.3062	
SSR	10.0481		4.34099		84.8836	

Note that rates of return to ED are highest for OTHER, that the gender differential is smallest for NONWH and that UNION has the largest impact for HISP individuals.

(d) For CPS78, the pooled regression yields an SSR of 81.3488, while the sum of the three SSR's in (c) above is 78.2299; the calculated F-statistic with 12,532 d.f. is 1.7675, which is larger than the critical value at typical significance levels. For CPS85, however, the pooled SSR is 101.306, while the sum of the three SSR's from (c) above is 99.27269; the calculated F-statistic with 12,516 d.f. is 0.8807, which is less than the critical value at usual significance levels. Hence the null hypothesis of parameter equality among the three racial groups is rejected for CPS78, and is not rejected for CPS85.

To test the null hypothesis that the parameters of the HISP sample were equal to those of the OTHER sample, one must obtain additional information on what is the SSR in a constrained regression involving these two sub-samples. That turns out to be 66.8373 for CPS78 and 89.9819 for CPS85; using the information in (c) above for the SSR for the two separate regressions (66.2935 and 89.22459), the F-statistic with 6,481 d.f. for CPS78 is 0.6523, while that with 6,455 d.f. for CPS85 is 0.6436; hence the null hypothesis of parameter equality between HISP and OTHER is not rejected in either sample, given usual significance levels.

(e,f) For CPS78, the OTHER-NONWH difference in mean LNWAGE is 0.20043; using OTHER parameters as weights, the difference in log-endowments is 0.04634, or 23.12% of the differential. When instead the comparison is between OTHER-HISP, the difference in LNWAGE is 0.18418, and using the OTHER parameters as weights, the difference in mean log-endowments is 0.15721, or 85.35% of the difference in LNWAGE.

With CPS85, the results are a bit strange. The OTHER-NONWH mean difference in LNWAGE is 0.12176, and using OTHER parameters as weights, the difference in log-endowments is 0.00141, or 1.16% of the differential in mean LNWAGE. When instead the comparison is between OTHER-HISP, the difference in mean LNWAGE is 0.26957 (larger than the OTHER-NONWH difference), and using the OTHER parameters as weights, the difference in mean log-endowments is 0.19593, or 88.66% of the difference in mean LNWAGE.

(g) With CPS78, the difference in OTHER-NONWH log-endowments using NONWH parameters as weights is 0.03708, or 18.50% of the difference in mean LNWAGE. When instead the comparison is between OTHER-HISP, using the HISP parameters as weights the difference in mean log-endowments is 0.14381, or 78.08% of the difference in mean LNWAGE.

For CPS85, the difference in mean OTHER-NONWH log-endowments using NONWH parameters as weights is -0.01384 (yes, a negative difference), or -11.37% of the difference in mean LNWAGE. When instead the comparison is between OTHER-HISP, using the HISP parameters as weights the difference in mean log-endowments is 0.17395, or 64.53% of the difference in mean LNWAGE.

(h) As a proportion of differences in LNWAGE, HISP individuals appear to bear less discrimination than do NONWH individuals, even though in 1985 differences in mean LNWAGE from OTHER individuals were larger for HISP than for NONWH individuals.

Exercise 7: Measuring and Interpreting Wage Discrimination by Gender

TASKS: Estimate parameters of a stylized human capital equation by OLS, and sort data by gender. Using dummy variables, Chow tests and the Blinder-Oaxaca procedure, obtain and compare alternative measures of wage discrimination by gender.

COMMENTS: Students might also want to compare and contrast the discussion on wage discrimination by gender in this chapter with the literature on comparable worth; for references, see the Further Readings citations at the end of Chapter 5 in the text.

(a) The estimated equation is given in Exercise 4 of this chapter, part (a). For CPS78, the estimated equation implies that holding other factors fixed, females earn only 73.6% as much per hour as males; for CPS85, the number is 79.3%.

(b,g) For CPS78, there are 207 females and 343 males, while in CPS85, there are 289 males and 245 females. For CPS78, sample means for males (females) are: 1.81292 (1.46241) for LNWAGE, 0.08455 (0.135270) for NONWH,

0.06997 (0.05797) for HISP, 0.34985 (0.23188) for UNION, 12.39942 (12.76329) for ED, 19.93294 (16.70531) for EX and 583.1516 (437.08213) for EXSQ. In CPS85, sample means for males (females) are: 2.16528 (1.93403) for LNWAGE, 0.13495 (0.11429) for NONWH, 0.04844 (0.05306) for HISP, 0.23529 (0.11429) for UNION, 13.01384 (13.02449) for ED, 16.96540 (18.83265) for EX and 434.56401 (513.10204) for EXSQ. The mean male-female difference in LNWAGE is 0.35050 in CPS78 and 0.23125 in CPS85—a considerable decline. Males, on average, have slightly less schooling than females in both samples. Although in CPS78 on average men have about 3.2 years more potential experience, in CPS85 women have about 1.9 years greater potential experience. Since women tend to have had more intermittent labor force participation, EXP is likely to be a more accurate measure of actual experience for men. The CPS78 sample has a larger percentage of female than male NONWH, but this is reversed in CPS85; the CPS85 sample has a smaller percentage of female than male HISP, but this too is reversed in CPS85. In both samples, a greater proportion of men than women work on union jobs.

   (c,g) The estimated OLS equations from CPS78 (absolute t-statistics in parentheses) by gender are, beginning with males,

$$LNWAGE = 0.4674 + 0.1724*UNION - 0.2967*NONWH - 0.0813*HISP + 0.0705*ED$$
$$ (4.10) \quad (3.98) \quad\quad (4.01) \quad\quad\quad (0.99) \quad\quad (9.13)$$

$$+ 0.0363*EX - 0.0005*EXSQ \quad\quad R^2 = 0.3897$$
$$(6.37) \quad\quad (4.02) \quad\quad\quad\quad\quad SSR = 45.7482$$

and for females,

$$LNWAGE = 0.3646 + 0.2763*UNION + 0.0119*NONWH + 0.0373*HISP + 0.0695*ED$$
$$ (1.88) \quad (4.09) \quad\quad (0.14) \quad\quad\quad (0.31) \quad\quad (5.22)$$

$$+ 0.0084*EX + 0.00001*EXSQ \quad\quad R^2 = 0.2239$$
$$(0.99) \quad\quad (0.03) \quad\quad\quad\quad\quad SSR = 31.8801.$$

For CPS85, the estimated OLS equation for males is of the form

$$LNWAGE = 0.6521 + 0.2069*UNION - 0.1595*NONWH - 0.0249*HISP + 0.0804*ED$$
$$ (4.04) \quad (3.24) \quad\quad (2.03) \quad\quad\quad (0.19) \quad\quad (7.47)$$

$$+ 0.0423*EX - 0.0006*EXSQ \qquad R^2 = 0.3071$$
$$(5.69) \qquad (3.91) \qquad \qquad SSR = 56.9970$$

while for females it turns out to be

$$LNWAGE = 0.2757 + 0.1815*UNION - 0.0315*NONWH - 0.1791*HISP + 0.1050*ED$$
$$(1.53) \quad (2.15) \qquad (0.37) \qquad (1.50) \qquad (8.81)$$

$$+ 0.0259*EX - 0.0004*EXSQ \qquad R^2 = 0.3037$$
$$(3.30) \qquad (2.34) \qquad \qquad SSR = 41.1471.$$

The effect of schooling by gender varies in the two samples, but it is unlikely the difference is ever statistically significant. The negative effect of NONWH on LNWAGE is larger for men than for women, and the effect of HISP varies in the two samples, but is never statistically significant. The effect of EX on LNWAGE is larger for males, and the age-earnings profile is flatter for females than for males, due perhaps to the mismeasurement of EX for females.

(d,g) The SSR in the pooled regression in CPS78 is 91.8124, and in CPS85 it is 107.178; the sum of the separate SSR in CPS78 is 77.6283, while that in CPS85 is 98.1441 (see the detailed SSR in (c) above). This yields a Chow test statistic with 7,536 d.f. in CPS78 of 13.991, and one with 7,520 d.f. in CPS85 of 6.838. In both cases, the null hypothesis of parameter equality by gender is decisively rejected at usual significance levels.

(e,f) The male-female difference in LNWAGE in CPS78 is 0.35051; using male parameter weights, the difference in log-endowments is 0.05533 (15.79%), while with female parameter weights the difference in log-endowments is 0.03505 (10%). Hence with CPS78, between 84.21 and 90% of the difference in LNWAGE by gender is "explained" by discrimination. Of that difference due to endowments, the EX variable appears to be particularly important, although UNION and NONWH contributions are also consequential. Using CPS85 data, we see that the male-female difference in LNWAGE is smaller at 0.23125. Now come some rather bizarre results. The male-female difference in log-endowments using the male parameter estimates is -0.00781 (-3.38% of the difference in LNWAGE), and is 0.00403 (1.74%) using female parameter weights.

(g) The rather strange results noted above suggest that between 1978 and 1985, although the difference in LNWAGE by gender declined, the difference in log-endowments declined even more, and the role of discrimination changed from 84.21 to 90% in 1978 to even higher levels of 98.26 to 103.38% in 1985. The 1985 results are simply quite strange, but that's what the data tell us!

Exercise 8: Heteroskedasticity in the Statistical Earnings Function

TASKS: Estimate traditional statistical earnings function by OLS, and compute heteroskedasticity-robust standard errors using the procedure of Halbert J. White [1980]; compare OLS and robust standard errors. If possible, do a GLS estimation based on estimated variances of auxiliary regression. Then test for homoskedasticity using the White test.

COMMENTS: Whether one can do the transformation suggested in part (b) of this exercise depends on whether all observations have strictly positive fitted values. Students might run into this problem by finding out they cannot take the square root of a negative number.

Note also that while many computer programs now provide robust standard errors as a simple option available to the user, if it is not available on your software, you might employ a computationally feasible way of obtaining robust standard errors as outlined in Karen Messer and Halbert J. White [1984].

(a) Parameter estimates and implicit standard errors are given in part (a) of Exercise 4. t-statistics based on robust standard errors for the constant, FE, UNION, NONWH, HISP, ED, EX, EXSQ variables for CPS78 turn out to be 4.96, 8.74, 5.51, 2.35, 0.50, 11.24, 6.22 and 3.41, respectively, while those for CPS85 are 5.10, 5.96, 4.66, 2.35, 0.94, 10.81, 5.77 and 4.07. In

CPS85, t-statistics on HISP, ED, EX and EXSQ are larger when based on implicit robust standard errors, while in CPS85 t-statistics on UNION, NONWH and HISP are larger. Hence it is not the case that all heteroskedasticity-robust standard errors are larger than the OLS-based biased estimates. Since the OLS estimates are biased and the bias is data-dependent, these results are consistent with theoretical expectations.

(b) For the CPS78 data, a regression was first run of RESIDSQ on a constant, ED, EX, EXSQ, NONWH, HISP, UNION and FE; the fitted values at observations 120 and 142 were negative, however. But when a similar regression was run with HISP, UNION and FE deleted (all of which had t-values less than unity in the first regression), all fitted values were positive. A weighted least squares regression gave results very similar to the OLS run:

$$\text{LNWAGE} = \underset{(4.79)}{0.5405} - \underset{(8.61)}{0.3181}\text{*FE} + \underset{(4.83)}{0.1866}\text{*UNION} - \underset{(3.41)}{0.1661}\text{*NONWH} - \underset{(0.76)}{0.0606}\text{*HISP}$$

$$+ \underset{(10.65)}{0.0746}\text{*ED} + \underset{(4.09)}{0.0228}\text{*EX} - \underset{(2.15)}{0.0003}\text{*EXSQ} \qquad R^2 = 0.3907.$$

The biggest change is in the NONWH standard error, which falls under GLS and now has a larger t-statistic (3.41 vs. 2.86).

For the CPS85 data, the residuals from the initial regression of RESIDSQ on a constant, FE, UNION, NONWH, HISP, ED, EX and EXSQ were all positive. Using these fitted values as weights, GLS results were again very similar to OLS findings:

$$\text{LNWAGE} = \underset{(4.81)}{0.5930} - \underset{(5.69)}{0.2287}\text{*FE} + \underset{(2.97)}{0.1761}\text{*UNION} - \underset{(2.14)}{0.1384}\text{*NONWH} - \underset{(0.82)}{0.0759}\text{*HISP}$$

$$+ \underset{(11.18)}{0.0915}\text{*ED} + \underset{(6.15)}{0.0334}\text{*EX} - \underset{(4.11)}{0.0005}\text{*EXSQ} \qquad R^2 = 0.3141.$$

The GLS t-statistics on FE, UNION, NONWH, EX and EXSQ are smaller than those based on OLS, but the GLS t-statistics on HISP and ED are larger.

(c) For both the CPS78 and CPS85 data sets, exact collinearity resulted unless the NONWH*HISP interactive dummy variable was omitted. With the 20 remaining regressors (plus a constant), the R^2 from the CPS78 regression is 0.05145, while that for 1985 was 0.013499; the $T*R^2$ χ^2 test statistics with 20 degrees of freedom are therefore 28.2975 for CPS78 and 7.2085 for CPS85. Since the 0.05 critical value is 31.410, the null hypothesis of homoskedasticity is not rejected in either sample, although this conclusion is a bit more uncertain in CPS78.

FINAL COMMENTS:

The data used in the exercises of this chapter were taken from random samples of CPS tapes issued by the U.S. Census Bureau. Data for other years are also available from the Census Bureau, and you might want to use other data for additional exercises. Also, in many countries the central statistical bureau conducts similar population surveys on a regular basis, and that data might be of particular usefulness for doing similar analyses on determinants of wage rates in other countries.

INSTRUCTOR'S NOTES FOR CHAPTER SIX:

EXPLAINING AND FORECASTING AGGREGATE INVESTMENT EXPENDITURES:
DISTRIBUTED LAGS AND AUTOCORRELATION

ECONOMETRIC PROCEDURES EMPLOYED IN THE EXERCISES OF CHAPTER SIX:

- Print out data, examine and comment on data trends, compute implicit depreciation rate for capital and compare with rates assumed in capital rental price construction; assess relative importance of replacement and net investment in gross investment

- Estimate using the OLS, Hildreth-Lu and iterative Cochrane-Orcutt procedures

- Check for AR(1) disturbances with lagged dependent variable using Durbin's m- and h-test statistics

- Employ classical hypothesis-testing procedures to choose a preferred specification, and then examine ex post forecasting properties using the root mean squared error (RMSE) criterion

- Estimate a model using the Almon polynomial distributed lag (PDL) procedure, do PDL-AR(1) estimation, compute and interpret the sum of the estimated PDL coefficients

- Do PDL and PDL-AR(1) estimation with and without end-point restrictions, and find a preferred specification using classical test procedures

- Conduct a "horse race" among alternative models of investment using the %RMSE and Theil inequality coefficient criteria

More-advanced procedures:

- Employ Box-Jenkins differencing procedures to make data series stationary; identify the order of the MA and AR processes using sample autocorrelations, partial autocorrelations, and Box-Pierce Q-statistics; then estimate ARIMA model and do static and dynamic ex post forecasts, comparing models using %RMSE criterion

- Estimate model with a lagged dependent variable and AR(1) disturbances by 2SLS-AR(1), using the Fair procedure to construct instruments

- Compute long-run price and output elasticities and their confidence intervals based on PDL-AR(1) estimates of a CES investment equation

GOALS FOR CHAPTER SIX:

To introduce students to five alternative models of investment behavior, to engage them in the estimation of distributed lag models with autocorrelated disturbances, and to involve them in choosing among alternative model specifications. Students will also come to the sobering conclusion that models that perform admirably in estimation may at times achieve only very limited success in the forecasting context.

GENERAL COMMENTS TO THE INSTRUCTOR:

This is a long chapter, for in it five alternative models of investment behavior are presented and compared. The chapter contains sufficient material to keep students busy for a full quarter, or for at least half a semester, particularly if some of the referenced readings are also assigned and discussed in detail. I have also found that teaching from this chapter is a somewhat humbling experience, for constructing a plausible, rigorous and stable econometric model of investment behavior remains an elusive goal.

Not all the material in this chapter need be covered, however. For instructors wanting to employ only some of the sections, I recommend having students work through Section 6.1 (definitions of variables and measurement issues), Section 6.2 on the accelerator model (including the introductory discussion of distributed lags and autocorrelation), only one or two other investment models (from among the time series/AR, cash flow, neoclassical and

Tobin's q models) and finally, Section 6.8 on the empirical comparison of the five models using static and/or dynamic ex post forecasting procedures.

I highly recommend that all students work through Exercise 1 in order to become familiar with the Kopcke data. Each of the following five exercises—Exercises 2 through 6—focuses on one of the five alternative models of investment behavior; your choice of which exercises to assign will likely depend on which of these models you cover in class.

The next three exercises employ slightly more advanced procedures. Exercise 7 deals with Box-Jenkins ARIMA models, Exercise 8 with simultaneity and autocorrelation and Exercise 9 with PDL-AR(1) estimation of Bischoff's putty-clay model of investment behavior.

The final exercise—Exercise 10—is a rather ambitious one, for it has students doing a "horse race" among alternative investment models on the same data, comparing the models using the %RMSE and Theil inequality coefficient criteria. My own experience, and from what I have learned from other instructors, suggests that Exercise 10 is best carried out by dividing the class into several groups, and having each group work on one or two of the five models.

There is one other important comment that should be made. Because the underlying KOPCKE data on investment has been revised and re-based to a different year from that originally employed in the three Kopcke studies, your students will not be able to replicate Kopcke's results as reproduced in Chapter 6. To make sure your students are doing their estimation correctly, I therefore include at the beginning of each of the exercise-specific comments below, for Exercises 2 through 6, the estimated model that results when the revised Kopcke data is used in estimating the models reported by him in his three studies. Your students should be able to replicate these results.

SPECIFIC NOTES ON THE EXERCISES IN CHAPTER SIX:

Exercise 1: Examining the Data

GOAL: To have students become familiar with the KOPCKE data base, interpret the plausibility of data trends, and speculate on the extent and possible consequences of multicollinearity.

TASKS: Print out data, examine trends of selected variables. Compute the rate of depreciation implicit in the capital stock construction, and check whether it is consistent with that used in the rental price of capital data. Assess relative importance of replacement and net in total gross investment. Compute simple correlations, and comment on possible multicollinearity.

SPECIFIC NOTES ON EXERCISE 1:

(a) Note that since the data in KOPCKE come in two panels, each with 140 observations on a number of variables, some computer software programs may require you to edit this file somewhat in order that its contents be read in properly.

(b) The ratio of IE to IS is about 1.38 at the beginning of the sample, and rises to 2.58 by 1986:4, indicating that equipment investment has been growing more rapidly than structures investment. Moreover, the ratio of KELAG to KSLAG also increases, from 0.66 to 0.97 over the sample. The equipment asset price deflator has grown relative to that for structures; their ratios at observations 1 and 140 are 1.26 and 1.42, respectively; the corresponding ratio of rental prices CE to CS also increases, 0.81 to 1.09. It is not clear, based on the relative price trends, why there has been a shift toward equipment and away from structures investment. Note that there's a change in trends, however, beginning in the early 1970s.

(c) Although the equipment-output intensity increases steadily from 1952:1 through 1986:4 and is almost equal to the structures-output intensity at the end of the sample, the behavior of the structures-output intensity is a

bit more erratic; at the end of the sample it is almost the same as that at
the beginning (0.588 vs. 0.590).   If one simply sums these two capital stocks
and divides by output, the overall capital intensity has increased, from 0.977
in 1952:1 to 1.155 in 1986:4.   In this sense, production in the U.S. has
become more aggregate-capital intensive.

(d) Tobin's q has a low value of 0.510 in 1979:1, another relatively low
value of 0.516 in 1974:4 and a high value of 1.032 in 1968:4.   The low values
are associated with oil price shocks from OPEC-I and OPEC-II.   The fact that q
was less than unity in 136 of the 140 observations and that nonetheless much
net investment occurred suggests that it is more prudent to state that
investment is an increasing function of q, rather than q must be greater than
one for net investment to occur.   The capacity utilization ratio was above 0.9
in all four quarters of 1966, the highest values it realized in the sample;
low values occurred in 1975:2 and in 1982:4, both in recessionary time
periods.   Extreme values of q do not correspond precisely with extreme values
of U, although movements appear to be positively correlated.   Relationships
between q and CE, and between q and CS, are less clear.

(e) The implicit 1953 and 1986 depreciation rates for equipment are
0.1219 and 0.1436, and particularly the latter is not far from the 15% rate
assumed by Kopcke in the construction of CE; for structures, the story is
similar—the implicit depreciation rates for 1953 and 1986 are 0.0599 and
0.0593, slightly larger than the 5% used in the construction of CS.   Hence
there is a problem of logical consistency, but how important it is in practice
is not clear.   Concerning replacement investment, as a proportion of total
investment replacement investment ranges from roughly 80 to 90% for equipment,
and 50-60% for structures.   Although in some years net investment in equipment
is negative and the replacement proportion of total investment is greater than
100% for equipment, for structures net investment is positive in each quarter.

(f) The Y's and lagged Y's are highly correlated with each other—simple correlations between Y and Y lagged for up to five lags are all greater than 0.99; for Tobin's q, the intercorrelations are not as large. Since lagged values of Y are often used as regressors in investment equations, problems of multicollinearity could be considerable, unless restrictions are placed on the parameters of the distributed lag process.

Exercise 2: Testing for Autocorrelation with Lagged Dependent Variables

GOALS: To acquaint students with special procedures required when one tests for the absence of autocorrelation in models with lagged dependent variables as regressors, and to alert them to problems with multiple local optima.

TASKS: Estimate accelerator model of investment by OLS, and use Durbin's m- and h-statistics to test for AR(0) as a special case of AR(1); then estimate model with lagged dependent variable as regressor using the Hildreth-Lu and iterative Cochrane-Orcutt estimation procedures.

ON REPLICATING KOPCKE'S REPORTED RESULTS: As was noted above and in the text, data revisions and data re-basing will prevent you from replicating Kopcke's reported results, reproduced in Chapter 6, Table 6.2. For equipment investment, the three estimated accelerator models (using sample observations 25 through 87, 9 through 104 and 17 through 112) are, respectively (absolute values of t-statistics are in parentheses):

$$IE = -193080 + 0.079*Y + 0.063*Y(-1) + 0.048*Y(-2) + 0.046*Y(-3) - 0.137*KELAG,$$
$$(6.17) \quad (4.37) \quad (3.48) \quad\quad (2.68) \quad\quad (2.43) \quad\quad (2.49)$$

an R^2 of 0.704, a Durbin-Watson of 2.0818 and a ρ estimate of 0.95 (22.71);

$$IE = -254800 + 0.085*Y + 0.060*Y(-1) + 0.043*Y(-2) + 0.032*Y(-3) + 0.024*Y(-4)$$
$$(5.77) \quad (5.53) \quad (4.71) \quad\quad (3.38) \quad\quad (2.16) \quad\quad (1.08)$$

$$+ 0.017*Y(-5) - 0.136*KELAG, \quad \rho = 0.976 \quad\quad R^2 = 0.628$$
$$(1.08) \quad\quad (2.71) \quad\quad\quad (43.84) \quad\quad\quad DW = 1.9464;$$

and

$$IE = -246140 + 0.084*Y + 0.063*Y(-1) + 0.046*Y(-2) + 0.033*Y(-3) + 0.024*Y(-4) +$$
$$\quad\quad\quad (5.56)\quad (7.17)\quad\quad (9.63)\quad\quad\quad\quad (6.37)\quad\quad\quad\quad (4.60)\quad\quad\quad\quad (3.61)$$

$$0.016*Y(-5) + 0.020*Y(-6) + 0.004*Y(-7) - 0.001*Y(-8) - 0.008*Y(-9) - 0.159*KELAG,$$
$$(2.37)\quad\quad\quad (1.27)\quad\quad\quad\quad (0.54)\quad\quad\quad\quad (0.18)\quad\quad\quad\quad (0.61)$$

with an R^2 of 0.702, a Durbin-Watson of 2.2993 and an estimate of ρ of 0.964

(35.21). Note that the above parameter estimates on the Y's are the distributed

lags (the "unscrambled" estimates), not the estimated "scrambled" polynomial

terms.

For structures, the estimated equations over the same three time periods

are as follows:

$$IS = 19600 + 0.026*Y + 0.019*Y(-1) + 0.022*Y(-2) + 0.023*Y(-3) + 0.019*Y(-4)$$
$$\quad\quad (2.03)\quad (1.74)\quad\quad (1.30)\quad\quad\quad (1.44)\quad\quad\quad\quad (1.50\ )\quad\quad\quad\quad (1.20)$$

$$\quad\quad - 0.103*KSLAG,\quad \rho = 0.822\quad\quad R^2 = 0.704$$
$$\quad\quad\quad (2.49)\quad\quad\quad\quad (11.35)\quad\quad DW = 1.8948;$$

$$IS = 73856 + 0.034*Y + 0.023*Y(-1) + 0.015*Y(-2) + 0.011*Y(-3) + 0.012*Y(-4)$$
$$\quad\quad (2.98)\quad (3.58)\quad\quad (3.38)\quad\quad\quad (2.64)\quad\quad\quad\quad (1.84)\quad\quad\quad\quad (1.60)$$

$$\quad\quad + 0.018*Y(-5) - 0.157*KSLAG,\quad \rho = 0.962\quad\quad R^2 = 0.345$$
$$\quad\quad\quad (1.76)\quad\quad\quad\quad (4.17)\quad\quad\quad\quad (34.56)\quad\quad DW = 2.0046;$$

and finally,

$$IS = 51921 + 0.033*Y + 0.025*Y(-1) + 0.019*Y(-2) + 0.015*Y(-3) + 0.012*Y(-4)$$
$$\quad\quad (3.23)\quad (4.07)\quad\quad (5.91)\quad\quad\quad (4.61)\quad\quad\quad\quad (3.38)\quad\quad\quad\quad (3.00)$$

$$\quad\quad + 0.011*Y(-5) + 0.010*Y(-6) + 0.009*Y(-7) + 0.008*Y(-8) + 0.007(Y(-9)$$
$$\quad\quad\quad (2.95)\quad\quad\quad\quad (2.58)\quad\quad\quad\quad (2.02)\quad\quad\quad\quad (1.68)\quad\quad\quad\quad (1.52)$$

$$\quad\quad + 0.006*Y(-10) + 0.003*Y(-11) - 0.209*KSLAG,\quad \rho = 0.923\quad\quad R^2 = 0.497$$
$$\quad\quad\quad (1.08)\quad\quad\quad\quad (0.34)\quad\quad\quad\quad (3.37)\quad\quad\quad\quad (23.43)\quad DW = 1.7914$$

SPECIFIC NOTES ON EXERCISE 2:

(a) The equations for equipment and structures estimated over the 1956:1

—1986:4 time period (observation numbers 17 through 140) look like this

(absolute values of t-statistics in parentheses):

$$IE = -10917 + 0.123*Y - 0.111*Y(-1) + 0.909*IE(-1)\quad\quad R^2 = 0.9952$$
$$\quad\quad (2.78)\quad (6.66)\quad\quad (5.35)\quad\quad\quad (22.00)\quad\quad\quad DW = 2.2288$$

$$IS = 1889.9 + 0.039*Y - 0.037*Y(-1) + 0.954*IS(-1)\quad\quad R^2 = 0.9828$$
$$\quad\quad (1.31)\quad (3.30)\quad\quad (3.02)\quad\quad\quad (25.52)\quad\quad\quad DW = 1.2322$$

For equipment, the implicit estimates (t-statistics) of μ, λ and δ are 1.351 (1.93), 0.091 (2.21) and 0.102 (2.10), respectively, while for structures they are 0.844 (1.04), 0.046 (1.23) and 0.036 (0.78). Both implicit estimates of δ are less than the 0.05 and 0.15 values assumed by Kopcke, but perhaps not significantly so. The implicit 1.35 estimate of μ for equipment is too large. The (biased) estimates of ρ implicit in the Durbin-Watson test statistic are -0.1144 and 0.3839, both of which are biased toward zero since a lagged dependent variable is present in the equation as a regressor.

(b) For equipment, it is possible to compute Durbin's h-statistic as equal to -1.309, which is not significant at usual confidence levels. For structures, Durbin's h-statistic is 4.702, which is statistically significant. When one estimates by OLS the residual equation as specified in Exercise 2 of the text, the coefficient estimate (asymptotic t-value) in the equipment equation is -0.1535 (-1.4767), and in the structures equation it is 0.4426 (4.8872). In this case, the Durbin h- and m-statistics are very similar, and their inference is consistent. In general, since the h-statistic cannot be computed whenever Var(b) > 1 (that does not happen here, however), the m-test is employed more frequently.

(c) For equipment, there is a strange pattern in that the SSR increases with ρ at 0.00 until $\rho = 0.50$, and then the SSR decreases, hitting its lowest value at $\rho = 1.00$; this leaves us with two local minima, one at 0.00 (where the standard error of the equation is 5101.99), and the other at 1.00 (this is the apparent global minimum, SER = 4691.28). With a finer grid at 0.01, the global minimum is attained at $\rho = 0.98$, where the t-statistic is 78.2588 and the SER is 4639.37. This inference is very different from that obtained earlier, and that obtained here is preferable.

For structures, the SER is also non-monotonic with respect to ρ, falling from $\rho = 0.00$ to 0.57-0.58, increasing until 0.63-0.64, then falling to a global minimum at $\rho = 0.82$ (where the SER is 2887.52 and the t-statistic is 7.257), and then increasing until $\rho = 1.00$. The inference is again quite different from that obtained earlier.

Incidentally, in both these Hildreth-Lu procedures, 123 observations are employed.

(d) Using the PC-TSP software which drops the first observation and leaves one with 123 observations, the iterative Cochrane-Orcutt procedure leads one to a local rather than global optimum; for equipment, the estimate (t-statistic) for ρ is -0.21125 (2.215), and for structures it is 0.5383 (3.070). Results may differ with other software, and depend on whether the estimation is over 123 or 124 observations.

Exercise 3: Regression Estimation of the Time Series/AR Model

GOALS: The purpose of this exercise is to have students estimate a time series/AR model by OLS, and choose a preferred specification based on results from hypothesis testing and properties of the estimated parameters.

TASKS: Estimate a simple time series having lagged dependent variables by OLS; compute % root mean squared errors (%RMSE) of the residuals; estimate a more general model and choose a preferred specification, checking for stationarity. Test for the particular specification employed by Kopcke as a special case of the preferred specification.

ON REPLICATING KOPCKE'S REPORTED RESULTS: As was noted above and in the text, data revisions and data re-basing will prevent you from replicating Kopcke's reported results, reproduced in Chapter 6, Table 6.7. For equipment investment, the three estimated time series/AR models (using sample observations 25 through 87, 9 through 104 and 17 through 112) are, respectively (absolute values of t-statistics are in parentheses):

$$IE = -1388.9 + 1.0269*IE(-1) \qquad R^2 = 0.989, \quad DW = 1.0947$$
$$\quad (0.794) \quad (74.099) \qquad \text{Durbin's m-statistic: } 3.70156$$

$$IE/KELAG = 0.0124 + 1.4148*IE(-1)/KELAG(-1) - 0.4901*IE(-2)/KELAG(-2)$$
$$(2.573) \quad (15.616) \qquad\qquad (5.410)$$

where the R^2 is 0.9222, the Durbin-Watson test statistic is 2.0767, and

Durbin's m-test statistic is -0.8875. Finally,

$$IE = 564.16 + 1.355*IE(-1) - 0.076*IE(-2) - 0.301*IE(-3) - 0.206*IE(-4)$$
$$(0.448) \quad (12.765) \qquad (0.429) \qquad (1.672) \qquad (1.111)$$

$$+ 0.391*IE(-5) - 0.162*IE(-6) \qquad R^2 = 0.9945, DW = 1.8637$$
$$(2.095) \qquad (1.459) \qquad \text{Durbin's m-statistic: } 2.77098.$$

For structures, the equations estimated over the same three time intervals are

$$IS = 907.43 + 0.9980*IS(-1) \qquad R^2 = 0.9806, \quad DW = 1.7111$$
$$(0.528) \quad (55.596) \qquad \text{Durbin's m-statistic: } 1.02695$$

$$IS/KSLAG = 0.0020 + 1.2011*IS(-1)/KSLAG(-1) - 0.2252*IS(-2)/KSLAG(-2)$$
$$(0.877) \quad (11.882) \qquad\qquad (2.195)$$

where the R^2 is 0.9449, the Durbin-Watson test statistic is 2.0652, and

Durbin's m-test statistic is -1.5451. Finally,

$$IS = 556.99 + 1.214*IS(-1) - 0.108*IS(-2) + 0.041*IS(-3) - 0.126*IS(-4)$$
$$(0.379) \quad (11.127) \qquad (0.633) \qquad (0.238) \qquad (0.709)$$

$$- 0.011*IS(-5) - 0.049*IS(-6) - 0.068*IS(-7) + 0.106*IS(-8)$$
$$(0.062) \qquad (0.283) \qquad (0.377) \qquad (0.868)$$

with an R^2 of 0.9820, a Durbin-Watson of 1.9877 and a Durbin m-statistic of

-1.05195.

SPECIFIC NOTES ON EXERCISE 3:

(a) There's a bit of unfortunate confusion in the text on this exercise.
The number of lags for the equipment equation should have been six, not eight.
Nonetheless, since eight is what was requested in the text, here are the OLS
results over the 1956:1-1979:4 (observations 17 through 112) time period,
where t-statistics are in parentheses:

$$IE = 71.324 + 1.374*IE(-1) - 0.136*IE(-2) - 0.271*IE(-3) - 0.140*IE(-4)$$
$$(0.058) \quad (12.83) \qquad (0.75) \qquad (1.53) \qquad (0.78)$$

$$+ 0.471*IE(-5) - 0.562*IE(-6) + 0.173*IE(-7) + 0.097*IE(-8) \quad R^2 = 0.9950$$
$$(2.58) \qquad (3.01) \qquad (0.88) \qquad (0.84) \qquad\qquad DW = 2.0285$$

and where Durbin's h-test statistic is -3.011. If one ignores the lag 7 and 8 terms, the results are roughly comparable to those reported by Kopcke, particularly in the time shape of the distributed lag coefficients. When the more recent data are added and estimation is from 1956:1 to 1986:4, results are:

$$IE = 385.07 + 1.236*IE(-1) + 0.170*IE(-2) - 0.619*IE(-3) + 0.434*IE(-4)$$
$$(0.300) \quad (13.19) \qquad\qquad (1.14) \qquad\qquad (4.12) \qquad\qquad (2.62)$$

$$- 0.384*IE(-5) - 0.005*IE(-6) + 0.230*IE(-7) - 0.057*IE(-8) \quad R^2 = 0.9947$$
$$(2.20) \qquad\qquad (0.03) \qquad\qquad (1.37) \qquad\qquad (0.55) \qquad\qquad DW = 1.9715$$

and Durbin's m-test statistic is 0.798. Note that the parameter estimates are very unstable, even changing sign in a number of cases.

(b) For the 1956:1-1979:4 era, the % mean squared error is 0.00082, while for 1956:1-1986:4 it increases to 0.00095. The %RMSE are therefore 0.0286 and 0.0308, respectively. Hence the variability of the residual increases when the more recent data are included, providing additional evidence of parameter instability.

(c) As noted in (a), there's a bit of confusion here. The exercise asks for m = 6, but it should have been 8, as in Kopcke. (Results for m = 8 are presented above in the "On Replicating Kopcke's Reported Results" section.) Nonetheless, here are the results for m = 6, first for 1956:1-1979:4 and then for 1956:1-1986:4:

$$IS = 597.13 + 1.227*IS(-1) - 0.115*IS(-2) + 0.034*IS(-3) - 0.154*IS(-4)$$
$$(0.41) \quad (11.40) \qquad\qquad (0.68) \qquad\qquad (0.20) \qquad\qquad (0.89)$$

$$- 0.003*IS(-5) + 0.009*IS(-6) \qquad R^2 = 0.9818, \ DW = 1.9737$$
$$(0.02) \qquad\qquad (0.08) \qquad\qquad \text{Durbin's m-statistic: -0.485}$$

and

$$IS = 1938.3 + 1.347*IS(-1) - 0.287*IS(-2) + 0.017*IS(-3) - 0.251*IS(-4)$$
$$(1.51) \quad (14.60) \qquad\qquad (1.85) \qquad\qquad (0.10) \qquad\qquad (1.49)$$

$$+ 0.086*IS(-5) + 0.073*IS(-6) \qquad R^2 = 0.9844, \ DW = 1.9986$$
$$(0.51) \qquad\qquad (0.07) \qquad\qquad \text{Durbin's m-statistic: -0.005}$$

Again there's a fair bit of parameter instability, although not as much as with the equipment equation. The % mean squared error for the two time periods is 0.00055 and 0.00068, again smaller than for the equipment equation and larger when the more recent data are included; the corresponding %RMSE are 0.0234 and 0.0260.

(d) For equipment, in all specifications the sum of the lag coefficients is very close to but slightly greater than unity; the specification with the highest adjusted R^2 is with m = 7. Incidentally, this is a useful exercise for demonstrating empirically that when the t-statistic on the single potentially excluded variable is greater (less) than one in absolute value, deleting that variable will increase (decrease) the adjusted R^2. Also, since there are lagged dependent variables, one should not use the Durbin-Watson test statistic here—it is biased. Durbin's m-statistic is more useful.

For structures, all specifications of m from 1 through 12 have sums of lagged coefficient that are less than unity, ensuring stationarity. The models with m = 2, 5 and 9 are quite attractive in terms of statistically significant coefficients and low Durbin m-test statistics. A parsimonious parameterization is for m = 2, where the estimated equation is

$$IS = 2126 + 1.3850*IS(-1) - 0.4024*IS(-2) \qquad R^2 = 0.983481, \ DW = 2.0572$$
$$\quad (1.68) \ (16.64) \qquad\qquad (4.86) \qquad\qquad \text{Durbin's m-test} = -0.777.$$

If one tests m = 2 against m = 6 (the preferred Kopcke specification in his last study) using traditional test procedures, the SSR in the two regressions are 0.114596E+10 and 0.110342E+10, yielding an F-statistic with 4,117 degrees of freedom of 1.13, which is not significant at usual confidence levels.

Exercise 4: Almon Lag Estimation of the Cash Flow Model

GOAL: To help students gain experience in using the Almon polynomial distributed lag procedure in the estimation of a cash flow model of investment spending.

TASKS: Estimate a cash flow model of investment using the Almon PDL technique with restrictions on the polynomial parameters; using the PDL-AR(1) procedure, test for AR(0). Estimate an unconstrained model by OLS, and then test for the PDL restrictions, with and without autocorrelation. Evaluate effects of multicollinearity. Test for alternative degrees of the PDL specification. Estimate using most recent data, and choose a preferred specification.

ON REPLICATING KOPCKE'S REPORTED RESULTS: As was noted above and in the text, data revisions and data re-basing will prevent you from replicating Kopcke's reported results, reproduced in Chapter 6, Table 6.3. For equipment investment, the two estimated cash flow models (using sample observations 25 through 87, and 17 through 112) are, respectively (absolute values of t-statistics are in parentheses):

$$IE = -60005 + 0.214*RC + 0.050*RC(-1) + 0.056*RC(-2) + 0.077*RC(-3)$$
$$(6.84)\quad(4.18)\qquad(1.10)\qquad\quad(1.70)\qquad\quad(1.94)$$

$$+\ 0.046*RC(-4) - 0.017*RC(-5) - 0.005*RC(-6) + 0.139*KELAG \quad R^2 = 0.8903$$
$$(1.39)\qquad\quad(0.35)\qquad\quad(0.09)\qquad\quad(8.52)\qquad\quad DW = 1.7406$$

Here the coefficients are on the unscrambled variables, and estimation is by maximum likelihood retaining the first observation ($\rho = 0.817$, $t = 10.72$). For the second cash flow model,

$$IE = -44134 + 0.267*RC + 0.191*RC(-1) + 0.133*RC(-2) + 0.101*RC(-3)$$
$$(2.44)\quad(6.79)\qquad(7.05)\qquad\quad(5.65)\qquad\quad(4.24)$$

$$+\ 0.097*RC(-4) + 0.126*RC(-5),\ \rho = 0.968 \qquad R^2 = 0.8903$$
$$(3.57)\qquad\quad(3.22)\qquad\quad(46.09)\qquad DW = 1.7452.$$

For structures, the analogous equations are as follows:

$$IS = 24418 + 0.098*RC + 0.042*RC(-1) + 0.070*RC(-2) + 0.057*RC(-3)$$
$$(2.46)\quad(2.07)\qquad(0.90)\qquad\quad(1.75)\qquad\quad(1.42)$$

$$+\ 0.004*RC(-4) + 0.036*RC(-5) + 0.024*KSLAG,\ \rho = 0.859 \qquad R^2 = 0.7965$$
$$(0.07)\qquad\quad(0.66)\qquad\quad(1.42)\qquad\quad(13.24)\qquad DW = 1.9474$$

and

$$IS = 44389 + 0.087*RC + 0.074*RC(-1) + 0.055*RC(-2) + 0.037*RC(-3)$$
$$(4.77)\quad(2.93)\qquad(3.85)\qquad\quad(3.32)\qquad\quad(2.20)$$

$$+\ 0.026*RC(-4) + 0.030*RC(-5),\ \rho = 0.962 \qquad R^2 = 0.4898$$
$$(1.35)\qquad\quad(1.00)\qquad\quad(41.56)\qquad DW = 1.7258.$$

SPECIFIC NOTES ON EXERCISE 4:

(a) Based on OLS estimation, the Durbin-Watson test statistics are 0.0655 for equipment and 0.0731 for structures; AR(0) is decisively rejected. When the iterative Cochrane-Orcutt procedure is employed, estimates of the cash flow model are as follows (with t-statistics in parentheses):

$$IE = -36820 + 0.264*RC + 0.187*RC(-1) + 0.130*RC(-2) + 0.098*RC(-3)$$
$$(1.20) \quad (6.49) \qquad (6.59) \qquad\qquad (5.21) \qquad\qquad (3.89)$$

$$+ 0.094*RC(-4) + 0.123*RC(-5), \quad \rho = 0.978 \qquad R^2 = 0.8903$$
$$(3.29) \qquad\qquad (3.03) \qquad\qquad (45.26) \qquad DW = 1.7585$$

and

$$IS = 50581 + 0.084*RC + 0.071*RC(-1) + 0.052*RC(-2) + 0.034*RC(-3)$$
$$(4.09) \quad (2.79) \qquad (3.62) \qquad\qquad (3.08) \qquad\qquad (2.00)$$

$$+ 0.023*RC(-4) + 0.026*RC(-5), \quad \rho = 0.960 \qquad R^2 = 0.3061$$
$$(1.17) \qquad\qquad (0.85) \qquad\qquad (33.73) \qquad DW = 1.7585.$$

Note the very large t-statistics on the estimated ρ, indicating that the null hypothesis of AR(0) disturbances is decisively rejected. For equipment, the distributed lag coefficient estimates are a bit larger here than reported by Kopcke (see Table 6.3), although they tend to follow a similar pattern; those for structures are generally smaller here, and also follow a similar pattern. The estimates of ρ are similar. For equipment, the sum of the distributed lag coefficients is 0.89586, implying that a $1 increase in real cash flow eventually results in an $0.89586 increase in equipment investment; for structures, the comparable sum is 0.29007.

(b) For equipment (structures), the maximized ln L assuming AR(0) with the PDL restrictions imposed is -1051.37 (-1002.54), and when the parameters are freed up the comparable ln L is -1051.34 (-1002.50); hence the likelihood ratio test statistic with one degree of freedom (seven parameters estimated in the unconstrained, six in the constrained model) is 0.06 (0.08), indicating that the null hypothesis on the validity of the PDL restrictions is not rejected. Assuming AR(1) disturbances, with the PDL restrictions imposed the sample ln L is -905.602 for equipment and -865.958 for structures, and when the PDL restrictions are relaxed the sample ln L increases to -903.698 for equipment and -865.180 for structures. The likelihood ratio test statistic with 1 d.f. is therefore 3.808 for equipment and 1.556 for structures; again, the null hypothesis is not rejected for structures at usual significance levels, but for equipment it is rejected at significance levels greater than about 5%. An interesting feature of these models is that when the PDL restrictions are imposed, much sharper estimates of the distributed lag coefficients emerge; i.e., the adverse effects of multicollinearity can be mitigated by employing (in some cases, empirically supported) PDL restrictions.

(c) Under AR(0), when the degree of the PDL is increased to four rather than three, no constraints are placed on the PDL parameters, and thus the sample log-likelihood is the same. The likelihood ratio test statistic is therefore identical to that in (b). This should also occur with AR(1) disturbances, although numerical convergence issues may slightly change the LR test statistic.

(d) In each model estimated for both structures and equipment, AR(0) as a special case of AR(1) is decisively rejected. For equipment, a rather nice specification turns out to be one with m = 6 and a third-degree polynomial, but with KELAG included as a regressor:

$$IE = -110870 + 0.311*RC + 0.163*RC(-1) + 0.103*RC(-2) + 0.095*RC(-3)$$
$$\quad\; (4.42)\quad (7.40)\qquad (5.39)\qquad\quad (3.93)\qquad\quad (3.52)$$

$$+ 0.099*RC(-4) + 0.078*RC(-5) + 0.079*KELAG, \; \rho = 0.951 \qquad R^2 = 0.6519$$
$$\;\; (3.18)\qquad\quad (1.80)\qquad\quad (3.60)\qquad\quad (34.23)\qquad\qquad DW = 2.4749$$

Models allowing longer m and larger d did not significantly improve the fit. For structures, it was rather difficult to come up with a nice specification, for the number of lags needed to be very small. Even with the relatively parsimonious m = 6 and d = 3 specification of Kopcke, a number of the distributed lag coefficients were insignificantly different from zero, as was the coefficient on KSLAG.

Exercise 5: Putty-Clay in the Neoclassical Model of Investment

GOALS: The purpose of this exercise is to engage students in estimating and interpreting parameters of a neoclassical investment equation, based on the Cobb-Douglas production function, and incorporating the putty-clay effects by allowing for differential impacts on investment of price and output changes.

TASKS: Construct price-output variables consistent with Bischoff's putty-clay specification, and estimate a PDL-AR(1) model. Then test whether the output responses differ from the price responses, using traditional hypothesis-testing procedures. Experiment with other specifications using the more recent data, and choose a preferred specification.

ON REPLICATING KOPCKE'S REPORTED RESULTS: As was noted above and in the text, data revisions and data re-basing will prevent you from replicating Kopcke's reported results, reproduced in Chapter 6, Table 6.4. For equipment investment, the three estimated neoclassical models (using sample observations 25 through 87, 14 through 104 and 17 through 112) are, respectively (absolute values of t-statistics in parentheses):

IE = -50271 + 0.013*X1E1 + 0.027*X1E2 + 0.024*X1E3 + 0.014*X1E4 + 0.001*X1E5
     (5.79)   (3.84)   (5.90)   (5.08)   (2.86)   (0.14)

- 0.014*X2E1 - 0.026*X2E2 - 0.025*X2E3 - 0.012*X2E4 - 0.000*X2E5 + 0.153*KELAG
  (3.91)   (5.55)   (4.86)   (2.39)   (0.04)   (10.36)

where the coefficients are on the scrambled variables (to conserve on space here), the R^2 is 0.935, the DW is 2.3670, and $\rho = 0.812$ (t = 10.97);

IE = -33021 + 0.014*X1E1 + 0.032*X1E2 + 0.018*X1E3 - 0.014*X2E1 - 0.032*X2E2
     (3.10)   (4.73)   (7.08)   (4.33)   (4.55)   (6.64)

      - 0.017*X2E3 + 0.151*KELAG, $\rho = 0.878$ $R^2 = 0.8725$
        (4.09)   (8.00)   (17.41)   DW = 2.005

and

$$IE = -31555 + 0.016*X1E1 + 0.034*X1E2 + 0.021*X1E3 - 0.016*X2E1 - 0.034*X2E2$$
$$(3.87) \quad (5.70) \quad\quad (8.58) \quad\quad (5.84) \quad\quad (5.42) \quad\quad (8.14)$$

$$- 0.020*X2E3 + 0.165*KELAG, \quad\quad \rho = 0.822 \quad R^2 = 0.9395$$
$$(5.58) \quad\quad (13.46) \quad\quad\quad (14.06) \quad DW = 2.186.$$

For structures, the equation estimated over the first time interval has the following form:

$$IS = 16390 - 0.0013*X1S1 + 0.0020*X1S2 + 0.0010*X1S3 + 0.0013*X1S4$$
$$(2.96) \quad (1.33) \quad\quad (4.51) \quad\quad (2.19) \quad\quad (2.55)$$

$$- 0.0014*X1S5 - 0.0128*KSLAG, \quad\quad \rho = 0.7157 \quad R^2 = 0.8769$$
$$(1.39) \quad\quad (0.74) \quad\quad\quad (8.07) \quad DW = 2.045$$

where coefficients are on the scrambled variables.

SPECIFIC COMMENTS ON EXERCISE 5:

(a) Notice that in this exercise we only use the equipment data.

(b) When estimated over observations 17 through 112 (1956:1-1979:4) with m = 13, d = 4 and AR(1) disturbances, the equation I obtained looks like this (the coefficients are on the scrambled variables, and t-statistics are in parentheses):

$$IE = -22120 + 0.016*X11 + 0.037*X12 + 0.025*X13 + 0.009*X14 - 0.017*X21$$
$$(3.08) \quad (5.81) \quad\quad (9.13) \quad\quad (6.35) \quad\quad (2.78) \quad\quad (5.81)$$

$$- 0.037*X22 - 0.025*X23 - 0.007*X24 + 0.166*KELAG, \quad \rho = 0.831 \quad R^2 = 0.939$$
$$(8.67) \quad\quad (6.11) \quad\quad (2.32) \quad\quad (13.08) \quad\quad\quad (14.08) \quad DW = 2.205$$

and the log of the sample maximized log-likelihood function is -895.362. Notice that the coefficients on the X2 variables are negative and statistically significant, implying that the differential impact on investment of output from that of price is significant. It is difficult to compare these results with those reported by Kopcke, since he does not report differential coefficients for the b's and c's.

(c) When the coefficients on the X2's are constrained to zero (and note there are only four such parameters, even though m = 13), the sample maximized log-likelihood with AR(1) disturbances is -925.569. Given the information in

(b) above, the likelihood ratio test statistic is 60.414, which is much larger than the χ^2 critical value with 4 d.f. at usual significance levels. Hence the putty-clay hypothesis of Bischoff is empirically significant in this data.

(d) I experimented with various combinations of m = 9 and m = 13, d = 4 or 5, and with zero end-point restrictions on the trailing price term. Using the 1956:1-1986:4 data, the same specification employed in Kopcke (iii) turned out to be rather nice. This looked like the following, where parameters are on scrambled coefficients and t-statistics are in parentheses:

$$IE = -30848 + 0.016*X11 + 0.036*X12 + 0.026*X13 + 0.011*X14 - 0.017*X21$$
$$\quad\quad (3.94) \quad (4.57) \quad\quad (7.59) \quad\quad (6.07) \quad\quad (3.17) \quad\quad (4.42)$$

$$\quad - 0.036*X22 - 0.027*X23 - 0.009*X24 + 0.156*KELAG, \quad \rho = 0.755 \quad R^2 = 0.950$$
$$\quad\quad (7.08\ ) \quad\quad (5.82) \quad\quad (2.61) \quad\quad (15.31) \quad\quad\quad (11.66) \quad DW = 2.485$$

With this specification, parameters are remarkably similar to those obtained over the earlier data set—see (b) above. Moreover, although increasing d from 4 to 5 slightly improved the fit, the null hypothesis that the two scrambled coefficients equaled zero could not be rejected. Imposing the restriction that the trailing term on the price variable was equal to zero yielded a t-statistic of about 1.5 in most cases, and thus I had a slight preference for the specification without this restriction imposed.

Exercise 6: Almon PDL End-Point Restrictions in Tobin's q Model

GOALS: The purpose of this exercise is to involve students in estimating and interpreting a Tobin's q investment equation using the Almon PDL procedure, and to test for the empirical validity of end-point restrictions.

TASKS: Construct q-variables, estimate a PDL-AR(1) investment equation, test whether trailing term is zero, estimate a slightly amended equation, and then choose a preferred specification based on more recent data.

ON REPLICATING KOPCKE'S REPORTED RESULTS: As was noted above and in the text, data revisions and data re-basing will prevent you from replicating Kopcke's reported results, reproduced in Chapter 6, Table 6.6. For equipment investment, the three estimated Tobin's q models (using sample observations 25 through 87, 9 through 104 and 17 through 112) are, respectively (with absolute values of t-statistics in parentheses):

$$IE = -86949 + 0.192*RFE1 + 0.187*RFE2 + 0.059*RFE3 + 0.042*RFE4$$
$$\quad (5.94) \quad (4.03) \qquad (3.96) \qquad (1.25) \qquad (0.84)$$

$$+ \; 0.088*RFE5 + 0.133*KELAG, \qquad \rho = 0.889 \quad R^2 = 0.825$$
$$\quad (1.79) \qquad (6.94) \qquad\qquad (15.30) \quad DW = 1.981;$$

$$IE/KELAG = 0.217 - 0.465*XE1 + 0.499*XE2 + 0.105*XE3, \; \rho = 0.985 \quad R^2 = 0.2679$$
$$\qquad (6.23) \quad (2.19) \qquad (4.63) \qquad (1.32) \qquad\qquad (56.41) \quad DW = 1.5075$$

where the coefficients on the XE variables are multiplied by E-07; and

$$IEU = -33288 - 0.018*XE1 + 0.004*XE2 + 0.017*XE3 + 0.247*KELAG, \; \rho = 0.7926$$
$$\qquad (4.63) \quad (1.22) \qquad (0.44) \qquad (3.67) \qquad (23.69) \qquad\qquad (12.67)$$

and where $R^2 = 0.9527$, DW = 2.1447. For structures, the models estimated using sample observations 9 through 104 and 17 through 112 are as follows:

$$IS/KSLAG = 0.094 - 0.120*XS1 + 0.135*XS2 + 0.053*XS3, \; \rho = 0.926 \quad R^2 = 0.3399$$
$$\qquad (30.82) \quad (2.13) \qquad (4.47) \qquad (2.56 \;) \qquad\qquad (23.92) \quad DW = 2.0650$$

where the coefficients on the XS variables are multiplied by E-07; and

$$ISU = \; 23433 - 0.002*XS1 - 0.003*XS2 + 0.007*XS3 + 0.085*KSLAG, \; \rho = 0.8772$$
$$\qquad (1.45) \quad (0.24) \qquad (0.67) \qquad (2.08) \qquad (5.51) \qquad\qquad (17.81)$$

and where $R^2 = 0.4299$, DW = 1.5666.

SPECIFIC COMMENTS ON EXERCISE 6:

(a) I've defined the equipment and structures variables as XE and XS.

(b) Using data from 1956:1-1979:4 (observation numbers 17 through 112), I obtained the following (using the ML AR(1) procedure in which the first observation is retained), with t-statistics in parentheses:

$$IE = -57917 - 0.048*XE1 + 0.059*XE2 - 0.004*XE3 + 0.059*XE4 + 0.282*KELAG$$
$$\qquad (2.17) \quad (2.41) \qquad (5.47) \qquad (0.39) \qquad (3.11) \qquad (9.08)$$

where the R^2 is 0.554, the DW = 1.7904, $\rho = 0.979$ (65.35), ln L = -919.882 and the coefficient estimates are on the scrambled variables. The unscrambled distributed lag coefficients are, starting with the current value and then lagging sequentially, -0.048 (2.41), 0.038 (4.07), 0.061 (5.31), 0.045 (5.53), 0.014 (1.70), -0.010 (0.86), -0.003 (0.30) and 0.059 (3.11). For structures, the equation looks like this:

$$IS = -1240.1 - 0.014*XS1 + 0.015*XS2 + 0.002*XS3 + 0.009*XS4 + 0.101*KSLAG$$
$$(0.06) \quad\quad (1.70) \quad\quad\quad (3.57) \quad\quad\quad (0.46) \quad\quad\quad (1.07) \quad\quad\quad (5.43)$$

where the R^2 = 0.434, DW = 1.7497, ρ = 0.973 (50.20) and the ln L = -877.350. The unscrambled distributed lag coefficients, beginning with the current term, are -0.014 (t = 1.698), 0.006 (1.58), 0.014 (3.17), 0.014 (3.76), 0.010 (3.38), 0.004 (0.98), -0.001 (0.15), -0.000 (0.04), and 0.009 (1.07).

(c) When the trailing term is set to zero, the ln L for the equipment equation is -925.311 and that for the structures equation is -878.276 (estimation is by the ML-AR(1) method retaining the initial observation). The implied likelihood ratio test statistics are 10.858 and 1.852, respectively. With 1 d.f., the null hypothesis that the mth term equals zero is rejected for the equipment equation, but is not rejected for the structures equation.

(d) Results will change, for means of the right-hand variables will change. Nonlinearities on the PDL coefficients will also affect estimates. Estimating by the ML-AR(1) method in which the first observation is retained, I obtained the following results for the revised equipment equation, where XEM ≡ Q*KELAG, and where t-statistics are in parentheses:

$$IE = -60110 - 0.062*XEM1 + 0.064*XEM2 - 0.006*XEM3 + 0.061*XEM4 + 0.142*KELAG$$
$$(2.24) \quad\quad (2.92) \quad\quad\quad (5.30) \quad\quad\quad (0.47) \quad\quad\quad (2.88) \quad\quad\quad (5.69)$$

where the R^2 is 0.536, the DW = 1.6938, ρ = 0.977 (60.99), ln L = -923.049 and the coefficient estimates are on the scrambled variables. The unscrambled distributed lag coefficients are, starting with the current value and then lagging sequentially, -0.062 (2.92), 0.037 (3.72), 0.066 (5.11), 0.049 (5.39), 0.015 (1.61), -0.012 (0.95), -0.005 (0.52) and 0.061 (2.88). There is little basis to choose between the two, although the coefficient on KELAG appears more reasonable in this modified equation. For structures, the equation looks like this (where XSM ≡ Q*KSLAG):

IS = 650.21 - 0.015*XSM1 + 0.015*XSM2 + 0.002*XSM3 + 0.008*XSM4 + 0.060*KSLAG
      (0.03)   (1.77)   (3.47)   (0.40)   (0.98)   (3.65)

where the R^2 = 0.433, DW = 1.7141, ρ = 0.971 (47.53), and the ln L = -878.274. The unscrambled distributed lag coefficients, beginning with the current term, are -0.015 (t = 1.77), 0.005 (1.48), 0.014 (3.07), 0.014 (3.66), 0.010 (3.27), 0.004 (0.92), -0.001 (0.21), -0.000 (0.14) and 0.008 (0.98). Except for the coefficient on KSLAG, the results are virtually identical to those in (b) above, and thus there is little to choose between them.

(e) I only experimented with the XEM and XSM variables, constrained the model to lie along a third-degree polynomial, let m vary from 5 to 9, and checked for trailing point restrictions. For equipment, a rather nice equation is the following, with m = 5 and the trailing point restriction imposed (the LR test for this restriction was 0.20):

IE = -26280 - 0.085*XEM1 + 0.063*XEM2 + 0.033*XEM3 + 0.146*KELAG, ρ = 0.924
     (1.69)   (2.74)   (2.63)   (2.02)   (7.47)   (28.60)

where the R^2 is 0.6034, DW = 1.8055 and ln L = -1246.81. The unscrambled distributed lag coefficients are, beginning with the current term, -0.085 (t = 2.74), 0.035 (1.58), 0.066 (3.21), 0.045 (3.55) and 0.010 (0.49).

For structures, among the specifications with which I experimented, none was particularly impressive. A modestly decent equation on the basis of statistical criteria was with m = 6 and with the trailing point restriction imposed (the LR test statistic for this restriction was 1.44), and it looked like this:

IS = 304601 - 0.029*XSM1 + 0.010*XSM2 + 0.006*XSM3 + 0.061*KSLAG, ρ = 0.941
     (2.08)   (2.40)   (1.30)   (1.19)   (4.83)   (32.09)

where the R^2 = 0.322, DW = 1.2874 and ln L = -1176.34. An interesting problem with this model, however, is that the sum of the distributed lag coefficients is negative (-0.0029737), implying that an increase in Tobin's q eventually results in a <u>decrease</u> in structures investment! This is a good example of the need to interpret the coefficients, and not just look at their t-values.

<u>Exercise 7: Box-Jenkins Identification, Estimation and Forecasting of an
            Investment Equation</u>

GOALS: The purpose of this exercise is to give students "hands-on" experience in modeling the investment data series using the Box-Jenkins time series approach. It is a somewhat open-ended exercise—other researchers may come to somewhat different conclusions—and thus I'll only present selected results here for parts (a) through (c). If you find that you come to some rather clear-cut conclusions with this data, please let me know the details. Finally, obtaining numerical convergence in moving average models is often problematic, and do not be surprised if you experience some difficulties in obtaining convergence with your statistical software.

TASKS: Using Box-Jenkins techniques, first transform the data to make them stationary using sample autocorrelation functions and the Box-Pierce portmanteau test; identify the order q of the MA process (examining the autocorrelation functions) and the order p of the AR process (observing the partial autocorrelations); then choose several preferred specifications, and estimate them. Use more recent data, re-do the above, and then compare models using <u>ex post</u> dynamic forecasting properties.

SPECIFIC COMMENTS ON EXERCISE 7:

(a) The IE data show a clear upward trend with time. To check on replication, note that with $d = 1$, the Box-Pierce Q-statistic is 17.9 at $m = 1$, and for $d = 2$ the same test statistic at $m = 1$ is 19.4; at $m = 2$, these statistics are 33.1 and 20.8, respectively. For $d = 0$, 3 and 4, the test statistics are considerably larger. Sample autocorrelations decline rather quickly with $d = 1$ or 2. I have a modest preference for $d = 1$ or 2.

For the IS data, the data also trend upward over time, but not as markedly as the IE data. Sample autocorrelation coefficients dampen even with d = 0, but are clearly tending toward zero as the lag length increases with d = 1. For d = 1, the Box-Pierce Q-statistic at m = 1 is 6.60. The d = 1 specification looks quite attractive.

(b) For the IE data, with d = 1, the sample autocorrelations at lag length 1 and 2 are quite large, while with d = 2 they are large at 1, and at 4 or 5 (recall that the investment data have been seasonally adjusted). The partial autocorrelation functions indicate that when d = 1, the first two partial autocorrelation coefficients are significant, while with d = 2, those at 1 and at 4 are significant. Possible choices for d = 1 are p = 2 and q = 2, and for d = 2, p = 4 and q = 1.

With the IS data and d = 1, the sample autocorrelation function at lag length 1 is significant, that at 2 is marginal, and the partial autocorrelation function is significant only at length 1. There are no clear spikes in the sample autocorrelation functions. Possible choices for the IS time series representation are for d = 1, p = 1 or 2 and q = 0.

(c) For the IE data, with d = 1 the p = q = 1 representation was quite nice; the AR parameter estimate (t-statistic) was 0.777 (6.83), while the MA parameter estimate was 0.360 (2.12), and the Box-Pierce Q-statistic was 0.55292. When d = 2, the p = 4 and q = 1 AR representation looked like this (t-statistics in parentheses):

$$\phi(B) = 1 - 1.063B - 0.421B^2 - 0.176B^3 - 0.276B^4$$
$$\quad\quad\quad (-4.88)\quad (-2.38)\quad\quad (-1.14)\quad\quad (-2.30)$$

and the MA parameter was -0.615 (t = -2.90). With this specification, the Box-Pierce Q statistic at m = 1 was 0.00082.

With the IS data, the ARIMA(1,1,1) specification was rather attractive; the AR coefficient (t-statistic) was 0.805 (5.20), the MA coefficient was

0.542 (2.64), and the Box-Pierce Q-statistic was 0.12140 at m = 1. However, another somewhat surprisingly attractive specification was that for the ARIMA (1,2,1) representation, which yielded an AR coefficient of 0.268 (t = 2.58), an MA coefficient of 0.974 (64.68) and a Box-Pierce Q-statistic of 0.10486.

Exercise 8: Estimation with Simultaneity and Autocorrelation

GOALS: The purpose of this exercise is to have students gain first-hand experience with instrumental variable estimation of several models in the presence of simultaneity and first-order autocorrelation.

TASKS: Estimate an accelerator equation by OLS, and allowing for AR(1) disturbances. Then estimate by 2SLS, and by 2SLS-AR(1), taking care to construct the set of instrumental variables. Compare the various estimates.

SPECIFIC COMMENTS ON EXERCISE 8:

(a) Based on the 1956:1-1986:4 time period (observations 17 through 140), the accelerator equation (6.15) was estimated by maximum likelihood allowing for AR(1) disturbances, retaining the first observation. For equipment, the estimate (t-statistic) of ρ was 0.978 (62.01), and for structures it was 0.953 (34.32). The AR(1) estimates on the current output and lagged capital stock differed substantially from the OLS estimates. If disturbances follow an AR(1) process, in the presence of essentially a lagged dependent variable (given the perpetual inventory method used to construct the capital stock), OLS estimates will be biased.

(b) Using as instruments a constant, Y(-1) through Y(-6), the lagged capital stock, lagged investment and the lagged capacity utilization rate, the 2SLS estimates under the AR(0) assumption differ quite a bit from the OLS estimates, particularly for coefficients on current output and lagged capital stock.

(c) With the same set of instruments as in (b), using the iterative Cochrane-Orcutt estimation procedure, the estimate of ρ (t-statistic) I obtained for the equipment equation is 0.964 (40.21) and for structures it is 0.958 (36.85); in both cases, there is strong evidence rejecting AR(0) in favor of the AR(1) alternative hypothesis. Parameter estimates differ considerably from OLS to 2SLS-AR(1); for example, in the equipment equation the OLS estimate on current output is 0.010, while the 2SLS-AR(1) estimate is 0.175, and comparable estimates on KELAG change sign from 0.100 to -0.255. In the structures equation, similar patterns emerge; the OLS estimate on current output is -0.026 and KSLAG it is -0.051, while the respective 2SLS-AR(1) estimates are 0.040 and 0.118.

NOTE: In this exercise, I have not suggested a Hausman specification test on whether the disturbances are correlated with Y. As an option, you might have students do this test.

Exercise 9: Levels and First Differences of the CES Capital Demand Equation with Autocorrelation

GOALS: The purpose of this exercise is to have students become involved in assessing the empirical evidence on the controversy surrounding the responsiveness of investment to changes in the user cost of capital, and in the level of output. The estimated model is based on the CES (not the Cobb-Douglas) function, and the sensitivity of results to various types of autocorrelated disturbances is examined. Students will also encounter problems with multiple local optima.

TASKS: Estimate several PDL-AR(0) neoclassical investment models in level form based on Bischoff's putty-clay specification. Then estimate the same model in first-difference form, which is equivalent to estimating a PDL-AR(1) model with $\rho = 1.00$. Next estimate the same model, but estimate ρ

rather than assume it is zero or one. Finally, estimate the model using several other AR and MA stochastic specifications. For all these estimated models, compute long-run price and output elasticities.

SPECIFIC COMMENTS ON EXERCISE 9:

(a) For the IE equation, coefficients on the lagged dependent variable were always statistically significant in the s = 1,2,3 equations when estimated using the PDL procedure with AR(0) disturbances. When s = 1 was imposed, Durbin's m-test statistics were significant; else they were insignificantly different from zero. Perhaps the best of the IE equations here was the following (scrambled coefficients, t-statistics in parentheses):

$$
\begin{aligned}
\text{LNKE} = &-0.074 - 0.003*\text{LNPE1} + 0.001*\text{LNPE2} - 0.001*\text{LNPE3} + 0.003*\text{LNPE4} \\
&\;(2.10)\quad (1.16) \qquad\quad (0.62) \qquad\qquad (0.41) \qquad\qquad (1.11)
\end{aligned}
$$

$$
\begin{aligned}
&+ 0.036*\text{LNY1} - 0.008*\text{LNY2} - 0.002*\text{LNY3} - 0.009*\text{LNY4} + 1.51*\text{LNKE}(-1) \\
&\;\;(4.84) \qquad\quad (1.89) \qquad\qquad (0.27) \qquad\qquad (1.39) \qquad\qquad (16.27)
\end{aligned}
$$

$$
\begin{aligned}
&- 0.338*\text{LNKE}(-2) - 0.193*\text{LNKE}(-3) \\
&\;\;(2.00) \qquad\qquad\quad (2.12)
\end{aligned}
$$

with an R^2 of 0.99999 (yes!), a Durbin's m-test statistic of -0.62 and an ln L of 648.759. However, the sum of the distributed lag coefficients on the price variables is positive (not negative) at 0.00108, while that for output is positive (0.013736) as should be the case. For the IS equation, the t-statistic on the s = 3 lagged variable was typically around -1.5, and when s = 1 the Durbin m-test statistic was significant, else it was not. None of the structures equations was particularly good, but one equation that was not too bad was the following (yet notice how long it takes for the price effects to become negative and significant):

$$
\begin{aligned}
\text{LNKS} = &\;\;0.019 + 0.000*\text{LNPS1} + 0.000*\text{LNPS2} + 0.001*\text{LNPS3} - 0.002*\text{LNPS4} \\
&\;(3.58)\quad (0.01) \qquad\quad (0.06) \qquad\qquad (1.35) \qquad\qquad (2.38)
\end{aligned}
$$

$$
\begin{aligned}
&+ 0.009*\text{LNY1} - 0.001*\text{LNY2} - 0.001*\text{LNY3} + 0.004*\text{LNY4} + 1.69*\text{LNKS}(-1) \\
&\;\;(3.46) \qquad\quad (0.96) \qquad\qquad (0.86) \qquad\qquad (1.39) \qquad\qquad (18.51)
\end{aligned}
$$

$$
\begin{aligned}
&- 0.569*\text{LNKS}(-2) - 0.139*\text{LNKS}(-3) \\
&\;\;(3.25) \qquad\qquad\quad (1.52)
\end{aligned}
$$

having a rather high R^2 of 0.999995, an ln L of 742.951 and a Durbin's m-test statistic of -0.29.

(b) Under the assumption that $\rho = 1.00$ in an AR(1) process, one estimates a first-differenced model. For equipment, when s = 3, typically the coefficient on s = 2 was insignificant; and when s = 1, Durbin's m-statistic became significant, else it was not. It was difficult to find a desirable specification, for in most cases most of the price coefficients were statistically insignificant, and in some cases the sum of the distributed lag coefficients on the price variables was positive rather than negative. One specification that was modestly acceptable was the following, for s = 2 and m = 11 (but even here it takes quite a while for the price coefficient to become near significant, and Durbin's m-test statistic is marginal at -1.906):

$$DLNKE = - 0.003*DLNPE1 - 0.001*DLNPE2 + 0.003*DLNPE3 - 0.005*DLNPE4 + 0.061*DLNY1$$
$$\quad\quad (1.10) \quad\quad\quad (0.62) \quad\quad\quad (0.12) \quad\quad\quad (1.50) \quad\quad\quad (5.84)$$

$$+ 0.018*DLNY2 + 0.013*DLNY3 - 0.000*DLNY4 + 0.607*DLNKE(-1) + 0.235*DLNKE(-2)$$
$$\quad (2.59) \quad\quad\quad (1.95) \quad\quad\quad (0.04) \quad\quad\quad (6.86) \quad\quad\quad\quad (2.83)$$

with an R^2 of 0.904493 and a sample ln L of 647.480. Another almost equally acceptable specification was that when s = 3 and m = 11, but to save space I'll not reproduce that here.

For structures, when the first-difference specification was employed, with s = 3, typically the coefficients on s = 2 and 3 were insignificant; in almost all specifications, most of the price variables were statistically insignificant as well. Of the various specifications with which I experimented, perhaps the best was the following, where m = 9 and s = 1:

$$DLNKS = - 0.002*DLNPS1 - 0.000*DLNPS2 - 0.001*DLNPS3 + 0.000*DLNPS4$$
$$\quad\quad (1.21) \quad\quad\quad (0.31) \quad\quad\quad (0.51) \quad\quad\quad (0.16)$$

$$+ 0.016*DLNY1 + 0.004*DLNY2 + 0.006*DLNY3 - 0.007*DLNY4 + 0.949*DLNKS(-1)$$
$$\quad (3.50) \quad\quad\quad (1.46) \quad\quad\quad (2.30) \quad\quad\quad (1.56) \quad\quad\quad (61.14)$$

which had an R^2 of 0.906649, a Durbin's m-test statistic of -1.33233 and a sample ln L of 736.744. With this specification, the pattern of the price and output distributed lag coefficients appeared quite plausible.

(c) The first time I did this I used the iterative Cochrane-Orcutt procedure and noticed that the estimates of ρ I obtained were almost always negative and close to zero. With a lagged dependent variable, what was happening was that the initial estimate of ρ was a biased one, and it sent the computational algorithm off into the wrong direction, where it converged at a local rather than global optimum. I then re-did this part of the exercise using the Hildreth-Lu technique, having a somewhat coarse grid step of 0.1 and running from $\rho = -0.9$ to $+0.9$. As you will see, the Hildreth-Lu procedure did much better than the iterative Cochrane-Orcutt method.

In particular, for the equipment equation all models with $s = 2$ or $s = 3$ had several optima, and the SER (sample ln L) was continuing to decrease (increase) when ρ hit 0.9. When $s = 1$, the global optimum was at 0.7 or 0.8. The preferred specification is the same as that in (b) above, $s = 2$ and $m = 11$, where with $\rho = 0.9$, the sample ln L equals 646.282; note that the sample ln L was slightly larger in the first-difference version at 647.480. Hence for the equipment equation, there certainly is support for the first-difference specification in which $\rho = 1.00$.

For structures, matters are even a bit more complicated. Again there is a local-global problem, and given the size and range of the grid, optima tend to congregate at either $\rho = -0.1$ to 0.0 or at $\rho = 0.9$. Based on the results of (b) above, when $s = 3$ and $m = 9$, the Hildreth-Lu procedure suggests a global optimum at $\rho = 0.9$, where the ln L of 737.825 is slightly greater than in the first-differenced model where ln L = 736.744. Parameter estimates at the two points are very similar, however.

(d) Given space constraints and the open-ended nature of this portion of the exercise, I will not present results here. I should emphasize, however, that issues of local and global optima must be carefully addressed when estimating and choosing amongst more general AR or MA specifications.

Exercise 10: A "Horse Race" Project Based on More Recent Data

GOALS: The purpose of this exercise is to engage students in a "horse race" among alternative investment models, comparing the models in terms of performance in estimation, static forecasts and dynamic forecasts.

TASKS: Using 1956:1-1981:4 data, for three of the five investment models, choose a preferred specification, experimenting with various lags and stochastic specifications. Then do an _ex post_ forecast, with both static and dynamic values for the lagged dependent variables. On the basis of the %RMSE and Theil inequality coefficient criteria, determine which models win the "horse race", for equipment and for structures investment.

NOTES ON EXERCISE 10: This is a rather open-ended exercise, and therefore I will not present results here. Recall that I have discussed alternative ways of designing this exercise for class use at the beginning of this chapter under the heading "General Comments to the Instructor." Good luck!

INSTRUCTOR'S NOTES FOR CHAPTER SEVEN:

<u>THE DEMAND FOR ELECTRICITY—STRUCTURAL AND TIME SERIES APPROACHES</u>

ECONOMETRIC PROCEDURES EMPLOYED IN THE EXERCISES OF CHAPTER SEVEN:

- Generate transformed variables, examine data trends, and compute simple correlations

- Do OLS and GLS allowing for heteroskedasticity, both "brute force" and simple way, if software permits the latter

- Compute White's heteroskedasticity-consistent robust standard errors

- Calculate implied elasticities for linear equation at sample means

- Verify empirically the numerical relationships among coefficients when an omitted variable bias exists

- Interpret standard error of regression, and compute a forecast

- Do GLS for AR(1) process—Hildreth-Lu, iterative Cochrane-Orcutt and maximum likelihood (retrieving first observation)

- Do in-sample forecast beginning in 1973, examine forecast errors

- Test for AR(1) disturbances in presence of lagged dependent variable, using Durbin's m- and h-tests

- Examine local-global minima problems for alternative computational algorithms in estimation of AR(1) model

- Assess why one-step Cochrane-Orcutt procedure is inappropriate in presence of lagged dependent variable

- Implement empirically a number of rather <u>ad hoc</u> forecasting procedures—single exponential smoothing, double exponential smoothing and Holt's 2-parameter exponential smoothing method

More-advanced procedures:

- Use Box-Jenkins time series techniques to test for stationarity, and examine simple and partial autocorrelations

- Do ARIMA(0,1,1) estimation and forecasting

- Insert these forecasts of exogenous variables into structural demand equation, and compare results with predicted demand given actual values of forecasted exogenous variables; re-do assuming price elasticity of demand for electricity is zero

GOALS FOR CHAPTER SEVEN:

To help students gain first-hand experience in constructing models of electricity demand, in replicating and interpreting classic electricity demand studies, and in using these and other models to construct forecasts using structural, extrapolative and time series approaches.

GENERAL COMMENTS TO THE INSTRUCTOR:

This chapter will be of particular value to instructors and students interested in exploring alternative forecasting procedures. The approach taken here is a somewhat eclectic one, exposing students to a variety of admittedly <u>ad hoc</u> and more structural approaches to forecasting, and letting them (or you) make judgments on the appropriate role of structural and time series considerations in the forecasting process. While my own bias is clearly toward the more structural approach, I have tried to be rather catholic in the exercises, and therefore the chapter should be useful even to those who prefer the time series approach.

The empirical application chosen in this chapter—forecasting electricity demand—is particularly instructive, for this is one industry in which forecasting is absolutely essential for rational long-term planning. Not surprisingly, over the last two decades the industry has changed considerably in the way in which it has constructed its electricity demand forecasts. Procedures which were only used by academics years ago are now widely implemented by industry practitioners.

I strongly recommend that you have all students do both Exercises 1 and 2, for examining the data provides a most helpful background prior to getting involved in estimation. For instructors particularly interested in forecasting, you will find Exercises 5, 7 and 8 to be most useful.

Exercises 1 through 7 employ tools typically taught up to and including generalized least squares procedures (although many econometrics courses do not deal with some of the more ad hoc forecasting procedures implemented in Exercise 7). Exercise 8 utilizes Box-Jenkins and transfer function procedures, and therefore is appropriate for students in a course emphasizing time series approaches.

SPECIFIC NOTES ON THE EXERCISES IN CHAPTER SEVEN:

Exercise 1: Examining Houthakker's U.K. Data on 42 Towns

TASKS: Print and examine data series, compute budget shares, ex post average price of electricity and intramarginal expenditure of electricity, compute and print a correlation matrix, calculate logarithmic transformations of variables.

COMMENTS: The purpose of this exercise is simply to help students become familiar with important features of the data used by Houthakker in his 1951 pioneering study on factors affecting the demand for electricity in 42 towns of Great Britain in 1937-38. Variations in prices among towns, the importance of the intramarginal electricity budget share, the relationship between marginal and ex post average price, are all examined. Students will find this preliminary data analysis to be of considerable help in understanding and interpreting the regression results they obtain in subsequent exercises.

(a) For the marginal electricity price in 1933-34 (MC4) as well as for MC6 and MC8, the smallest value was 0.33 and the largest was 0.75. The relative variation in gas prices is slightly less, from 4.2 to 11.0. One would expect electricity demand to vary directly with the price of gas when both types of cookers are available, since they are substitutable goods.

(b) The variation in INC is considerable, over fivefold from a minimum of 279 to a max of 1422. A look at the data suggests there is a positive relationship between INC and KWH, although being able to infer partial relationships from simple data trends is notoriously difficult. The budget share for electricity is very small—a mean of 0.89%, with a minimum of 0.396% to a maximum of 1.396%.

(c) The mean of the <u>ex post</u> average price AVGPE is about twice as large as the MC8 marginal price—1.02782 vs. 0.50024, reflecting the effects of a fixed charge independent of the amount of consumption of electricity (a two-part tariff of the form EXPEN = A + B*KWH, where A and B > 0). Hence AVGPE = A/KWH + B depends on the amount of KWH consumed—clearly this <u>ex post</u> average price is endogenous, depending on the KWH consumed. This implies a simultaneous equations problem in estimation, for not only does KWH depend on price, but price depends on KWH.

(d) The simple correlation matrix on the untransformed data looks like

	KWH	INC	MC6	GAS6	CAP
KWH	1.00000				
INC	0.76678	1.00000			
MC6	-0.27386	0.12703	1.00000		
GAS6	-0.01321	0.14375	0.32111	1.00000	
CAP	-0.03832	-0.31314	-0.04836	-0.03772	1.00000

while that for the log-transformed variables is

	LNX	LNM	LNPE2	LNPG2	LNH
LNX	1.00000				
LNM	0.77383	1.00000			
LNPE2	-0.28376	0.07842	1.00000		
LNPG2	0.02168	0.12129	0.36403	1.00000	
LNH	0.10979	-0.33500	-0.15794	-0.00212	1.00000.

These correlation coefficients look very similar—there are no sign changes, and magnitudes are roughly the same for the original and log-transformed data.

Exercise 2: Examining the Nelson-Peck NERC U.S. Time Series Data

TASKS: Print and examine data series, plot KWH vs. GNP and compute their simple correlations over various time periods, relate R^2 to simple correlation coefficient squared. Compute and interpret logarithmic first differences, calculate sample means, and comment on consistency with "double in ten" formula. Compare correlation matrix in level and first-differenced logarithmic form.

COMMENTS: The purpose of this exercise is to have students become familiar with important features of the data underlying the Nelson-Peck study of electricity demand forecasting in the U.S. from 1951 to 1984; this preliminary data analysis will be of considerable help to students in understanding and interpreting the regression results of subsequent exercises. In particular, students assess the variability over time in real electricity prices and real GNP, and multicollinearity among real GNP, electricity consumption and the real price of electricity.

(a) The real price of electricity declines steadily from 3.12 cents per KWH in 1951 to a low of 1.83 in 1970, then increases steadily to 2.96 in 1982, where it tends to stabilize, having a 2.92 value at the end of the sample, slightly less than the 3.12 at the beginning of the sample. Scale economies (see Chapter 3) might have contributed to this, as did the promotional pricing strategies adopted by electric utilities.

(b) Simple correlations between KWH and GNP are 0.99590 for 1951-84, 0.99281 for 1951-73 and 0.99019 for 1974-84. These are very high (note the somewhat unusual case that the correlation within the time sub-periods is less than that over the entire time period), and suggest that electricity demand is very closely related to GNP. Based on even a simple bivariate regression of KWH on a constant and GNP, the R^2 would be very, very high—simply the square of these three sample correlations for the three time periods—0.99182, 0.98567 and 0.98048.

(c) Sample means are 0.07486, -0.02376 and 0.03511 for LNK1, LNP1 and LNG1, respectively, implying that the double-ten rule for LNK1 (consistent with about 7%) is borne out in this 1951-73 data. For 1974-84, however, the sample mean of LNK1 falls to 0.02593. The simple correlation between LNP1 and LNK1 changes considerably in time periods, from -0.76133 (1952-84) to -0.59483 (1952-73) and -0.61175 (1974-84); that between LNK1 and LNG1 in the same time periods is 0.62241, 0.54493 and 0.87450—hence this correlation is largest post-1973. There are no sign changes in correlations over the various sub-periods. Moving to first differences in log-transformed data results in a lower correlation between the GNP and KWH variables than when one retains the levels data in natural units. The reverse occurs for correlations between the price and consumption data—these negative correlations increase (in absolute value) when first-differenced logarithmic transformations are applied.

Exercise 3: Replicating Houthakker's U.K. Study

TASKS: Compute transformed variables, do OLS and compare results with those of Houthakker. Do GLS by doing OLS on suitably transformed data, and compare OLS and GLS parameter estimates and standard errors. Compute heteroskedasticity-robust standard errors, and then do GLS the automated way, making sure the automated results are numerically equivalent to the "brute force" estimates. Compute elasticities based on an estimated linear equation, evaluated at a particular point. Do OLS estimation on a log-transformed model, and then compare GLS estimates with those reported by Houthakker.

COMMENTS: In this exercise students attempt to replicate (with considerable success) the econometric findings reported by Houthakker in a pioneering study that ingeniously utilized the very limited computational facilities of the EDSAC computer at Cambridge University.

(a) You should be able to replicate the OLS results. These OLS estimates are similar to Houthakker's GLS estimates for all parameters except that on GAS6, but its standard errors are very large for both OLS and GLS.

(b) The GLS results you obtain should match those reported in the exercise, and correspond very closely (but not quite exactly) with the GLS results reported by Houthakker. Incidentally, standard errors on PRECIP, GAS6 and CAP are all smaller with GLS than with OLS. Since the OLS estimates are biased, and the sign of the bias is in general unknown, the results here are not entirely unexpected, although the finding of larger standard errors under GLS is perhaps a bit more common. The heteroskedasticity-robust standard errors for the five coefficients (in the same order they appear in the equation in the text) are 458.6, 0.201, 157.6, 31.56 and 91.61, which except for INC, are all larger than the GLS estimates, and in most cases are smaller than the OLS biased standard error estimates. The GLS estimated income elasticity is 2.341*500/1171 = 0.9996, which is very close to the 1.01 estimate reported by Houthakker. The own-price elasticity estimate is equal to -604/(0.5*1171) = -1.032 (recall that PRECIP ≡ 1/MC6), which is close to Houthakker's -1.04 estimate. Since the sample means of MC6 and KWH are 0.54 and 1271—very similar to the 0.50 and 1171 values suggested by Houthakker—the elasticity estimates are unlikely to differ much when computed at the sample mean.

(c) In doing the log-log regression, make sure students take the log of MC6, not the log of PRECIP ≡ 1/MC6. You should be able to replicate the OLS results reported in this exercise. The heteroskedasticity transformation is not quite correct in this case, unless the original town data had been computed with geometric rather than arithmetic means for the relevant

variables. Your estimated GLS equation coefficients (standard errors) should
be: -1.0529 (0.533) for the constant; 1.1697 (0.088) for LNM; -0.8789 (0.189)
for LNPE2; 0.2075 (0.118) for LNPG2; and 0.1755 (0.033) for LNH. The R^2 from
the weighted residuals is 0.8719, while that from the unweighted is 0.8124.
These are very close to the GLS results reported by Houthakker (reproduced in
Section 7.5 in the text), although his 0.934 R^2 value remains a mystery (its
square, however, is 0.8724, which is very close to the 0.8719 R^2 value for the
weighted residuals given above). Most of the GLS estimated standard errors
are smaller than the biased OLS estimates—a slightly unusual result. On this,
see the discussion in part (b) above.

Exercise 4: Omitted Variable Bias—Intramarginal Electricity Price

TASKS: Generate variables and logarithmic transformations, do OLS on
equation with variable omitted, on an auxiliary regression equation, and then
on an equation with the LNF variable included. Verify the numerical
relationship among coefficient estimates in the omitted variable case. Then
do regression with ex post average price included, and incorporate the effect
of including intramarginal expenditure by redefining a variable and doing OLS
on the transformed model. Assess importance of omitted variable bias.

COMMENTS: Very frequently in applied work one must worry about the
effects of omitting a potentially important variable from the regression
equation. In this exercise, the omitted variable bias issue is addressed in
the context of electricity demand, where Taylor [1975] has argued that omitted
variable bias could be important. The purpose of this exercise, therefore, is
to help practitioners obtain a better understanding of factors affecting the
magnitude of the omitted variable bias.

(a) See Exercise 1(c).

(b) The sample mean of SH is 0.00443, with a minimum value of 0.00141 and a maximum value of 0.00685. Multiplying this sample mean by an income elasticity of 1.0 yields an a priori estimate of $b_{y2.K}$ equal to 0.00443—a very small number indeed.

(c) This OLS equation should look something like this (absolute values of t-stats in parentheses):

$$\text{LNF} = -2.460 + 0.429*\text{LNM} - 0.173*\text{LNPE2} + 0.224*\text{LNPG2} - 0.010*\text{LNH} \quad R^2 = 0.308$$
$$\quad\quad (2.72) \quad\quad (3.56) \quad\quad\quad (0.55) \quad\quad\quad\quad (0.92) \quad\quad\quad\quad (0.19)$$

Note that unlike the modern U.S. and Canadian case, here the coefficient on LNPE2 is negative (-0.173), but small.

(d) The estimated bias of $b_{y1} - b_{y1.K} = b_{21}b_{y2.K}$ in this case is -0.173*0.00443, or simply -0.000766. Hence in this context one expects the omitted variable bias to be very small indeed.

(e) This difference is slightly larger than predicted in (d), but still is very small. Specifically, the difference in estimates of the marginal electricity price elasticity is -0.90201 - (-0.89233) = -0.00968. The reason for the difference from that expected is that the economic theory argument in terms of income share times income elasticity is an approximate one, and in this case the income elasticity is slightly larger than unity.

(f) We would expect roughly the same result, since the argument is an algebraic one. The estimated (average) price elasticity of demand with LNF excluded is -0.91235 (t = 6.535), and the coefficient on LNAVPE in an auxiliary regression with LNF as dependent variable is 0.76762 (t = 3.589); however, the estimated average price elasticity of demand with LNF included jumps to -1.33170 (t = 14.80). The reason for this is that the estimate of $b_{y2.K}$ is 0.54625—much larger than that expected on the basis of economic theory (see part (d) above). The evidence given here is consistent with that reported by Bohi, although with LNF excluded (as is customarily the case), the magnitude of the difference is marginal.

(g) The estimated equation with LNINCM replacing LNM is (absolute values of t-statistics in parentheses)

LNX = -0.181 + 1.062*LNINCM - 0.904*LNPE2 + 0.054*LNPG2 + 0.185*LNH
      (0.29)   (12.93)   (4.24)   (0.32)   (5.18) R^2 = 0.837

which is very similar to the results reported in (e)—where the price elasticity estimate of -0.892 was obtained when LNF was explicitly included as a regressor.

(h) In this particular case, the omitted variable bias appears to be quite small, although the results in (f) are a bit surprising.

Exercise 5: The Fisher-Kaysen Specification with U.S. Time Series Data

TASKS: Generate logarithmic first-differenced data, estimate and interpret OLS estimates of Fisher-Kaysen equation, use parameter estimates to conduct an informal forecast given assumed growth rates in exogenous variables, re-estimate assuming AR(1) process in the disturbances; then re-do the above using data only through 1973, not through 1984.

COMMENTS: The purpose of this exercise is to have students assess the rather simple but insightful Fisher-Kaysen specification of electricity demand, using aggregate U.S. time series data from the Nelson-Peck study. Both estimation and forecasting techniques are employed. The short-run, long-run distinction implicit in the Fisher-Kaysen specification is highlighted.

(a) See Exercise 2(c) for details.

(b) The estimated coefficients (absolute values of t-statistics) are 0.04469 (6.528) for the constant, -0.43502 (4.5832) for LNP1 and 0.41215 (2.2362) for LNG1. The long-run growth in equipment stocks is about 4.5% per year, while the short-run price and "income" elasticities are estimated at -0.44 and 0.41, respectively; the latter are conditional on the stock of "white goods." The price elasticity estimate is quite large, given its short-run interpretation, and while the income elasticity is about the same value in absolute terms, its estimate is a bit more plausible.

(c) Compute this using "back of the envelope" procedures as -0.44*-0.02 + 0.42*0.04 + 0.04469 = 0.07029—which is very consistent with the "double-ten" formula.

(d) The Durbin-Watson test statistic is 0.9574, which either rejects or is inconclusive, depending on the significance level chosen. When ML estimation of an AR(1) model is employed (retaining the first observation), the price elasticity drops to -0.17592 (t = 2.075) and that for the income elasticity increases to 0.78804 (6.161); the ML estimate of ρ = 0.736 (6.174). When the iterative Cochrane-Orcutt method is employed instead (losing the first observation), the price elasticity estimate becomes -0.17001 (1.995) and the income elasticity estimate is 0.79478 (6.196); the estimate of ρ = 0.75698 (6.553). One of the reasons there's so little difference here between ML and iterative Cochrane-Orcutt is that the ML estimated residual for the first observation (actually, observation number 2 here since first differences are employed) is very small—only 0.009. Hence whether one retains or drops the first observation doesn't make much difference in this data set. The price elasticity estimates under AR(1) become a bit more plausible, but the income elasticity estimates become less so.

(e) Using only 1952-73 data, the OLS estimates are 0.0493 (5.93) for the constant term, -0.410 (2.53) for LNP1 and 0.450 (2.08) for LNG1—virtually the same as those in (b) above. The ML-AR(1) corresponding values are 0.040 (3.99), -0.261 (1.75) and 0.792 (4.74), with an estimate of ρ equal to 0.630 (0.17), while the iterative Cochrane-Orcutt estimates are 0.039 (3.26), -0.257 (1.68) and 0.800 (4.71), with a ρ estimate of 0.660 (4.03). These estimates are remarkably robust over the 1952-73 and 1952-84 time periods, as Nelson and Peck noted. Using the OLS estimates, compute the forecast informally as

-0.41*-0.024 + 0.45*0.035 + 0.0493 = 0.07489—hence a 7.5% AAGR forecast may well have been justified given these assumptions. Incidentally, the ML-AR(1) forecast is -0.26*-0.024 + 0.79*.035 + 0.040 = 0.07389—which is very similar to the OLS forecast. Both these forecasts are almost identical to the 7.5% NERC forecast made in 1973. For the OLS revised forecasts, compute it assuming γ is unchanged: -0.41*.042 + 0.45*.025 + 0.0493 = 0.04333—which is much smaller, and is a forecast value not attained by NERC forecasts until 1978-1979. Since growth in the purchases of "white goods" also depends on growth in GNP, forecasters could well have revised downward their estimate of the intercept term in the Fisher-Kaysen specification.

(f) The attractive property of the Fisher-Kaysen specification is its simplicity. However, its short-run elasticity estimates are a bit volatile and implausible in this data set, and it cannot help us much in the long run, for there is no reason to expect the stock of electricity-using durable goods to increase at a constant rate into the future.

Exercise 6: Partial Adjustment Specifications with U.S. Time Series Data

TASKS: Specify and estimate a partial adjustment model, test for the absence of first order autocorrelation in the presence of a lagged dependent variable, and discover the sensitivity of parameter estimates to alternative computational techniques, including problems of local and global optima.

COMMENTS: This is an important and instructive exercise, for in it students discover some of the "nightmare" problems that wreak havoc in estimation of time series models. The application is to annual U.S. time series data on electricity consumption from Nelson and Peck, and employs the traditional partial adjustment hypothesis.

(a) The estimated equation (7.9) for 1952-84 data (one observation is lost because of the lagged dependent variable being a regressor) is

$$\begin{aligned}
\text{LNKWH} = &-0.712 + 0.754*\text{LNKWH}(-1) - 0.128*\text{LNPE} + 0.375*\text{LNGNP} \quad R^2 = 0.9988 \\
&(2.60) \quad (15.54) \qquad\qquad\quad (4.64) \qquad\qquad (4.22) \qquad\qquad \text{DW} = 1.6915
\end{aligned}$$

where absolute values of t-statistics are in parentheses. The short-run price and income elasticities are -0.128 and 0.375, respectively, each of which is statistically significantly different from zero. Since 1 - 0.754 = 0.246, dividing these short-run elasticity estimates by 0.246 yields long-run elasticity estimates equal to -0.520 for price and 1.524 for income; the former is somewhat smaller in absolute value than conventional _ex post_ average price estimates found in the literature, while the latter is larger. There are large negative residuals in 1952 and 1974, and a large positive residual in 1955—these may well correspond with cyclical macroeconomic events not fully captured by the partial adjustment hypothesis.

(b) The implied (and biased) OLS estimate of ρ based on the 1.6915 DW test statistic is 0.154, which would suggest nonrejection of the null hypothesis. The OLS estimate of ρ is typically biased toward zero in the presence of a lagged dependent variable.

(c) Durbin's h-statistic cannot be employed since the term within the square root is negative—see Exercise 2(b) of Chapter 6 for the formula. Using Durbin's m-statistic procedure, one obtains an estimate of ρ equal to 0.13472, with a t-value of 0.741; the null hypothesis that $\rho = 0$ is therefore not rejected at usual significance levels.

(d) Using the Hildreth-Lu technique with step size of 0.05 and the 1953-84 data, the standard error of the equation based on various values of ρ is

ρ	STD. ERROR OF EQN	ρ	STD. ERROR OF EQN
0.50	0.0170718	0.75	0.0166926
0.55	0.0169069	0.80	0.0167442
0.60	0.0167779	0.85	0.0167569
0.65	0.0166963	0.90	0.0165628
0.70	0.0166689	0.95	0.0162404
		1.00	0.0198079

which indicates local minima at $\rho = 0.70$ and $\rho = 0.95$, the latter being the apparent global minimum. Since at $\rho = 0.95$ the standard error of ρ is 0.0552 and the t-value is 17.2105, the null hypothesis of no autocorrelation is decisively rejected, calling into question the power of the Durbin m-test statistic procedure. With a finer grid of 0.01, standard errors of the equation for different estimates of ρ are 0.0166700 ($\rho = 0.69$), 0.0166689 (0.70) and 0.0166699 (0.71), while near the other local minimum, the values are 0.0162799 ($\rho = 0.93$), 0.0162126 (0.94) and 0.0162404 (0.95). Hence the apparent global optimum is at $\rho = 0.94$, where the short-run price and income elasticities are estimated to be -0.17002 (t = 2.72) and 0.72278 (7.21), and the coefficient estimate on the lagged dependent variable is 0.146 (1.48), implying long-run price and income elasticity estimates of -0.199 and 0.846, respectively. While estimates under AR(1) are preferred statistically, none of the estimated elasticities is particularly plausible—under the AR(1), short-run price elasticity estimates are plausible, but long-run ones are not, for example. Note that the AR(1) standard error estimate on the lagged dependent variable is about twice as large as that under OLS—hence with the AR(1) model, moving from short- to long-run estimates increases considerably the uncertainty of the long-run elasticities. That may well be an accurate conclusion.

(e) The estimate of ρ after one step of the iterative Cochrane-Orcutt procedures is but 0.07595, with a standard error of 0.1736, suggesting nonrejection of the null hypothesis. Note that since a lagged dependent variable is present, this initial estimate of ρ is a biased one. When one iterates the Cochrane-Orcutt procedure until convergence is obtained, one obtains an estimate of ρ equal to 0.674 (after 12 iterations), and the ML algorithm (retrieving the first observation) converged at $\rho = 0.644$ (after 30 iterations). Note that this is a local, not a global optimum, indicating that considerable care must be exercised in checking for the presence of multiple local optima in these types of models.

(f) Earlier it was noted that the OLS residual at the first usable observation (1952, the first observation available when a lagged dependent variable is a regressor) was quite large at -0.04094 (it turned out to be the second largest residual in absolute value). One might therefore expect AR(1) estimation procedures that retained the first observation to differ from those that do not. This is in fact what happens. Although the converged value changed very slightly depending on the starting value of ρ chosen (0.0, 0.50, 0.90, 0.95 and 0.98), the sample log-likelihood was maximized at a ρ estimate of 0.668197 (ln L = 83.7989), whereas with the Hildreth-Lu procedure noted above, the apparent global optima was reached at a much different estimate of $\rho = 0.94$.

(g) The final choice is not clear. But the ML estimates (retaining the first observation) when $\rho = 0.668$ are not bad for price, although still uncomfortably large for income; the short-run price and income elasticities are -0.206 (t = 3.83) and 0.710 (t = 6.30), respectively, and the long-run estimates turn out to be -0.487 for price and 1.679 for income. What is clear, however, is that AR(0) is not a good assumption in this case.

Exercise 7: Forecasting Using Extrapolation and Smoothing

TASKS: Compute forecasts of electricity demand using a number of extrapolative techniques, including a constant growth extrapolation based on a simple regression equation, single exponential smoothing, double exponential smoothing and the Holt two-parameter smoothing method.

COMMENTS: The purpose of this exercise is to engage students in considering the forecasts that would have been made in the 1970s and 1980s, based on the data available at that time, had forecasters used a variety of extrapolation and smoothing techniques.

It is worth noting that not all the standard statistical software packages include commands for carrying out these various extrapolative and smoothing techniques in an automated manner. In this particular exercise, I have done the procedures using commands in the MicroTSP software package.

(a,b) Answers are given in the text of the exercise, where the computational algorithm chooses a value of α that minimizes the sum of squared forecast errors within the specified sample. Note also that these forecasts look rather similar to those generated by NSF.

(c) Since the forecasts based on double smoothing adapt more quickly, and since the NSF forecasts do not display a rapid adjustment by electric utility forecasters, it is unlikely that they employed double smoothing procedures.

(d) Holt's procedure produces negative forecasts more quickly, because it is rather sensitive in picking up trends, and the data in the late 1970s and early 1980s began to reveal a negative trend.

(e) Most econometricians prefer structural forecasts, since they incorporate the most important features of economic theory (e.g., the effects of price and income on electricity demand).

Exercise 8: Combined Structural, Time-Series Forecasting of Electricity Demand

TASKS: Examine data for stationarity and do differencing until stationarity is attained. Estimate an ARIMA(0,1,1) model using Box-Jenkins techniques, compute short- and long-run elasticity estimates. Forecast exogenous variables assuming they follow an ARIMA(0,1,1) process, and then carry out the forecast conditional on these forecasted regressors. Compare results to NERC summary forecasts. Attempt to discern whether forecast error is caused primarily by a failure to forecast exogenous variables properly, or by a breakdown in the equation used to forecast electricity demand directly.

COMMENTS: The purpose of this exercise is to involve students in implementing empirically a combined structural, time series (Box-Jenkins) model of demand for electricity along the lines of that published by Nelson-Peck [1985]. It should be noted that this type of computation could be carried out in a number of alternative ways; see Nelson-Peck or time series textbooks for further details.

(a) For LNKWH and using 1951-73 data, autocorrelation functions are significant and decline monotonically for five time periods, but when LNK1 first-differenced data are employed the first autocorrelation coefficient is insignificant, as are others, and the Box-Pierce Q-statistic is but 1.895. Similar results occur with the price and output data.

(b) Using 1954-73 data, the iterative Cochrane-Orcutt estimated equation should look like this (with absolute values of t-statistics in parentheses):

$$LNK1 = 0.0275 - 0.2625*LNP1 - 0.1742*LNP1(-1) + 0.8653*LNG1 \quad R^2 = 0.7264$$
$$\quad (2.02) \quad (1.78) \quad\quad (1.42) \quad\quad\quad (5.27)$$

with a ρ estimate of 0.6863 (t = 4.029). Short-run implied price and income elasticity estimates are -0.26 and 0.87, respectively, while the long-run price elasticity estimate turns out to be -0.3178. These elasticity estimates correspond quite well with those in the literature, summarized in Section 7.5.

(c) If in fact the process generating LNG1 and LNP1 followed an MA(1) form, then these forecasts would be rational.

(d) The results are very similar at about 6.8%.

(e,f and g) See Nelson-Peck [1985] and Nelson-Peck-Uhler [1987] for further details.

FINAL COMMENTS:

Since most electric utilities are regulated, data on electricity prices and consumption are typically publicly available. Your students might want to get in touch with local regulatory authorities to do a forecasting exercise such as those done in this chapter. At the national level in the U.S., data are available from the U.S. Department of Energy, Energy Information Administration. See the text for further references.

Finally, for those inclined to do causality testing, the data on electricity consumption and GNP can be used for such exercises (although the advertising-sales relationship is examined in the causality context in Chapter 8 of this textbook); a number of articles on electricity-GNP causality have appeared in <u>The Energy Journal</u> over the past five years or so. See various issues of that journal for further details.

INSTRUCTOR'S NOTES FOR CHAPTER EIGHT:

CAUSALITY AND SIMULTANEITY BETWEEN ADVERTISING AND SALES

ECONOMETRIC PROCEDURES EMPLOYED IN THE EXERCISES OF CHAPTER EIGHT:

- Evaluate potential simultaneous equations bias in OLS estimation

- Do OLS and 2SLS structural estimation, perform the Hausman specification test; also do nonlinear least squares

- Show that standard errors obtained from 2SLS are not the same as those obtained from "brute force" 2-step OLS estimation

- Check whether parameters in equations are identified

- Compare OLS estimates with varying periodicity of data—annual, quarterly and monthly

- Estimate 90% duration levels for advertising

- Use the Griliches procedure for choosing among alternative distributed lag and autocorrelation specifications—the Koyck lingering effects, current effects with AR(1) and brand loyalty with AR(1)

- Work through logical consistency issues in models for which the dependent variables are shares

- Do Box-Jenkins checks for stationarity, examine the autocorrelation and partial autocorrelation functions, check the cross-correlograms of residuals, infer causality and do ARMA estimation

- Do bivariate transfer function estimation of final form

- Evaluate models using out-of-sample forecasting procedures

- Estimate aggregate sales-advertising model by OLS, OLS-AR(1), 2SLS, 2SLS-AR(1); perform the Hausman specification test

- Evaluate effects of cigarette ad ban using nonlinear estimation

- Estimate a pooled cross-section time series model using the Kmenta cross-sectionally heteroskedastic and time-wise autoregressive specification

GOALS FOR CHAPTER EIGHT:

In this chapter a number of economic issues concerning the causes and effects of advertising are examined. Econometric issues addressed here include problems in the measurement of advertising quantity and price, issues of simultaneous equations specification and identification, procedures for implementing the Hausman specification test and testing for Granger causality, constructing logically consistent market share models, accounting properly for autocorrelation when attempting to measure the cumulative or lingering effects of advertising with alternative distributed lag specifications, and dealing with problems of temporal aggregation.

GENERAL COMMENTS TO THE INSTRUCTOR:

This chapter is a rather detailed one, and covers a number of topics of particular interest to students in the bridge areas between marketing and economics. It is therefore of interest to students in business and economics. Moreover, it is not necessary to cover all the sections of the chapter—they are reasonably independent, and thus you might assign only some of the sections if you are short on time. On the other hand, some instructors have taken a great deal of time with this chapter (about half a semester), and have gone into the various topics in considerable detail. Hence the material in this chapter can be used in a variety of ways to meet your interests and time constraints.

Unlike the other chapters in which the first exercise overviews the principal data sets, in this chapter there are more than the usual number of data sets (seven), and therefore in this chapter what data analysis there is occurs within each of the exercises. Moreover, the exercises need not be done in the order they appear.

One econometric technique suited to the advertising-sales issue but not covered in this chapter is that of co-integration. Instructors interested in this procedure might want, however, to employ some of the data on the data diskette in designing additional exercises. I would appreciate hearing from you if you find that you are able to design such an exercise effectively.

SPECIFIC NOTES ON THE EXERCISES IN CHAPTER EIGHT:

Exercise 1: Assessing Price and Quantity Endogeneity in a Sales-Advertising Model for Oranges

TASKS: The goal here is to have students gain experience in dealing with potential simultaneous equations biases. Estimate a model by OLS, do the Hausman specification test for exogeneity, then do 2SLS. Show that, while parameter estimates are identical, the standard errors obtained from 2SLS are not the same as those obtained from a "brute force" two-step OLS estimation.

COMMENTS: The data set used here is that by Marc Nerlove and Frederick Waugh in their study of the effects of advertising by two voluntary trade associations. Following Nerlove-Waugh, employ the 1910-59 annual data, excluding the war years 1942-46.

(a) The nonlinear least squares coefficient estimates (t-statistics in absolute values) are -0.7195 (7.397) for η, 0.6646 (6.879) for β, 0.1678 (2.316) for γ and 0.0743 (2.124) for δ. The sum of γ and δ is 0.24218 (4.947). These results match Nerlove-Waugh.

(b) This can be shown easily by simply subtracting LQTY from both sides, leaving LPRI ≡ log(REV/QTY) as the dependent variable. This results in the coefficient on LQTYC being more negative by one; i.e., -1.3899 rather than -0.3899. Note that the standard error on this coefficient is unaffected.

(c) The implicit assumption must be that supply is perfectly inelastic, which is a rather suspicious assumption.

(d) The new equation looks something like the following (absolute t-values in parentheses):

$$LQTY = -5.3255 - 0.4151*LPR + 0.6900*LINC + 0.3266*LNa + 0.0305*LNA$$
$$(10.42) \quad (7.39) \quad\quad (9.41) \quad\quad\quad (6.66) \quad\quad\quad (1.19)$$

with an R^2 of 0.9676. The price elasticity estimate is closer to zero, the income elasticity estimate is about the same, the estimate of γ is about twice as large, while that of δ is only half as large. On <u>a priori</u> grounds, it is not clear which specification is preferred—that with quantity, or that with price as exogenous; there's good reason to believe that they are both endogenous, in which case both equations yield biased OLS estimates.

(e) Recognizing that the underlying rationale here is weak at best, I think it is still of interest to do the Hausman test, if only to help students gain computational facility with it. The coefficient estimate on LQTYFIT is 1.3758, and the t-value is 2.0991, which is slightly larger than the asymptotic t-value at a 95% significance level (1.96). Hence the null hypothesis that LNQTY is exogenous (that it is uncorrelated with the equation disturbance term) is rejected, and this undermines the Nerlove-Waugh model.

(f) Just identified, due to the usual order condition. The estimated 2SLS equation should look like this (absolute t-values in parentheses):

$$LPR = 4.297 + 0.4698*LQTY - 0.4243*LINC - 0.7766*LNa + 0.1577*LNA$$
$$(0.59) \quad (0.39) \quad\quad (0.47) \quad\quad\quad (1.17) \quad\quad\quad (1.76)$$

and has an R^2 of 0.292. This equation is much worse; for example, coefficients on the price and income variables have the wrong sign. (You'd get much better results if you treated the log of population as an instrument.)

(g) The double-OLS and 2SLS parameter estimates are identical, but the standard errors differ. Results are (with double-OLS standard errors in parentheses and 2SLS in square brackets):

$$LPR = 4.297 + 0.4698*LQTY - 0.4243*LINC - 0.7766*LNa + 0.1577*LNA$$

$$\begin{array}{ccccc} (6.0510) & (0.9889) & (0.74560) & (0.54825) & (0.074288) \\ [7.3219] & [1.1966] & [0.90220] & [0.66340] & [0.089890] \end{array}$$

Note that the 2SLS are always larger than the double-OLS standard errors—the common factor of proportionality is 1.2100. This occurs because when 2SLS computes the residuals, it uses the actual value of the LQTY regressor rather than the fitted value LQTYFIT to compute the fitted value of LPR. The 1.2100 factor arises because it is the ratio of the standard error of the regression in the 2SLS model relative to that in the double-OLS model; i.e., 1.2100 = 0.335722/0.277449.

Exercise 2: Estimating 90% Duration Levels for Advertising with Annual and Monthly Data for the Lydia E. Pinkham Medicine Company

TASKS: Construct and comment on advertising-sales ratios of Pinkham data. Replicate Palda's OLS results, and compute a 90% duration interval. Then re-estimate using annual, monthly and quarterly data covering the same time period. Evaluate whether results are consistent with the data interval bias hypothesis put forward by Darral Clarke [1976].

COMMENTS: This is a most interesting exercise, for it raises issues of temporal aggregation, issues which are very important but are not often addressed in the econometric literature. Moreover, the Lydia E. Pinkham data set originally developed by Kristian Palda has become legendary; for humorous reading, take a look at the history of the Pinkham Company in Palda [1964] and Pollay [1979].

(a) Means, mins and maxes for advertising-sales ratios in the annual Palda data are 0.51191, 0.30734 and 0.84972, while for the monthly data they are 0.48518, 0.01868 and 1.57896. These high ratios are simply astounding. As measured by the standard deviation, there is more variation in the monthly data (0.23864 vs. 0.10307). For annual data, the maximum value occurred in

1934, while the minimum occurred only two years later in 1936. In the monthly data, there appears to be a rather high ratio of advertising to sales in December in some years, although not in 1916; often November has a rather high value as well.

(b) See the footnote in the text (in Exercise 2(b)) for detailed estimation results.

(c) The implied 90% duration interval is 55.410 months, with a standard error of 14.897 months. Palda's estimate is virtually identical. The estimate implies that it takes 55.41 months to achieve 90% of the cumulative effects of advertising on sales.

(d) With these 42 annual observations, the estimated coefficient on the lagged dependent variable is 0.5168, giving a 90% duration interval of about 41.86 months, and a standard error of 18.303 months. These estimates display some variability, but not excessively so.

(e) With the monthly data from 1907:2 to 1926:12 and 1937:2 to 1960:6, the estimated equation looks like this (absolute t-values in parentheses):

$$MSALES = 25990 + 0.686*MSALES(-1) + 0.321*MADV - 13987*MDUM1$$
$$(6.84) \quad (27.28) \qquad\qquad (11.24) \qquad\quad (4.16)$$

$$+ 6934*MDUM2 - 6538*MDUM3$$
$$(2.56) \qquad\quad (1.85)$$

with an R^2 of 0.8412, and an implied 90% duration interval equal to only 6.0999 months, with a standard error of 0.592 months. This is much smaller than that based on annual data—41.86 months in (d) above—and is also consistent with the data interval bias hypothesis of Clarke.

(f) Based on the quarterly data from 1907:1 to 1926:4 and 1937:1 to 1960:2, the estimated equation has the form (absolute t-values in parentheses)

$$QSALES = 44952 + 0.766*QSALES(-1) + 0.290*QADV - 26838*QDUM1$$
$$(3.02) \quad (20.31) \qquad\qquad (5.23) \qquad\quad (2.11)$$

$$+ 24005*QDUM2 - 17681*QDUM3$$
$$(2.41) \qquad\qquad (1.32)$$

with an R^2 of 0.913 and an implied 90% duration interval of 25.977 months (SE of 4.81 months). These results are perfectly consistent with Clarke's data interval bias hypothesis—41.86 months based on monthly data, 25.98 for quarterly data, and 6.10 for monthly data. He's right. But why?

Exercise 3: Choosing Between Current and Lingering Effects Models

TASKS: Estimate by OLS a Koyck distributed lag model, a current effects model with AR(1) disturbances, and a more general brand loyalty model with AR(1) disturbances. Choose among these three models using a procedure outlined by Zvi Griliches [1967].

COMMENTS: This is a useful exercise in choice among alternative model specifications. The application is to measuring the carryover effect of current advertising on future sales. Although the exercise allows students to choose between the annual and monthly Palda data sets, here I'll only present results based on the annual data.

(a) Based on the 1912-1960 annual data, Palda's re-estimated equation looks like this (absolute t-values in parentheses):

SALES = 256.05 + 0.607*SALES(-1) + 0.533*ADV - 82.14*DUM1
        (2.56)   (7.15)   (3.76)   (0.68)

        + 217.1*DUM2 - 202.2*DUM3
          (3.11)   (2.90)

with an R^2 of 0.915.

(b) The iterative Cochrane-Orcutt procedure yields the equation

SALES = 1324.0 + 0.666*ADV + 586.8*DUM1 + 459.6*DUM2 - 220.4*DUM3
        (5.69)   (5.95)   (1.91)   (1.99)   (1.34)

with an estimate of ρ = 0.8710 (t = 12.41), and an R^2 of 0.536 on the ρ-transformed variables. The sum of squared residuals here is smaller than in (a) above (1259520 vs. 14420000), and, not surprisingly, estimates on the effects of advertising are slightly higher in this current effects model.

(c) The more general Griliches specification, when estimated by OLS over the same 1912-1960 time period, yields the equation

SALES = 235.53 + 0.602*ADV - 0.375*ADV(-1) + 0.763*SALES(-1)
        (2.46)   (4.37)   (2.37)   (7.33)

        - 64.0*DUM1 + 192*DUM2 - 118*DUM3
          (0.55)   (2.85)   (1.56)

with an R^2 of 0.925 and a sum of squared residuals equal to 1271780. Since the coefficient on lagged sales is statistically significant, this undermines support for the Koyck specification used by Palda. The product of the advertising and lagged sales coefficients, 0.602*0.763 = 0.459, is somewhat larger than the negative of the lagged advertising coefficient (0.375), but they are not that different. Hence on the basis of this Griliches criterion, there is more support for the current effects with autocorrelation model than there is for the Koyck specification.

(d) The estimated brand loyalty model with AR(1) disturbances, based on the 1912-1960 data, is of the form (using the iterative Cochrane-Orcutt estimator)

SALES = 775.32 + 0.300*SALES(-1) + 0.573*ADV + 508.3*DUM1
        (2.94)   (2.62)   (4.93)   (1.73)

        + 444.6*DUM2 - 183.4*DUM3
          (1.95)   (1.21)

with a ρ estimate of 0.811 (t = 9.14) and a sum of squared residuals equal to 1082690. Since ρ appears to be very statistically significant, there is not much support for the lingering effects model; and since the coefficient on lagged sales is also statistically significant, there is not much support for the current effects model with autocorrelated disturbances. Based on this annual data, therefore, the brand loyalty model appears to be significantly superior to the more restrictive lingering effects with AR(0) and current effects with AR(1) disturbances. These results are not entirely consistent, but neither are they clearly inconsistent with those obtained in (c) above.

Exercise 4: Avoiding Embarrassment with Consistent Market Share Specifications

TASKS: Construct market advertising variables for each firm as (us/others), and realize that when these are regressors in market share equations, fitted shares will not sum to unity. Then do it right. Realize what the problem is here—any regressor should be in at least two equations.

COMMENTS: Share models are common in the literature, and are certainly so in the marketing literature. Yet the adding-up problem with seemingly appropriate share specifications is a rather common one. In this exercise students will find out more about this problem, and how to get around it. The application is to cigarette advertising and sales for Camels, Lucky Strike and Chesterfield from 1931 to 1949, based on data used by Nicholls and Borden.

(a) Note that 1932 was a bad year for advertising by Reynolds (for Camels). During the Depression, sales of Camels fell, while those of Lucky Strike increased, although both fell in 1931 to 1932. For both brands, advertising fell. During World War II, sales of both brands rose, but Camels increased the least; expenditures on advertising decreased for all brands.

(b) The OLS equation estimated for 1932 to 1949 is

$$\text{SHCAM} = 0.1514 + 0.0340*\text{WCAM} - 0.0002*\text{RLINC} + 0.6878*\text{SHCAM}(-1)$$
$$\phantom{\text{SHCAM} = }(1.986) \quad (1.422) \qquad\quad (1.331) \qquad\qquad (4.564)$$

(c) The OLS equation estimated for 1932 to 1949 is

$$\text{SHLUC} = 0.0905 + 0.0210*\text{WLUC} + 0.0003*\text{RLINC} + 0.6646*\text{SHLUC}(-1)$$
$$\phantom{\text{SHLUC} = }(1.351) \quad (2.472) \qquad\quad (1.938) \qquad\qquad (5.088)$$

In 1932, the FITCAM and IMPCAM shares are 0.42629 and 0.39753—quite different, while for FITLUC and IMPLUC they are 0.60247 and 0.57371, respectively. SUMSH is largest at 1.02876 in 1932, and smallest at 0.98624 in 1934. That the SUMSH value is as close as it is to one is coincidental—this type of model specification has a big problem, for shares do not sum to unity.

(d) The coefficients on the LWCAM and LWLUC variables are identical at 0.03623, and the same is true for the coefficients on the lagged dependent variable at 0.66497; the LWCAM and LWLUC variables sum to zero at each observation, while the sum of the lagged shares is unity at each observation. Now the implicit and fitted shares are identical, and appropriate shares sum to unity. When ASHCAM and ASHLUC replace LWCAM and LWLUC, the coefficients in each estimated equation equal 0.16033, and those on the lagged dependent variable equal 0.66635 in each equation; note that these two sets of regressors each sum to unity at each observation.

(e) SUMSH varies from a low of 0.97101 in 1945 to a high of 1.01805 in 1949. Inconsistency is also demonstrated in 1945, when IMPCHE is 0.30716, but FITCHE is 0.27817.

(f) Now the inconsistency re-emerges in the three-brand case. The value of SUMSH ranges from 0.97760 in 1945 to 1.02310 in 1933. Note that the sum of the LWCAM, LWLUC and LWCHE variables at each year is no longer a constant, nor is it zero. Consistency will still not emerge, however, when the ASHCAM, ASHLUC and ASHCHE variables are instead used as regressors, even though the sum of these three variables at each observation is always unity; one constraint that will ensure consistency is to constrain the coefficient on the lagged share to be the same in all three equations. Procedures for doing that are discussed in Chapter 9 of the text, in the context of estimating parameters in systems of equations with cross-equation restrictions imposed.

Exercise 5: Using Granger's Method to Determine Causality Between Aggregate
            Advertising and Aggregate Sales

TASKS: Do Box-Jenkins checks for stationarity, examine the autocorrelation and partial autocorrelation functions, employ the Box-Pierce Q-statistic, check the cross-correlogram of residuals, estimate models using ARIMA procedures, compare these models using the mean squared error of ex post forecasts, and infer causality.

COMMENTS: In this exercise, I employ the nominal advertising series ADN and the corresponding nominal consumption series UCGN, which is not seasonally adjusted.

(a) After first and fourth differencing (the latter to account for seasonality), based on 1957:2 to 1970:4 data, the log-differenced variable for nominal consumption LUCG41 was found to follow an MA process of the form (absolute values of t-stats in parentheses)

$$(1-B)(1-B^4)\text{LNUCG}_t = \underset{(0.414)}{0.0009643} + (1 - \underset{(1.429)}{0.1994B^2} - \underset{(5.543)}{0.7670B^4})\,\epsilon_{\text{UCGN},t}$$

which is quite close to the results presented in Eq. (8.47) in the text. The Box-Pierce Q-statistic for eight lags is insignificant at 1.639, and the first autocorrelation coefficient is insignificant at -0.051, as are all the others. If one includes an MA(3) coefficient, its t-statistic is only -0.508.

For the advertising variable, based on 1956:2-1970:4 data, the first-differenced variable LADN1 was found to follow an MA(5) process of the form

$$(1-B)\text{LNADN}_t = \underset{(3.136)}{0.00908} + (1 - \underset{(2.167)}{0.2958B^5})\,\epsilon_{\text{ADN},t}$$

for which the Box-Pierce Q-statistic for eight lags was 2.742, and each of the autocorrelation coefficients was less than the 0.130 standard error. Another equation with an MA(1) term added as well results in an MA(1) coefficient with a t-statistic of -0.940; with an AR(1) term added instead, the t-statistic on that coefficient is but -0.834.

(b) Based on these pre-whitened residuals, the cross-correlogram is constructed. The cross-correlograms between $\epsilon_{\text{ADN},t}$ and $U_{\text{CGN},t-k}$ indicate sample correlations of 0.058, 0.080, -0.183, -0.150, -0.122, 0.044, 0.046 and 0.035 for k = -8 to -1, respectively; 0.470 at k = 0; and 0.179, -0.041, 0.201, -0.177, 0.197, -0.121, -0.146 and -0.097 for k = 1 to 8; the standard error is 0.135. Hence the correlation at k = 0 is clearly significant, while that at k = 1 (0.179) is marginal. The k = 0 and k = 1 results tend to suggest that consumption causes advertising. As Ashley et al. concluded, there seems to be no sensible lag structure to put together for the advertising causing sales hypothesis.

Then regress the residual from the advertising equation (RESA1) on the consumption residual lagged (RESC1(-1)), allowing for an AR(1) process. Based on the 1957:4-1970:4 data, this yields an estimated equation of the form

$$RESA1 = no\ constant + 0.3527*RESC1(-1) - 0.2039*RESA1(-1)$$
$$\qquad\qquad\qquad\qquad (1.685) \qquad\qquad\qquad (1.325)$$

where absolute values of t-statistics are in parentheses.

(c) A rather pleasing equation we ended up with had the form, based on 1958:1-1970:4 data,

$$(1-B)LNADN_t = 0.00924 + (1-B)(0.0260B)LNUCGN_t + (1 - 0.0260B^5)\eta_{ADN,t}$$
$$\qquad\qquad (2.957) \qquad\qquad (1.042) \qquad\qquad\qquad (2.052)$$

for which the residual had a Box-Pierce Q-statistic for eight lags of 3.231, and for which only the eighth lag had a slightly larger autocorrelation coefficient than the 0.138 standard error. Since causation is unidirectional from consumption to advertising, the preferable final form for the advertising equation turns out to be that in (a) above.

(d) For advertising causes consumption, the preferred equation is somewhat similar to (8.50) and has the form (based on 1957:2-1970:4 data)

$$(1-B)(1-B^4)LNUCGN_t = 0.0411 - 0.0132(1-B)LNADN_t + (1 - 0.1432B^2 - 0.7589B^4)\eta_{UCGN,t}$$
$$\qquad\qquad\qquad (1.090) \qquad (1.070) \qquad\qquad\qquad\qquad (1.053) \qquad (5.585)$$

for which the Box-Pierce Q-statistic for eight lags is 0.703, and all autocorrelations are less than half their 0.135 standard error.

(e) The results obtained here are a bit strange. The RMSE of the 1971:1-1975:4 forecast based on the bivariate relationship that lagged advertising and lagged consumption cause consumption is larger than the univariate from lagged consumption to consumption (0.019921 vs. 0.018235); this result is possible but not very attractive. Nonetheless, it surely indicates that adding advertising does not help us to forecast consumption!

On the other hand, the corresponding RMSE for the univariate of lagged advertising causing advertising is 0.025729, while that for the bivariate relationship that lagged consumption and lagged advertising cause advertising is 0.028192, which is about 9.57% larger. This can be marginally significant, depending on the significance level.

The results seem to suggest, therefore, that (perhaps) consumption causes advertising, but evidence of reverse causality is very weak indeed.

Exercise 6: Estimating a Simultaneous Equations Model of Aggregate Sales and Aggregate Advertising

TASKS: Employ OLS and 2SLS estimation procedures with and without first order autocorrelation. Test for exogeneity using the Hausman specification test. Assess the nature of simultaneity and perhaps causality by examining quarterly aggregate U.S. consumption and aggregate advertising expenditures from the 1956:1-1974:4 time period.

COMMENTS: In this exercise the classic results reported by Schmalensee are replicated, and then the robustness of his consumption causes advertising but not the reverse finding is examined using updated data.

(a) OLS results for the three equations estimated from 1956:2 to 1967:3 are (absolute values of t-statistics in parentheses):

$$CGR_t = \begin{array}{c} 0.1140 \\ (2.727) \end{array} + \begin{array}{c} 0.2338*YPCR_t \\ (6.603) \end{array} + \begin{array}{c} 0.5086*CGR_{t-1} \\ (4.808) \end{array} - \begin{array}{c} 0.0017*ADV(-1) \\ (0.490) \end{array} \qquad \begin{array}{l} R^2 = 0.9887 \\ DW = 1.6730 \end{array}$$

$$CGR_t = \begin{array}{c} 0.1629 \\ (4.394) \end{array} + \begin{array}{c} 0.2086*YPCR_t \\ (5.996) \end{array} + \begin{array}{c} 0.3828*CGR_{t-1} \\ (4.248) \end{array} + \begin{array}{c} 0.0072*ADV \\ (2.323) \end{array} \qquad \begin{array}{l} R^2 = 0.9900 \\ DW = 1.5691 \end{array}$$

$$CGR_t = \begin{array}{c} 0.1548 \\ (4.410) \end{array} + \begin{array}{c} 0.2029*YPCR_t \\ (5.792) \end{array} + \begin{array}{c} 0.4052*CGR_{t-1} \\ (4.778) \end{array} + \begin{array}{c} 0.0068*ADV(+1) \\ (2.491) \end{array} \qquad \begin{array}{l} R^2 = 0.9901 \\ DW = 1.9970 \end{array}$$

If advertising "caused" consumption, one would expect the highest positive coefficient when ADV(-1) was a regressor and the lowest positive coefficient when ADV(+1) was a regressor; but the exact opposite occurs. If causality went from consumption to advertising, one would expect the opposite pattern, which is what in fact is observed. These results are consistent with those reported by Schmalensee.

(b) The three coefficient estimates (absolute values of asymptotic t-statistics in parentheses) on the fitted value variable in the three expanded equations are for YPCRFIT1, -0.10662 (1.513); for YPCRFIT2, -0.10616 (1.538); and for YPCRFIT3, -0.14221 (2.105). The inference is not overwhelmingly clear-cut, but with all t-values greater than 1.5, it is probably best to be cautious and consider estimation treating YPR as endogenous. Also, there's a long tradition in consumption function estimation of treating income as endogenous.

(c) 2SLS results for the three equations estimated from 1956:2 to 1967:3 are (absolute values of t-statistics in parentheses):

$$CGR_t = \underset{(1.828)}{0.0856} + \underset{(3.934)}{0.1880}*YPCR_t + \underset{(4.768)}{0.6081}*CGR_{t-1} - \underset{(0.358)}{0.0013}*ADV(-1) \quad \begin{array}{l} R^2 = 0.9900 \\ DW = 1.8104 \end{array}$$

$$CGR_t = \underset{(3.430)}{0.1401} + \underset{(3.426)}{0.1622}*YPCR_t + \underset{(4.318)}{0.4673}*CGR_{t-1} + \underset{(2.572)}{0.0084}*ADV \quad \begin{array}{l} R^2 = 0.9895 \\ DW = 1.6616 \end{array}$$

$$CGR_t = \underset{(3.051)}{0.1225} + \underset{(2.770)}{0.1374}*YPCR_t + \underset{(4.881)}{0.5241}*CGR_{t-1} + \underset{(2.861)}{0.0085}*ADV(+1) \quad \begin{array}{l} R^2 = 0.9893 \\ DW = 2.2148 \end{array}$$

The same pattern observed in (a) emerges with 2SLS estimates, but the 2SLS coefficient on current valued ADV in the second equation is larger and certainly more significant than in the OLS equation of (a). Simultaneity may be present. But if it is, estimating the equation in this way yields inconsistent parameter estimates, for ADV is presumed to be exogenous here.

(d) The 2SLS results when the ADV variable in its various time forms is also treated as endogenous (or correlated with the disturbance term) are as follows:

$$CGR_t = \underset{(1.295)}{0.0748} + \underset{(3.940)}{0.1890}*YPCR_t + \underset{(4.005)}{0.6386}*CGR_{t-1} - \underset{(0.467)}{0.0029}*ADV(-1) \quad \begin{array}{l} R^2 = 0.9883 \\ DW = 1.8616 \end{array}$$

$$CGR_t = \underset{(2.729)}{0.1269} + \underset{(3.457)}{0.1647}*YPCR_t + \underset{(4.067)}{0.5029}*CGR_{t-1} + \underset{(1.376)}{0.0064}*ADV \quad \begin{array}{l} R^2 = 0.9895 \\ DW = 1.7085 \end{array}$$

$$CGR_t = \begin{array}{c} 0.1273 \\ (2.993) \end{array} + \begin{array}{c} 0.1347*YPCR_t \\ (2.671) \end{array} + \begin{array}{c} 0.5116*CGR_{t-1} \\ (4.509) \end{array} + \begin{array}{c} 0.0094*ADV(+1) \\ (2.393) \end{array} \quad \begin{array}{c} R^2 = 0.9892 \\ DW = 2.2288 \end{array}$$

Notice that the coefficient on current-valued ADV in the second equation is positive but insignificantly different from zero, while that on ADV(+1) in the third equation remains positive and statistically significant. To this point, therefore, Schmalensee's evidence points in favor of consumption causing advertising, but there is not much support for the reverse causality. However, these results are all contingent on the absence of serial correlation. So let's consider that next.

(e) When the model is estimated by 2SLS with both YPCR and ADV treated as endogenous and disturbances are permitted to follow an AR(1) process, the three values of ρ obtained (t-values in parentheses) are 0.5975 (4.943), 0.3989 (2.885) and 0.0826 (0.549). Hence autocorrelation appears to be present in the lagged and current-valued ADV equations. But if one examines the coefficients on the three ADV terms, they are 0.0088 (t = 1.176), 0.0050 (1.030) and 0.0073 (1.846). Notice that even with AR(1) permitted, the 2SLS estimates do not provide support for causality from advertising to consumption, but do provide some support for the reverse causality.

Two other comments here. First, in part (e), the estimation requires dropping one more observation, so the estimation is from 1956:3 to 1967:3. Second, with AR(1) disturbances in 2SLS estimation with a lagged dependent variable, care must be taken in forming the instruments, as has been shown by Ray Fair. (See the references in Chapters 6 and 10 for a full citation to his 1970 _Econometrica_ article on this matter.) The estimation done here with 2SLS-AR(1) incorporates the Fair procedure for forming instruments.

(f) To check robustness, I have also re-done parts (a) through (e) above using the entire data available—from 1956:2 to 1975:3 for (a) through (d), and 1956:3 to 1975:3 for (e). Qualitatively, the results are unchanged, although a few differences emerge. In particular, the t-value on current ADV in the second regression is persistently significant until AR(1) is permitted, when the t-value falls to 1.74; however, in all cases the coefficient on ADV(+1) is significant, even when AR(1) disturbances are permitted—in that case the t-value is 2.64. Finally, with this updated data, in all three equations the AR(1) coefficient is statistically significant. In brief, Schmalensee's results seem to hold up reasonably well with these updated data.

Exercise 7: Evaluating the Effects of the Cigarette Broadcast Ban

TASKS: Replicate the OLS results reported by SKM, compute correlations among variables, do an ex post forecast based on an OLS equation, estimate a variety of models by nonlinear least squares, and test hypotheses using the likelihood ratio test statistic.

COMMENTS: The purpose of this exercise is to help students interpret the controversial empirical findings reported by Schneider, Klein and Murphy (SKM) concerning the apparent ineffectiveness of the 1971 broadcast ban on cigarette advertising in the U.S.

Part (f) of this exercise is rather open-ended, and could serve as a useful short term paper, as a take-home exam or as a class exercise involving several teams.

(a) You should be able to replicate the results reported in Eq. (8.60) in the text. Based on this 1930-70 estimated equation and 1971-78 actual values of the exogenous variables, the 1978 forecast for per capita consumption is 6389.64, compared to an actual value of 3592.00, implying a 77.9% prediction error. Clearly, the model is not reliable.

(b) The 1930-78 results you obtain should look something like this (absolute values of t-statistics in parentheses):

$$\begin{aligned}
\text{LSALESPC} = \ & 0.0434 + 0.0167*\text{D53} - 0.0742*\text{D64} - 0.3116*\text{D71} - 0.1288*\text{DF} \\
& (0.03) \quad (2.34) \qquad (1.05) \qquad\quad (5.05) \qquad\quad (1.95)
\end{aligned}$$

$$\begin{aligned}
& + 1.2523*\text{LINCPC} - 0.1899*\text{LRPRICE} - 0.1547*\text{LASTOCK} \qquad R^2 = 0.9497 \\
& \quad (16.31) \qquad\qquad (0.72) \qquad\qquad\quad (1.84) \qquad\qquad\qquad \text{DW} = 0.6220
\end{aligned}$$

Note the negative coefficient on LASTOCK and the low t-value on LRPRICE.

(c) If the logic of their model is correct, then the coefficient on this log-fitted value should be unity by definition. Using nonlinear least squares procedures, you should be able to replicate these results, as discussed in the exercise.

(d) The simple correlation coefficient between LNI and LINCPC is 0.95954. Given this collinearity, it may be difficult to obtain precise estimates of the coefficients when both variables are included as regressors. The simple correlation between LINCPC and LINCPC2 is 0.99956, while that between LNI and LINCPC2 is 0.95090. The coefficients (t-statistics) on LINCPC and LINCPC2 are 4.6456 (1.568) and -0.2511 (1.146); the implied income elasticity rises from 1.3545 in 1930 to a high of 1.497 in 1933, and then declines monotonically to a low value of 0.7795 in 1978. Despite this trend in the income elasticity, this is not a particularly good specification, and is not a viable alternative to that in (b); the price elasticity estimate of -0.32 is insignificant (t = 1.12), the coefficient on LASTOCK has the wrong sign, although it is insignificant (-0.103, t = 1.09), and the coefficients on the DF and D64 dummy variables are insignificant.

(e) The nonlinear least squares estimated equation using 1930-78 data looks something like this (convergence took a rather large number of iterations):

$$\begin{aligned}
\text{LSALESPC} = \ & -0.465 - 0.094*\text{DF} - 0.003*\text{SHFIL} - 0.027*\text{SHLOW} - 1.019*\text{LTPERCIG} \\
& (0.11) \quad (1.51) \qquad (0.83) \qquad\quad (2.01) \qquad\qquad (1.41)
\end{aligned}$$

$$\begin{aligned}
& + 1.102*\text{LINCPC} - 1.197*\text{LRPRICE} + 0.135*\text{LNI} + 0.065*\text{LOG}(\text{ASTOCK}+0.396*\text{ASTOCK2}) \\
& \quad (2.96) \qquad\qquad (5.31) \qquad\qquad (0.31) \qquad (0.66) \qquad\qquad\qquad (0.18)
\end{aligned}$$

with an R^2 of 0.9598, a Durbin-Watson test statistic of 0.9419, and a sample maximized log-likelihood of 55.6867. Note that the income elasticity estimate is still large (1.102), that the 0.135 estimate on LNI is quite different from unity (but not quite different at a 95% significance level, given its standard error), and that the 0.396 estimate of r is very imprecise. With the 0.462 income elasticity estimate constraint imposed, the nonlinear least squares estimated equation I obtained looked like this:

LSALESPC = 2.703 - 0.076*DF - 0.002*SHFIL - 0.023*SHLOW - 1.290*LTPERCIG
           (0.66) (1.21)   (0.59)   (1.57)   (1.77)

  + 0.462*LINCPC - 1.202*LRPRICE + 0.893*LNI + 0.042*LOG(ASTOCK+0.264*ASTOCK2)
   (----)   (5.32)   (10.09)   (0.53)   (0.10)

with an R^2 of 0.957, a Durbin-Watson of 0.9560 and an ln L of 53.7732. Note that while the other coefficients have not changed that dramatically, the coefficient on LNI has increased substantially to almost unity (with a very small standard error relative to the earlier run), and that the coefficients on both the advertising stock variables have insignificant t-statistics. Incidentally, the null hypothesis that the income elasticity estimate equals 0.462 is 2*(55.6867 - 53.7732) = 3.8270, which is just barely less than the 0.05 critical value of 3.8416.

(f) In addition to the possibilities noted in the text, students might want to examine the role of autocorrelation in this model.

Exercise 8: Distinguishing the Sales Effects of Advertising Quality and Advertising Quantity

TASKS: Examine data. Then estimate a time series of cross-sections by OLS for each cross-section, by GLS, and then carry out Kmenta's cross-sectionally heteroskedastic and time-wise autoregressive specification.

COMMENTS: The empirical focus of this exercise is the estimation of a model in which the effects on sales of advertising quality are empirically distinguished from those of advertising quantity. Students should be reminded that the quality variable used is based on experts' judgments ex post, and thus the results should be interpreted rather cautiously.

(a) There's not much variation over time in LY within Region 1, but there is more so in Regions 2 through 5. Somewhat surprisingly, there's a fair bit of between-region variation in LPR—see observations 8, 39-44 and 54, for example. The zero values in ADR may correspond to data errors, missing observations, or some other problem, and they could obviously affect results substantially; the authors provide no discussion on this issue. LQUAL displays considerable variability over the sample.

(b) The five OLS region-specific estimated equations have the form (absolute values of t-statistics in parentheses):

	CONSTANT	LY(-1)	LPR	LADR	LQUAL	DMR	PJF	PND	R^2	DW
1	12.30 (6.76)	.069 (0.52)	-.406 (2.08)	.012 (1.07)	.181 (1.18)	-.178 (3.77)	-.074 (1.30)	-.276 (5.78)	.575	2.145
2	12.40 (6.76)	.074 (0.58)	-.755 (3.32)	-.023 (0.55)	.214 (1.32)	-.147 (3.06)	-.124 (2.11)	-.253 (4.68)	.504	2.076
3	15.40 (8.07)	-.167 (1.22)	-.634 (2.51)	.029 (2.32)	.539 (2.75)	-.068 (1.35)	-.153 (2.28)	-.267 (4.33)	.478	2.044
4	9.15 (5.71)	.193 (1.51)	-.684 (2.33)	.010 (0.69)	.212 (0.44)	-.166 (2.72)	-.013 (0.16)	-.381 (5.41)	.525	2.129
5	9.92 (5.95)	.151 (1.14)	-.546 (2.47)	.018 (1.64)	.408 (2.19)	-.127 (2.47)	-.001 (0.02)	-.248 (4.42)	.513	2.130

The short-run price elasticities vary considerably from -0.406 to -0.755, advertising elasticities from -0.023 to +0.029, and quality elasticities from 0.181 to 0.539. The implied long-run price elasticities for Regions 1 through 5 are -0.436, -0.815, -0.543, -0.848 and -0.643, respectively, while those for advertising quantity are 0.013, -0.025, 0.025, 0.012 and 0.021. (Note that for Region 3, the negative estimate of η^* implies that short-run elasticities are larger in absolute value than corresponding long-run elasticities.) In Regions 3 and 5, the statistically significant coefficient on LQUAL implies that advertising quality has a significant positive impact on sales.

(c) Estimates of ρ (t-values in parentheses) for Regions 1 through 5, based on a Hildreth-Lu procedure with grid steps of 0.05, are -0.20 (1.46), 0.55 (4.70), 0.10 (0.72), -0.20 (1.46) and -0.20 (1.46), respectively. Note that in most cases the estimated ρ is insignificantly different from zero. In Region 2 where ρ is significant the GLS estimates deteriorated; in particular, the estimate of η^* was negative and significant.

(d) You should be able to replicate the results reported at the end of Section 8.4. (I used the software program called SHAZAM for this purpose.) One could also estimate this model in different ways, such as treating it as a five-equation system to be estimated using the iterative Zellner estimator. The important result is that advertising quality has an elasticity estimate about 20 times as large as advertising quantity.

(e) You'll find that some of the results are affected considerably, but the quality elasticity is still much larger than the quantity elasticity.

FINAL COMMENTS:

Data on firm-specific price, quantity and advertising variables are often difficult to obtain. Some electric utilities have instituted energy conservation programs that rely heavily on promotional information advertising; since electric utilities are typically regulated, that data might be available to you for analysis. More traditional marketing data might also be made available by the Marketing Science Institute; for further details, see footnote 21 on page 438 in the text.

INSTRUCTOR'S NOTES FOR CHAPTER NINE:

MODELING THE INTERRELATED DEMANDS FOR FACTORS OF PRODUCTION:
ESTIMATION AND INFERENCE IN EQUATION SYSTEMS

ECONOMETRIC PROCEDURES EMPLOYED IN THE EXERCISES OF CHAPTER NINE:

- Examine data, generate variables, and assess their trends

- Do OLS estimation of bivariate Cobb-Douglas and CES models

- Compare iterative Zellner-efficient (IZEF) and equation-by-
  equation OLS estimates of input-output demand equations derived from
  the generalized Leontief cost function

- For a singular equation system, do equation-by-equation OLS and verify adding-up conditions; also confirm numerical invariance of
  parameter estimates to which equation is deleted in IZEF and I3SLS
  estimation

- Compute substitution elasticities, check that monotonicity and
  curvature conditions are satisfied by the estimated model

- Compare elasticity estimates based on generalized Leontief and
  translog cost functions

- Compute and compare likelihood ratio, Lagrange Multiplier and Wald
  test statistics, and attest to inequality relationship among them

- Compute a generalized R^2 statistic for a system of equations, and
  relate it to the likelihood ratio test statistic that all slope
  coefficients are simultaneously equal to zero

- Estimate an interrelated factor demand model with vector AR(1)
  disturbances, and test for the AR(0) null hypothesis

- Estimate a model of cost and production allowing for non-neutral
  technical change, and estimate the implied rate of multifactor
  productivity growth

GOALS FOR THE EXERCISES IN CHAPTER NINE:

To help students gain experience with, and an empirical understanding of, econometric issues frequently encountered when estimating demand equations for factors of production, using system estimation techniques with cross-equation constraints. The data for the exercises is from a 1975 study by Berndt and Wood, who reported the controversial finding that energy and capital inputs in U.S. manufacturing were complementary rather than substitutable inputs.

GENERAL COMMENTS TO THE INSTRUCTOR:

The exercises in this chapter are quite straightforward, and introduce students to the issues commonly encountered when estimating parameters in systems of equations. It would be best if all students work through Exercise 1, for by doing that they become familiar with the data used in subsequent exercises.

Although the econometric issues involved are largely similar, rather than having models in which all inputs are assumed to adjust instantaneously, one could instead specify restricted cost functions in which some inputs are fixed and others are variable. You might want to adapt the exercises to have students look at these types of models as an alternative. See Section 9.7 in the text for further details.

SPECIFIC NOTES ON THE EXERCISES IN CHAPTER NINE:

Exercise 1: Inspecting the Berndt-Wood KLEM Data for U.S. Manufacturing

TASKS: Examine time trends of variables, generate several new variables for later use, and interpret intercorrelations among them. Verify accounting relationship between gross output and value-added.

COMMENTS: The purpose of this exercise is to help students become familiar with features of the Berndt-Wood KLEM data set for U.S. manufacturing over the 1947-1971 time period.

(a) All input quantities increased from 1947 to 1971, although in some years decreases occurred. Nominal input prices also generally increased, although P_K decreased after 1959.

(b) The relative price of labor increased most rapidly, while PKP actually fell; PEP and PMP were relatively flat. Tax policy (investment incentives) affected PKP, and regulation of energy prices likely restrained growth in PEP.

(c) From 1947 to 1971, labor intensity fell and capital intensity increased, energy intensity was roughly constant, and materials intensity fell.

(d) PLP had the largest standard deviation and PMP the least. Simple correlations among the four input-output coefficients are all positive; correlations between input-output coefficient and that factor's relative price are negative for all inputs except E; there are positive correlations between KY and PEP, and between LY and PEP, but all other correlations between an input-output coefficient and another input's relative price are negative. It is rather difficult to infer partial input substitutability or complementarity merely by looking at simple correlations.

(e) Real unit cost fell, indicating perhaps the effects of productivity growth and/or economies of scale.

(f) You should be able to verify this relationship. Which output measure is preferable depends in large part on which inputs one is including—if one includes intermediate inputs such as materials and energy, then the output measure should be a gross output one; but if one includes only the primary inputs of capital and labor, then the appropriate output measure is value-added.

Exercise 2: Single Equation Estimation of CES and Cobb-Douglas Forms

TASKS: Run a set of bivariate regressions, and interpret slope coefficient estimates in terms of Cobb-Douglas or CES parameters. Test Cobb-Douglas and fixed input-output coefficient technologies as special cases. Attest to numerical relationship among alternative σ estimates.

COMMENTS: The purpose of this rather simple exercise is to engage students in estimating and interpreting parameters of the Cobb-Douglas and CES production functions.

(a) The point estimate of α_K is 1.0543, which according to Eq. (9.4) should be the share of capital costs in value-added; a share of greater than 1.0 does not make sense, and implies a negative share for labor. The low Durbin-Watson test statistic of 0.5203 is troubling as well; finally, if input quantities are endogenous, then LNQKQL may be correlated with the equation disturbance term, yielding a simultaneous equations bias.

(b) Point estimates of σ involving ln K as a regressor are typically found to be smaller in the time series literature; those patterns are present here. The t-statistics corresponding to the null hypothesis that $\sigma = 0$ in the three equations are 5.304, 34.814 and 8.416—all result in rejection at traditional significance levels, yielding no support for the fixed coefficient, zero-price elasticity specification. When the null hypothesis is instead that $\sigma = 1$, it is barely rejected at the 95% significance level for the first equation (t = 2.136), it is rejected more strongly for the labor equation (t = 2.546), and it is rejected quite strongly for the capital/labor equation (t = 4.417). Hence there's not much support for the Cobb-Douglas either, although the point estimate of σ based on the labor demand equation is quite close to one at 0.932.

(c) The R^2 from the reciprocal regressions should be the same—0.550173, 0.981377 and 0.754867. The analytical relationships can be verified numerically; the three implicit estimates of σ are 1.296, 0.950 and 0.869.

Exercise 3: Comparing Equation-by-Equation and IZEF Estimates

TASKS: Estimate system of generalized Leontief (GL) and translog (TLOG) input equations using equation-by-equation OLS. Compare these OLS estimates to IZEF (iterative Zellner-efficient) estimates, when no cross-equation restrictions are imposed. Verify the adding-up relationship among parameters in the share equations of the TLOG.

COMMENTS: The purpose of this exercise is to have students consider when systems estimators are likely to give rather different results from equation-by-equation OLS estimates, in part by looking at the residual cross-products matrix, and/or whether the set of regressors is the same in each equation.

(a) Results should match those reported in Table 9.1 of the text. Note that residuals across equations are positively contemporaneously correlated (a cyclical phenomenon?), implying that equation-by-equation OLS will differ from IZEF. In this particular case, each of the IZEF standard errors is smaller than its OLS counterpart.

(b) You should be able to replicate results reported in Table 9.2 of the text. In this case the equation-by-equation OLS and IZEF parameter estimates coincide numerically, for the same set of regressors appears in each equation and there are no cross-equation constraints. Depending on the computer software, the IZEF standard errors may be smaller than the OLS ones, for OLS-based estimates typically adjust for degrees of freedom, while IZEF standard error estimates are often asymptotic estimates and are not adjusted for degrees of freedom. Your results will depend on the software you use here.

Exercise 4: Special Issues in Estimating Singular Equation Systems

TASKS: Estimate system of translog share equations using equation-by-equation OLS and confirm the adding-up relationships among parameter estimates. Then estimate by IZEF a three-equation share system with symmetry

constraints imposed where the implicit fourth equation is deleted; confirm
empirically that IZEF parameter estimates are invariant to equation deleted.
Show that this invariance does not occur with 3SLS, but that it does re-emerge
if the 3SLS procedure is iterated (I3SLS).

COMMENTS: This is an important exercise, for it addresses the adding up
and lack of invariance conditions that can easily result in embarrassing
situations where results do not satisfy important a priori relationships.   It
is worth noting that the estimation of share equations is not confined to
studies of production and cost; as was discussed in Chapter 8, for example,
share equations often appear in the marketing literature.

(a) You should be able to replicate results reported in Table 9.2.

(b) You should find that directly and indirectly estimated parameters
(and standard errors) are numerically invariant to the equation deleted. My
computer program "blew up"—FATAL ERROR, it said when I attempted to estimate
the singular equation system.

(c) The 3SLS results typically lack invariance to the equation deleted.
For example, you will find that with the M share equation deleted, the 3SLS
estimates of γ_{LE} and γ_{EE} are -0.0019224 and 0.037537, while with the K share
equation deleted, the 3SLS estimates are instead -0.00033198 and 0.050249,
respectively. Upon iterating the 3SLS estimator, however, numerically
invariant parameter estimates emerge.

(d) This type of specification would not make sense, for since the sum
of the four parameters must be zero, if three are set to zero, then the fourth
must also be zero. Except in rather unusual cases (see Exercise 4 in Chapter
8), a regressor cannot appear in only one of the share equations if the
adding-up properties are to hold.

Exercise 5: Substitution Elasticities and Curvature Checks

TASKS: Estimate GL system of input-output equations by IZEF, compute fitted input-output coefficients and various elasticities, and check whether the monotonicity and curvature conditions are satisfied at each observation. Do the same with the system of translog share equations.

COMMENTS: This exercise requires writing a fair bit of computer code instructions, but it is a useful one. Incidentally, alternative computational formulae can be used to compute the Allen and traditional price elasticities.

(a) You should be able to replicate the reported results. The fitted a_i are all positive, and while K and E, and K and M, are complements, all other inputs are substitutable. All own-price elasticities are less than one in absolute value, indicating price-inelastic factor demands.

(b) Although all own-Allen elasticity estimates are negative, the 2x2 determinants for K and L, for K and M and for L and M have negative values at many observations, thereby violating the necessary curvature conditions. Similarly, the 3x3 determinants involving all possible sets of three inputs have at least some positive values, again counter to the necessary curvature requirements. The determinant of the estimated 4x4 matrix should be very close to zero.

(c) You should be able to replicate the results reported in Table 9.2. All fitted cost shares are positive; all own-price elasticities of demand are negative, but demand is price-inelastic; and all input pairs except K and E are substitutes.

(d) Curvature checks are satisfied at all observations.

(e) The elasticity estimates are roughly similar for the GL and TLOG specifications, although there is a sign reversal with K and M indicating complementarity with the GL and substitutability with the TLOG.

Exercise 6: Obtaining Statistical Inference in Equation Systems

TASKS: Estimate either the GL or TLOG demand system using various weighting matrices, and then compute the likelihood ratio (LR), Wald (W) and Lagrange Multiplier (LM) test statistics for the null hypothesis that the off-diagonal zero restrictions are valid. Compare test results, and verify the inequality relationship $W > LR > LM$.

COMMENTS: This exercise provides a rather dramatic example of the numerical inequality relationship among alternative asymptotically equivalent test procedures. To do this exercise, it will be necessary that students can retrieve and then employ in further estimation the weighting matrices implied by various estimates of the residual covariance matrix. For some statistical software packages, this is not feasible.

(a) For the TLOG, the sample maximized ln L here is 344.566, whereas with the GL it is 397.557.

(b,c) For the TLOG, the Wald statistic (computed as T*difference in trace = 604.581 - 75.000) is 529.581, while for the GL it is (T*difference in trace = 596.807 - 100) equal to 496.807. When the constrained TLOG model is estimated by IZEF = ML, the sample maximized ln L is 287.419; hence the LR test statistic is 114.294. When the constrained GL model is estimated by IZEF = ML, the sample maximized ln L is 376.044; hence the LR test statistic is 43.026. With the TLOG and the GL, the degrees of freedom are 6; hence the null hypothesis is rejected in either model, given usual significance levels, for both the LR and the Wald test statistics.

(d) For the TLOG, the LM test statistic turns out to be 75.000 - 25.5425 = 49.4575, while for the GL it is 100.000 - 89.2390 = 10.7710. At the 0.05 and 0.01 significance levels, this implies rejection for the TLOG, but nonrejection of the null hypothesis for the GL.

(e) The inequality for the GL is (496.807 > 43.026 > 10.771), and for the TLOG it is (529.581 > 114.294 > 49.458); it therefore is consistent with that expressed in Eq. (9.38). There is conflict in inference at usual significance levels for the GL, but not for the TLOG.

Exercise 7: Goodness of Fit in GL or Translog Equation Systems

TASKS: Estimate either a GL or TLOG model with symmetry and constant returns to scale imposed, and then estimate it with all slope coefficients constrained to zero. Then compute the generalized R^2 for an equation system, and relate it to the likelihood ratio test statistic of the null hypothesis that all slope coefficients are simultaneously equal to zero.

COMMENTS: The purpose of this exercise is to have students construct a measure of goodness of fit in equation systems and, more generally, to encourage them to think through the relationship between goodness of fit and the results of particular hypothesis tests.

(a) You should be able to replicate results as given in the text. Sample log-likelihoods are given in parts (b,c) of Exercise 6 in this chapter of the Instructor's Resource Guide.

(b) The generalized R^2 for the TLOG model is 0.98967, while for the GL it turns out to be 0.82112. See the discussion in the previous exercise; the null hypothesis is not rejected for the GL, but it is for the TLOG at usual significance levels.

Exercise 8: Estimated Interrelated Factor Demand Models with Vector Autocorrelation

TASKS: Assuming that the autocovariance matrix is diagonal, estimate either a GL or TLOG model allowing for a vector AR(1) process, and then test the null hypothesis of AR(0) using the likelihood ratio test procedure.

COMMENTS: The purpose of this exercise is to help students understand that testing for autocorrelation in systems of equations is a relatively straightforward extension of the single-equation test procedure.

(a,b) For the TLOG estimated over the 1948-71 time period, the sample maximized ln L is 335.427, and the estimate of a common ρ parameter is 0.276, with a t-value of 2.49; the $\rho = 0$ constrained run over the same sample yields an ln L of 333.133, implying an LR test statistic of 4.588 (or an asymptotic t-statistic of 2.142). The null hypothesis of no autocorrelation is therefore rejected at a 95% level of confidence, but not at the 99% level. The parameter appearing most sensitive to allowing for autocorrelation is γ_{EE}, which changes from 0.020978 to 0.01696 when the AR(1) process is permitted; other parameters do not change as much.

For the GL estimated over the same time period, the sample maximized ln L is 419.104, and the estimates of ρ in the K, L, E and M equations (t-statistics in parentheses) are 0.849 (9.35), 0.894 (19.42), 0.910 (19.02) and 0.074 (0.40), respectively. On the basis of these asymptotic t-statistics, the AR(1) process appears to be statistically significant. This conjecture is verified by the LR test procedure; for the $\rho = 0$ constrained run, the sample maximized ln L is 389.799, implying a likelihood ratio test statistic equal to 58.610, which is significantly larger than the χ^2 critical value with four degrees of freedom at usual significance levels. For the GL model, parameters in the L, E and M input-output equations are quite sensitive to whether autocorrelation is permitted—some estimates even change sign.

Incidentally, the final estimates of ρ in both these models do not appear to correspond that well with implicit estimates of ρ based on the equation-specific Durbin-Watson test statistics.

Exercise 9: Obtaining Estimates of Multifactor Productivity Growth

TASKS: Specify a constant returns to scale translog cost function with non-neutral technical progress, and estimate an equation system consisting of the three share equations and the unit cost function. Obtain implicit estimates of the annual rate of multifactor productivity (MFP) growth, and test for Hicks-neutral technical progress using the LR test procedure.

COMMENTS: The purpose of this exercise is to engage students in setting up a model that permits biased technical progress, and then having them estimate the implied rate of multifactor productivity growth.

(a) With the M share equation deleted, 1947-71 IZEF parameter estimates (t-statistics) of the various time-related parameters turn out to be as follows: α_t, -0.24043 (1.091); α_{tt}, -0.00012 (1.065); γ_{Kt}, -0.00033 (1.493); γ_{Lt}, -0.00146 (1.480); γ_{Et}, -0.00031 (1.064); and the implicit estimate of γ_{Mt} is 0.00210. The sample maximized ln L is 425.164.

(b) The bias of technical progress is K, L and E-saving, but M-using. The null hypothesis of no technical progress (that all these t-related parameters are simultaneously equal to zero) is decisively rejected; the LR test statistic is 58.804, much larger than the χ^2 critical value for five degrees of freedom at any reasonable significance level. However, the null hypothesis of Hicks-neutrality is not rejected; the LR test statistic with three d.f. is 4.088 (the sample maximized ln L for the Hicks-neutral run is 423.120), which is less than the χ^2 critical value at usual significance levels.

(c) The estimated values of this derivative vary from -0.00476 in 1947 to -0.00851 in 1971, they increase in absolute value over time, and their mean is -0.00664. The negative of this rate of annual cost diminution corresponds to the rate of multifactor productivity growth, which is here found on average to be about 0.664% per year. Note that since the α_t and α_{tt} parameters are both negative, the rate of MFP growth is found to be accelerating over the 1947-71 time period.

FINAL COMMENTS:

The Berndt-Wood KLEM data employed in the exercises of this chapter have also been used in numerous other contexts. For the U.S., more recent KLEM-type data for total and a number of two-digit manufacturing industries are occasionally available on an unofficial basis from the U.S. Bureau of Labor Statistics, Division of Productivity Research, Washington, DC 20212. Contact Michael Harper, Chief (202-523-9261), for further information.

INSTRUCTOR'S NOTES FOR CHAPTER TEN:

<u>PARAMETER ESTIMATION IN STRUCTURAL AND REDUCED FORM
EQUATIONS OF SMALL MACROECONOMETRIC MODELS</u>

ECONOMETRIC PROCEDURES EMPLOYED IN THE EXERCISES OF CHAPTER TEN:

- Perform single-equation estimation of Klein's Model I, using OLS, 2SLS, OLS-AR(1) and 2SLS-AR(1) procedures

- Do 2SLS in two ways—one as a two-step "brute force" OLS procedure, the other directly; demonstrate that while the two procedures yield numerically equivalent parameter estimates, their standard error estimates differ; then compare the procedures in terms of how residuals are computed

- Develop the notion of an information set and do 2SLS estimation consistent with the error orthogonality condition of the rational expectations hypothesis (REH); given the information set, show why this 2SLS estimation is consistent with, but does not fully incorporate, the REH

- Estimate models with alternative AR(q) expectational processes using appropriate information set variables

- Test for the exogeneity of certain variables in Klein's Model I using the Hausman specification test

- Test for serial correlation of disturbances in a simultaneous equations model with lagged dependent variables using Durbin's m-test and the Breusch-Godfrey generalization of Durbin's test

- Demonstrate the numerical equivalence of indirect least squares, 2SLS and 3SLS parameter estimates in a just-identified model

- Compare 2SLS, 3SLS and I3SLS parameter estimates of an over-identified model, and comment on the role of the contemporaneous disturbance covariance matrix

- Estimate a structural model by full information maximum likelihood (FIML), and compare results with maximum likelihood (ML) estimation of a reduced form model with overidentifying restrictions imposed; test for the empirical validity of these overidentifying restrictions using the likelihood ratio test criterion

- Compute an ML estimate of the government spending impact multiplier, and construct a confidence interval for it

More-advanced procedures:

- Demonstrate that the determinant of the Jacobian from a structurally recursive model is equal to one; estimate a variant of Klein's Model I using successive least squares and by ML; and check on Prucha's argument that FIML and iterative Zellner-efficient standard error estimates in a structurally recursive model are not equivalent

- Replicate Taylor's iterative minimum distance estimation of a two-equation reduced form model incorporating restrictions from the REH; test for the empirical validity of these restrictions, and interpret test results

GOALS FOR THE EXERCISES IN CHAPTER TEN:

The goal of these exercises is to have students confront and deal with issues of estimation and inference in the simultaneous equations of small macroeconometric models.

GENERAL COMMENTS TO THE INSTRUCTOR:

In this chapter I have focused attention on the most basic issues involved in estimation and inference in simultaneous equations models. The literature on simultaneous equations estimation with non-static expectations is large and ever-growing. Much of it is quite technical, and therefore it is not possible to introduce students to all of the important issues simply by having them work through the ten exercises of this chapter. I expect that many instructors will find it useful to use the data in CHAP10.DAT for other purposes than those embodied in the exercises I have put together. My goal here is a rather humble one: Introduce students to the now-classic issues.

Subsequent to my writing the text, Professor Christopher L. Gilbert of the University of London, Queen Mary and Westfield College, kindly provided me with some of the data apparently originally used by A.W. Phillips in his classic article. For your possible use in a supplementary exercise, I attach a "hard copy" of the data given me by Professor Gilbert; the data set is found at the end of this chapter.

In order to do subsequent exercises in this chapter, it is necessary that students work through Exercises 1 and 2 first, for in them they construct variables required for later use. The contents of the ten exercises are briefly summarized in the text at the beginning of Section 10.6; I will not repeat that summary here.

SPECIFIC NOTES ON THE EXERCISES IN CHAPTER TEN:

Exercise 1: OLS, 2SLS and GLS Estimation of Klein's Model I

GOALS: The purpose of this exercise is to have students replicate other researchers' estimation of Klein's 3-equation Model I of the U.S. economy, using a variety of single-equation structural estimation methods.

TASKS: Generate variables, and verify national income accounting identities. Estimate the three equations of Klein's Model I by OLS, 2SLS, OLS-AR(1) and 2SLS-AR(1); compare and interpret results; and comment on the set of instruments that must be used to obtain consistent estimates in 2SLS-AR(1) estimation with a lagged dependent variable.

(a) This is straightforward.

(b) You should be able to replicate the OLS results in Table 10.3.

(c) The set of instruments used is of course that set of regressors that emerges when the reduced form of the equation system is solved out analytically. Assuming no serial correlation, these 2SLS estimates are consistent. The OLS and 2SLS of β_1 and β_2 differ considerably. For further discussion, see the footnote in this section of the exercise.

(d) The AR(1) parameter is significant only in the consumption equation (based on iterative Cochrane-Orcutt estimation).

(e) The instrument list must be expanded to include lagged values of the instruments, for correlation with both the once- and twice-lagged parts of the AR(1) disturbance on y_{t-1}—i.e., $u_{t-1} = \rho u_{t-2} + \epsilon_{t-1}$—must be taken into account. Again, only in the consumption equation is the AR(1) term insignificant. On the choice between OLS and 2SLS, see the discussion in Exercise 4 of this chapter.

Exercise 2: The Two Steps of 2SLS—A Lucas-Rapping Faux Pas?

GOALS: The purpose of this exercise is to help students better appreciate the 2SLS estimation procedure, and why its standard error estimates and residuals differ from those obtained at the second stage of a "brute force" two-step OLS estimation procedure. Incidentally, you might inform students that the result, that parameter estimates of these two procedures are equivalent, does not in general hold when the equation becomes nonlinear.

TASKS: Construct a number of variables, and attempt to replicate the 2SLS estimation of the three equations of the Lucas-Rapping model. Note that standard error estimates, R^2 and Durbin-Watson values differ from those reported by them. Then do reduced form estimation, retrieve fitted values, and re-do the 2SLS estimation by doing OLS with $\hat{y}$ replacing y as a regressor; and verify that now the Lucas-Rapping results can be replicated. Do this for all three equations, and interpret these findings. Comment on why these two estimation procedures give different standard errors, and why the 2SLS rather than the "brute force" two-step OLS procedure is appropriate.

(a) The 2SLS standard error estimates you obtain in the labor supply equation (10.36) should be (in the same order the variables appear in the exercise) 0.173, 0.597, 0.598, 0.206 and 0.639. In the labor demand Eq. (10.37) the 2SLS standard error estimates I obtained were 0.446, 0.102, 0.095 and 0.032, while those in the unemployment equation (10.38) were 0.009, 0.075, 0.210 and 0.054. The R^2 values in these three 2SLS estimated equations are 0.75296, 0.99536 and 0.92844, respectively, while the Durbin-Watson test statistics are 1.8232, 1.5623 and 1.5475.

(b,c) My experience has been that students enjoy doing this "detective" work on such an important and classic study.

(d) See your econometric theory textbook for details.

(e) Results are not affected qualitatively; but standard error estimates are always larger with 2SLS, with the ratio of the 2SLS to the second-step OLS estimated standard error equaling their relative values of their standard error of the regression.

Exercise 3: REH-Consistent Estimation Using 2SLS

GOALS: The purpose of this exercise is to engage students in several alternative procedures for obtaining consistent (but not necessarily efficient) estimates of models with rational expectations, employing the notion of an <u>information set</u>.

TASKS: Construct variables used by Taylor, consider the notion of an information set, and comment on how it changes when expectational disturbances are serially correlated. Under the AR(0) assumption, do 2SLS estimation, and demonstrate consistency with the residual (error) orthogonality condition of the REH. Then adjust the information set under AR(1) disturbances, and re-do the 2SLS estimation. Finally, estimate the two-equation model by 3SLS under the AR(0) assumption. An optional portion has students estimating the model with MA(1) disturbances, which in some special cases is consistent with the REH.

(a) This is relatively straightforward. Sample means of YDEV, RM1 and INF over the 91 observations are -0.01908, 0.80745 and 0.00875.

(b) It is worthwhile emphasizing to students why the concept of an information set is so very critical in models with rational expectations.

(c) The 2SLS results I obtained here were as follows (absolute values of t-statistics in parentheses):

$$YDEV = -0.041 + 1.258*YDEV(-1) - 0.406*YDEV(-2) + 0.635*RM1 - 0.585*RM1(-1)$$
$$\quad\ (0.56)\quad (10.66)\qquad\qquad (4.07)\qquad\qquad (3.18)\qquad\qquad (2.11)$$

$$+ 0.231*INF - 0.0001*TIME \qquad R^2 = 0.9203$$
$$\ (0.24)\qquad\quad (1.51)\qquad\qquad DW = 2.1585$$

Concerning the discussion here, I have found it useful to have students verify numerically that the sample correlation between a fitted value regressor in 2SLS and the residual is always zero. Precisely how expectations are formed is not worked out in this procedure—hence while it is consistent with the REH, it does not fully incorporate it. Estimates are roughly similar to those reported by Taylor and reproduced in Eq. (10.60), although the 2SLS coefficient estimate on INF here is considerably smaller.

The 2SLS estimates of the inflation equation are as follows:

$$INF = 0.0026 + 0.770*INF(-1) + 0.020*YDEV \qquad R^2 = 0.59577$$
$$\quad (3.15)\quad\ (11.22)\qquad\qquad (1.26)\qquad\qquad DW = 2.5636,$$

and, when the restriction is imposed, the constrained 2SLS equation is

$$ACCEL = 0.00056 + 0.0215*YDEV \qquad R^2 = 0.0161$$
$$\qquad (0.96)\qquad (1.26)\qquad\qquad DW = 2.8859.$$

Both estimates on the YDEV regressor are larger than that reported by Taylor, but the 2SLS standard errors here are also much larger.

(d) The three 2SLS equations estimated using IS_{t-2} turn out to be:

$$YDEV = -0.087 + 1.249*YDEV(-1) - 0.409*YDEV(-2) + 0.598*RM1 - 0.483*RM1(-1)$$
$$(1.09) \quad (5.22) \quad\quad\quad (1.83) \quad\quad\quad\quad (1.21) \quad\quad\quad (0.86)$$

$$- 0.480*INF - 0.0001*TIME \quad\quad R^2 = 0.9170$$
$$(0.44) \quad\quad\quad (1.28) \quad\quad\quad\quad DW = 2.1551$$

where the estimated coefficient on the INF regressor is now negative rather

than positive; for the unrestricted inflation equation,

$$INF = 0.0011 + 0.969*INF(-1) + 0.030*YDEV \quad R^2 = 0.60454$$
$$(1.15) \quad (11.41) \quad\quad\quad (1.65) \quad\quad\quad DW = 2.5636$$

where the coefficient on INF(-1) is larger and now very close to zero; and for

the restricted inflation equation,

$$ACCEL = 0.00083 + 0.0294*YDEV \quad\quad R^2 = 0.0258$$
$$(0.96) \quad\quad (1.26) \quad\quad\quad\quad DW = 2.6320$$

where the coefficient on YDEV is larger, but statistically insignificant.

(e) The 3SLS estimates are also consistent with error-orthogonality.

You might have students demonstrate that. The 3SLS estimates I obtained

without the restriction imposed were

$$YDEV = -0.071 + 1.208*YDEV(-1) - 0.375*YDEV(-2) + 0.622*RM1 - 0.531*RM1(-1)$$
$$(1.02) \quad (10.75) \quad\quad\quad (3.95) \quad\quad\quad\quad (3.27) \quad\quad\quad (2.01)$$

$$- 0.096*INF - 0.0001*TIME \quad\quad R^2 = 0.9208$$
$$(0.11) \quad\quad\quad (1.62) \quad\quad\quad\quad DW = 2.0627$$

for the output equation, and, for the inflation equation,

$$INF = 0.0026 + 0.770*INF(-1) + 0.020*YDEV, \quad R^2 = 0.59584$$
$$(3.20) \quad (11.42) \quad\quad\quad (1.28) \quad\quad\quad DW = 2.5636.$$

When the restriction is imposed on the inflation equation, the 3SLS estimates

turn out to be as follows:

$$YDEV = -0.075 + 1.201*YDEV(-1) - 0.370*YDEV(-2) + 0.620*RM1 - 0.523*RM1(-1)$$
$$(1.09) \quad (10.68) \quad\quad\quad (3.90) \quad\quad\quad\quad (3.26) \quad\quad\quad (1.98)$$

$$- 0.222*INF - 0.0001*TIME \quad\quad R^2 = 0.9202$$
$$(0.25) \quad\quad\quad (1.62) \quad\quad\quad\quad DW = 2.0479$$

for the output equation, and, for the restricted inflation equation,

$$ACCEL = 0.00056 + 0.0215*YDEV$$
$$(0.97) \quad\quad (1.28) \quad\quad\quad\quad DW = 2.8859.$$

Note that these 3SLS estimates are not that different from the 2SLS ones.

(f) See your econometric theory (or, perhaps, macroeconomic theory) textbook for further details, or consult references given in the text.

Exercise 4: Testing for Exogeneity Using Hausman's Specification Test

GOALS: The purpose of this exercise is to have students gain experience in implementing a test of the null hypothesis that the disturbance term in a stochastic equation is uncorrelated with a regressor (or a set of regressors). In the context of simultaneous equations, this Hausman test corresponds to the null hypothesis of exogeneity of regressors, when the alternative hypothesis is that they are endogenous.

TASKS: Estimate the three equations of Klein's Model I by OLS, then run three additional OLS regressions where "suspicious" regressors are the dependent variable, and retrieve fitted values. Next do OLS estimation of expanded equations, where the fitted value of a suspicious variable is added as a regressor. Test whether coefficients on the fitted value regressors are simultaneously equal to zero, using large-sample test statistics.

(a) You should be able to replicate the Table 10.3 results.

(b) The unrestricted reduced form parameter estimates are given in Table 10.4 of the text.

(c) The three expanded OLS regressions I ran looked like this (absolute values of t-statistics are in parentheses):

$$CN = 16.555 + 0.356*C + 0.707*P + 0.216*P(-1) + 0.454*WFIT - 0.690*PFIT$$
$$\quad\ (15.50)\ (1.50)\quad\ (3.71)\quad\ (2.49)\quad\ \ (1.89)\quad\ \ \ (3.23)$$

where the R^2 is 0.98913 and the SSR = 10.2338;

$$I = 20.278 + 0.725*P + 0.616*P(-1) - 0.158*KLAG - 0.575*PFIT$$
$$\quad\ (4.31)\quad\ (7.78)\quad\ (6.07)\quad\quad\ (7.01)\quad\quad\ (4.03)$$

with an R^2 of 0.965919 and a SSR equal to 8.59948; and

$$W1 = 15.507 + 0.671*P + 0.720*P(-1) + 0.597*T - 0.134*PFIT$$
$$\quad\ (10.13)\ (3.52\ )\quad\ (4.57)\quad\quad\ (10.95)\quad\ (0.53)$$

with an R^2 of 0.954594 and an SSR equal to 36.0934.

(d,e) The SSR in the restricted CN equation is 17.8795; the χ^2 value is therefore $[(17.8795 - 10.2338)/10.2338]*15 = 11.207$, which is significant at usual confidence levels. The large-sample t-statistic on PFIT in the I equation is also large and significant, while that on the PFIT term in the W1 equation is not. Hence the null hypothesis of exogeneity of the "suspicious" regressors is rejected in the CN and I equations, but is not rejected in the W1 equation of Klein's Model I.

(f) See your econometric theory text for further details.

Exercise 5: Testing for Serial Correlation in the Lucas-Rapping Model

GOALS: The purpose of this exercise is to have students gain experience in testing for various types (AR and/or MA) of serial correlation in the presence of a lagged dependent variable, using Durbin's m-test and the Breusch-Godfrey procedure.

TASKS: Retrieve residuals from the OLS estimation of reduced form equations, then run additional regressions with the residual as dependent variable, and test whether the coefficient on the lagged residual equals zero. Then generalize this Durbin procedure by testing for the absence of serial correlation when the alternative hypothesis is either an AR(2) or an MA(2) specification, by testing whether the coefficients on the two lagged residuals are simultaneously equal to zero. Do the same set of tests with 2SLS estimation of the structural equations, but add appropriately lagged instruments to ensure consistency of the estimation process.

(a) The equality of the standard error estimates is coincidental, as can be seen by checking your computer output and looking at the standard error estimates with additional digits reported.

(b) Under the alternative hypothesis, a regressor (in particular, the lagged dependent variable) is correlated with the error term. The coefficient estimate on RESY3(-1) was -0.2525, with a standard error estimate of 0.2691; the null hypothesis that the coefficient equals zero is not rejected at usual significance levels. In the other equation, the coefficient estimate on RESY1(-1) was 0.52384, and the standard error estimate was 0.3175, leaving a large-sample t-ratio of 1.6499, which is not significant at the most typical confidence levels.

(c) When the constrained regression with RESY3 as dependent variable was run, the ln L was 97.3720 (34 observations), and when the RESY3(-1) and RESY3(-2) regressors were included, it increased to 99.7764; twice the difference is 4.8088, which is less than the 0.05 χ^2 critical value with 2 d.f. of 5.99; hence the null hypothesis on the absence of serial correlation is not rejected for this equation. For the equation with RESY1 as dependent variable, the two sample log-likelihoods are 104.755 and 98.6799; minus twice the difference is 12.1502; and this likelihood ratio test statistic is larger than the χ^2 critical value at usual significance levels. Hence the null hypothesis on the absence of serial correlation is rejected, and second order serial correlation appears to be statistically significant.

(d) The 2SLS coefficient estimate (t-statistic) on the RESY1A(-1) variable was 0.171 (0.81), on the RESY2A(-1) variable it was 0.350 (1.77), and on RESUA(-1) it was 0.278 (1.42). Hence using this modified Breusch-Godfrey procedure in the 2SLS context, the null hypothesis on the absence of serial correlation is not rejected for each of the three equations. Incidentally, as a check on robustness, I also estimated this using an AR(1) procedure, with instruments adjusted using the Fair procedure. The AR(1) estimated coefficients (t-statistics) I obtained for the Y1, Y2 and U equations were

0.35 (2.19), 0.38 (2.43) and 0.26 (1.59), respectively. Hence the inference in the first two equations depends on which test procedure is employed.

Exercise 6: The Equivalence of Alternative Estimators in Just-Identified Models

GOALS: The purpose of this exercise is to have students demonstrate that OLS-based indirect least squares, 2SLS, 3SLS and I3SLS parameter estimates are numerically equivalent when each of the structural equations is just-identified.

TASKS: Using the necessary order conditions, demonstrate that each of the two equations in a revised Klein's Model I is just-identified. Estimate the structural equations by 2SLS and 3SLS, and verify the numerical equivalence of parameter estimates. Then estimate the reduced form equations by OLS, and solve for unique estimates of the structural parameters (indirect least squares). Discuss why doing Zellner's "seemingly unrelated" equation system estimation procedure would yield numerically equivalent parameter estimates.

(a) In each equation, the number of excluded exogenous variables (one) is just equal to the number of included endogenous variables appearing as regressors (one). The 2SLS estimates I obtained are as follows (absolute values of t-statistics in parentheses):

$$CN = 54.056 - 0.234*I + 0.789*T \qquad R^2 = 0.3928$$
$$ (24.88) \quad (0.170) \quad (2.844) \qquad DW = 0.3362$$

and

$$I = 25.349 - 0.047*CN - 0.108*KLAG \qquad R^2 = 0.0454$$
$$ (1.70) \quad (0.25) \quad (1.17) \qquad DW = 0.5578$$

(b) Although parameter estimates coincide with those in (a) above, in some computer programs the 3SLS standard error estimates do not make a finite sample degrees of freedom adjustment. If your program does not do that, the six t-statistics you should obtain (in the same order as parameters appear in (a) above) are 26.773, -0.183, 3.060, 1.825, -0.272 and -1.256.

(c) The v's are i.i.d. There are six reduced form parameters and six structural parameters to be estimated. The OLS estimates of the reduced form Eqs. (10.72) and (10.74) are as follows:

$$CN = 48.652 + 0.02554*KLAG + 0.7975*T \qquad R^2 = 0.5270$$
$$(1.85) \qquad (0.19) \qquad\qquad (3.71) \qquad\qquad DW = 0.3186$$

and

$$I = 23.085 - 0.1091*KLAG - 0.0371*T \qquad R^2 = 0.1411$$
$$(1.37) \qquad (1.30) \qquad\qquad (0.27) \qquad\qquad DW = 0.5841$$

The implicit ILS estimates of the structural parameters are numerically identical to the 2SLS and 3SLS estimates. Since the OLS estimates are linear in the reduced form parameters but nonlinear in the structural parameters, it is difficult to derive standard error estimates of the structural parameters from the reduced form, unless one does nonlinear least squares on the reduced form.

(d) Since the same regressors appear as right-hand variables in each of the reduced form equations and there are no cross-equation binding constraints, OLS, ZEF and, for that matter, IZEF estimates coincide.

(e) They are equivalent.

Exercise 7: Comparing 2SLS, 3SLS and I3SLS in an Over-identified Model

GOALS: Compare small-sample estimates of three simultaneous equations estimators—2SLS, three-stage least squares (3SLS) and iterative 3SLS (I3SLS), using either Klein's Model I or the Lucas-Rapping model.

TASKS: Estimate model by 2SLS, look at residual covariance matrix, and speculate whether 3SLS will differ much from 2SLS. Then estimate by 3SLS and compare results; also estimate by I3SLS. Comment on results, and choose a preferred estimation procedure.

(a) With Klein's Model I, the 2SLS residual correlation between CN and I is 0.364, between CN and W1 is -0.546, and between I and W1 is 0.237. In the Lucas-Rapping model, the 2SLS residual correlation between the labor demand and labor supply equations is 0.449, that between labor supply and U is -0.758, and that between labor demand and U is -0.299. In each of these cases, some of the correlations are modest, and thus we might expect some difference in parameter estimates and gains in efficiency from moving to the 3SLS "systems" estimator.

(b) The 3SLS estimates I obtained for Klein's Model I are given in Table 10.3 in the text. For the three-equation Lucas-Rapping model, the 3SLS estimates I obtained were as follows (absolute values of t-statistics in parentheses):

$$Y1 = 0.181 + 1.608*Y3 - 1.662*Y3(-1) + 0.804*X1 + 0.772*Y1(-1) \quad R^2 = 0.7299$$
$$\quad (1.53) \quad (3.24) \qquad (3.32) \qquad\quad (4.54) \qquad (10.09) \qquad DW = 1.7920$$

for labor supply,

$$Y2 = 1.722 - 0.411*Y4 + 0.633*Y2(-1) - 0.253*X4 \qquad R^2 = 0.9950$$
$$\quad (4.49) \quad (4.69) \qquad (7.74) \qquad\quad (8.77) \qquad DW = 1.6446$$

for labor demand, and, for the unemployment equation,

$$U \ = 0.041 - 0.524*X1 - 0.506*Y5 + 0.800*U(-1) \qquad R^2 = 0.9236$$
$$\quad (4.82) \quad (7.71) \qquad (2.67) \qquad (16.31) \qquad DW = 1.7004$$

Note that there are no sign changes on estimated slope coefficients from the Lucas-Rapping 2SLS estimates reported in Eqs. (10.36)-(10.38) in the text.

If one does 3SLS only on the labor supply and demand equations (as is suggested in the exercise), the 3SLS estimates turn out to be as follows:

$$Y1 = -0.119 + 1.835*Y3 - 1.833*Y3(-1) + 0.802*X1 + 0.684*Y1(-1) \quad R^2 = 0.7314$$
$$\quad (0.75) \quad (3.57) \qquad (3.57) \qquad\quad (4.51) \qquad (7.59) \qquad DW = 2.0452$$

for labor supply, and, for labor demand,

$$Y2 = 1.646 - 0.387*Y4 + 0.648*Y2(-1) - 0.250*X4 \qquad R^2 = 0.9949$$
$$\quad (4.26) \quad (4.37) \qquad (7.88) \qquad\quad (8.59) \qquad DW = 1.6929$$

(c) The I3SLS estimates I obtained for Klein's Model I are given in Table 10.3 in the text. For the three-equation Lucas-Rapping model, the I3SLS estimates I obtained were as follows (absolute values of t-statistics in parentheses):

$$Y1 = 0.366 + 2.111*Y3 - 2.205*Y3(-1) + 0.858*X1 + 0.765*Y1(-1) \quad R^2 = 0.6713$$
$$(3.41) \quad (4.29) \qquad (4.42) \qquad\quad (4.68) \qquad\quad (10.57) \qquad\quad DW = 1.8052$$

for labor supply,

$$Y2 = 1.607 - 0.397*Y4 + 0.658*Y2(-1) - 0.262*X4 \qquad R^2 = 0.9948$$
$$(5.11) \quad (5.52) \qquad (9.80) \qquad\quad (10.20) \qquad\quad DW = 1.5760$$

for labor demand, and, for the unemployment equation,

$$U = 0.050 - 0.543*X1 - 0.703*Y5 + 0.761*U(-1) \qquad R^2 = 0.9103$$
$$(6.03) \quad (8.45) \qquad (4.01) \qquad (16.49) \qquad\quad DW = 1.8766$$

If one does I3SLS only on the labor supply and demand equations (as is suggested in the exercise), the I3SLS estimates turn out to be as follows:

$$Y1 = -0.083 + 1.958*Y3 - 1.961*Y3(-1) + 0.720*X1 + 0.765*Y1(-1) \quad R^2 = 0.7258$$
$$(0.46) \quad (4.23) \qquad (4.24) \qquad\quad (4.47) \qquad\quad (8.97) \qquad\quad DW = 2.0242$$

for labor supply, and, for labor demand,

$$Y2 = 1.475 - 0.346*Y4 + 0.685*Y2(-1) - 0.289*X4 \qquad R^2 = 0.9940$$
$$(4.48) \quad (4.57) \qquad (9.77) \qquad\quad (10.59) \qquad\quad DW = 1.6795$$

Again, there are no sign changes on these estimated slope coefficients from the 2SLS estimates reported by Lucas-Rapping. As to choice among these alternative estimators, see your econometric theory textbook for a discussion of small-sample properties based on Monte Carlo studies, and their sensitivity to misspecification.

Exercise 8: Maximum Likelihood Structural and Reduced Form Estimation of Klein's Model I

GOALS and TASKS: The purpose of this exercise is to have students estimate Klein's Model I by full information maximum likelihood (FIML) of the structural equations, to solve out analytically for the implied reduced form, to estimate the reduced form by maximum likelihood (ML) with nonlinear restrictions imposed, and to verify that the structural FIML estimates are numerically equivalent to the reduced form ML estimates. The empirical validity of the overidentifying restrictions is also tested using the likelihood ratio test procedure.

(a) The FIML estimates are given in Table 10.3 of the text. After eight iterations, I obtained a sample ln L of -83.4665.

(b) This is tedious but straightforward.

(c) I had some problems obtaining convergence, and in fact the sample log-likelihood and maximized sample ln L are not quite the same (they should be the same); the sample ln L I obtained was -83.3246. I have not been able to track down the difference, but it could be simply an issue of tightness of convergence criteria in the different computational algorithms. The estimated value of the government spending impact multiplier is 0.640 (t = 2.671), based on the reduced form parameter estimates. Since it is an impact (not dynamic) multiplier, this value of less than one is plausible, given the model structure.

(d) The sample ln L under the alternative hypothesis in the unrestricted reduced form is -63.7675.

(e) The likelihood ratio test statistic with 12 d.f. is 39.1142, which is greater than the χ^2 critical value at usual significance levels. Hence the null hypothesis that the over-identifying restrictions in Klein's Model I are empirically valid is rejected. This result is not surprising, for this model is admittedly more a teaching tool than a realistic description of the U.S. economy from 1921 to 1941.

(f) The LR test statistics should be equal, provided that the accounting identities are preserved when the model is rewritten in alternative ways.

Exercise 9: Estimation of a Structurally Recursive Model

GOALS: The purpose of this exercise is to have students work through relations among alternative estimators in the special case of structurally recursive models.

TASKS: Demonstrate that the Jacobian matrix of Klein's Model I cannot be triangularized, and then show that in an alternative structurally recursive version of Klein's Model I, the Jacobian is triangular. Obtain consistent estimates of this model using the method of successive least squares. Discuss properties of successive least squares when the contemporary disturbance covariance matrix is diagonal, and when it is nondiagonal. Then estimate the model by FIML. Finally, estimate the model using the IZEF estimator, and comment on the comparison of the FIML and IZEF parameter estimates, and their standard errors.

(a,b) This is straightforward.

(c) The OLS estimate of the revised investment Eq. (10.63') is as follows (absolute values of t-statistics in parentheses):

$$I = 24.908 + 0.745*P(-1) - 0.179*KLAG$$
$$\quad (3.59) \quad (8.66) \quad\quad\quad (5.12)$$
$$R^2 = 0.8328$$
$$DW = 2.0511$$

The OLS estimation of the revised Eq. (10.76) yields

$$Y = 25.110 + 0.471*Y(-1) + 1.527*JFIT$$
$$\quad (3.18) \quad (2.95) \quad\quad\quad (4.20)$$
$$R^2 = 0.8590$$
$$DW = 1.4717.$$

Finally, the OLS estimates of Eq. (10.64') are

$$W1 = - 0.766 + 0.351*EFIT + 0.276*E(-1)$$
$$\quad\quad (0.21) \quad (1.64) \quad\quad\quad (1.85)$$
$$R^2 = 0.8614$$
$$DW = 1.2823.$$

These OLS estimates are consistent, and if the contemporaneous disturbance covariance matrix were diagonal, they would also be efficient.

(d) The method of successive least squares is like an IV estimator, although it differs from 2SLS in the nature of the instruments that are actually employed at each successive stage, and thus in general it is not equivalent to 2SLS equation-by-equation estimation.

(e) The FIML estimates (absolute values of t-statistics) I obtained are:

$$CN = 13.051 + 0.231*Y + 0.487*Y(-1)$$
$$\quad\quad (2.00) \quad (1.06) \quad\quad (2.03)$$
$$SSR = 90.7519$$
$$DW = 2.0691$$

$$I = 21.275 + 0.881*P(-1) - 0.172*KLAG$$
$$\quad (1.67) \quad (3.36) \quad\quad\quad (2.89)$$
$$SSR = 48.5283$$
$$DW = 1.0072$$

$$W1 = -2.064 + 0.387*(Y + TX - W2) + 0.262*E(-1) \quad SSR = 24.9216$$
$$\quad (1.20) \quad (4.91) \quad\quad\quad\quad\quad (2.89) \quad\quad DW = 1.1932$$

Differences from the successive least squares estimates in most cases are modest.

(f) The differences in implied t-statistics can be substantial. Based on the IZEF parameter and standard error estimates, the implied t-statistics are always larger; specifically, for the nine parameters estimated in (e) above, the t-statistics (in the same order the parameters appear there) are 4.88, 2.57, and 4.75; 3.68, 11.86 and 6.11; and 1.35, 9.90 and 5.54. Note that the relative magnitudes differ by coefficient, even within the same equation. See the Prucha article on reasons why the FIML standard error estimates are preferable.

Exercise 10: Replicating the Estimation of Taylor's REH Model

GOALS: To have students implement empirically the iterative minimum distance (in this case, maximum likelihood) estimation procedure used by Taylor in estimating parameters of his two-equation reduced form model, and to compare results using a more restrictive stochastic specification.

TASKS: Assuming disturbances are serially independent, estimate Taylor's two-equation reduced form model by IZEF (= ML), and test for the empirical validity of the cross-equation restrictions. Write up the computer code to generate alternative transformed variables using a two-dimensional grid, estimate the transformed model, and from the alternative estimates choose that set that minimizes the criterion function in Eq. (10.55). Compare results with those reported by Taylor. Test for the over-identifying REH restrictions.

Note: This is a rather computer intensive exercise, and it can be carried out in a number of different ways. For that reason, specific results are not reported here.

FINAL COMMENTS:

As I noted in the general comments earlier, some of the U.K. data apparently originally used by A.W. Phillips in his classic study on inflation and unemployment have been provided me by Professor Christopher L. Gilbert of the University of London, Queen Mary and Westfield College. For your possible use in supplementary exercises, I reproduce Gilbert's data set below:

PHILLIPS'S U.K. DATA ON INFLATION AND UNEMPLOYMENT, 1861-1913

YEAR	WDOT	U	YEAR	WDOT	U
1861	0.00	3.70	1888	0.00	4.15
1862	0.00	6.05	1889	3.17	2.05
1863	2.90	4.70	1890	4.08	2.10
1864	4.20	1.95	1891	0.00	3.40
1865	2.70	1.80	1892	0.00	6.20
1866	3.92	2.65	1893	-1.01	7.70
1867	-1.29	6.30	1894	0.00	7.20
1868	-2.63	6.75	1895	-1.02	6.00
1869	0.00	5.95	1896	1.02	3.35
1870	3.92	3.75	1897	1.01	3.45
1871	2.53	1.65	1898	1.98	2.95
1872	10.66	0.95	1899	1.94	2.05
1873	7.57	1.15	1900	3.77	2.45
1874	4.08	1.60	1901	-0.93	3.35
1875	0.00	2.20	1902	0.00	4.20
1876	-1.01	3.40	1903	-0.94	5.00
1877	-1.02	4.40	1904	-0.95	6.40
1878	-3.11	6.25	1905	0.00	5.25
1879	-2.13	10.70	1906	1.89	3.70
1880	0.00	5.25	1907	0.00	3.95
1881	0.00	3.55	1908	0.00	8.65
1882	0.00	2.35	1909	0.00	8.70
1883	1.07	2.60	1910	0.00	5.10
1884	0.00	7.15	1911	0.93	3.05
1885	-1.07	8.55	1912	2.74	3.15
1886	0.00	9.55	1913	3.54	2.10
1887	0.00	7.15			

INSTRUCTOR'S NOTES FOR CHAPTER ELEVEN:

WHETHER AND HOW MUCH WOMEN WORK FOR PAY:
APPLICATIONS OF LIMITED DEPENDENT VARIABLE PROCEDURES

ECONOMETRIC PROCEDURES EMPLOYED IN THE EXERCISES OF CHAPTER ELEVEN:

- Generate transformed data, compute means and standard deviations, sort data, and compare means across sub-groups

- Estimate a truncated normal regression equation (estimate by OLS an hours-worked equation in which hours of nonworkers are set to zero)

- Compute elasticities of hours worked with respect to wage rate and to income

- Compare OLS (a linear probability model), probit and logit estimates of a labor force participation equation; check how results match with Amemiya's approximation rule

- Relate a Tobit model of labor supply to the conditional OLS procedure, and compare results; decompose the effect of a regressor on hours worked into the change in hours worked for those already working weighted by the probability of working, and the change in the probability of working weighted by the expected value of hours worked for those who work

- Explore issues of over-, just- and under-identification in a reduced form model of labor supply; test for the empirical validity of the over-identifying restrictions

- Empirically implement the Heckit generalized Tobit estimator, using the inverse Mills ratio as a regressor, and compute robust standard errors

- Incorporate taxes into a model of labor supply using the linearized budget constraint specification; estimate using the Heckit multistage procedure

More-advanced procedures:

- Specify and estimate an extended Tobit simultaneous equations model in which parameters of the wage rate, reservation wage and labor force participation decisions are simultaneously estimated using the method of full information maximum likelihood with cross-equation parameter constraints imposed

GOALS FOR THE EXERCISES IN CHAPTER ELEVEN:

The goal of the exercises in this chapter on limited dependent variable techniques is to engage students in first-hand experience in implementing and interpreting first and second generation limited dependent variable procedures in order to measure factors affecting female labor force participation and hours worked.

GENERAL COMMENTS TO THE INSTRUCTOR:

The exercises of this chapter are relatively straightforward, and except for Exercise 8, they do not involve detailed computer programming, given the "canned" procedures widely available in software programs today. It is quite important (indeed, necessary) that all students do Exercise 1, for in it students construct a number of variables that are used in subsequent exercises. Exercises 2 and 3 involve OLS, probit and logit estimation procedures, while Exercise 4 deals with Tobit estimation. (Since several introductory econometric theory textbooks discuss logit and probit, but not Tobit estimation, I have designed separate exercises for the logit-probit and for the Tobit procedures.) Issues of identification are addressed in the reduced form model of Exercise 5, the multistage Heckit generalization of the Tobit procedure is implemented in Exercise 6, tax effects on labor supply are incorporated within a Heckit framework in Exercise 7, and a structural multiequation model is estimated by full information maximum likelihood in Exercise 8.

SPECIFIC NOTES ON THE EXERCISES IN CHAPTER ELEVEN:

<u>Exercise 1: Inspecting Mroz's 1975 Panel Study of Income Dynamics Data</u>

GOALS: The purpose of this exercise is to have students become familiar with salient features of the data series in the MROZ data file. Students also construct several variables used in subsequent exercises of Chapter 11.

TASKS: Compute, print out and compare sample means in MROZ data file with values reported by Mroz. Compare arithmetic means of selected variables for working women with those not working for pay. Compute several variables for later use, estimate a wage equation for working women, and use these parameter estimates to predict wage of those women not working for pay.

(a) You should be able to compute sample means for these variables, as discussed in the exercise.

(b) For working women, the sample means of KL6 and HW are 0.14019 and 4.29684, while for nonworking women, these means are 0.36615 and 6.13815; with on average a greater number of children under age six at home and with husbands having higher wages, one would expect that the nonworking women have higher reservation wages. An interesting feature of the data is that although years experience (AX) is larger for working than nonworking women (13.03738 vs. 7.46154 years), this is not due to nonworking women being younger—in fact, they are on average slightly older (43.28308 vs. 41.97196 years old).

(c) Make sure students save the PRIN variable for later use.

(d) The means and standard deviations of the LWW variable for working women are 1.19107 and 0.72320. The OLS equation you obtain should look like:

$$\text{LWW} = -0.5231 - 0.0002*\text{WA} + 0.1057*\text{WE} + 0.0411*\text{AX} - 0.0008*\text{AX2} + 0.0546*\text{CIT}$$
$$\qquad (1.880) \quad (0.040) \qquad (7.354) \qquad (3.108) \qquad (1.983) \qquad (0.794)$$

where absolute values of t-statistics are in parentheses, the R^2 is 0.1581, and the standard error of the regression is 0.6675. The mean of FLWW for nonworkers is 0.97456, while the mean of LWW for working women is 1.19017;

this difference is substantial, and indicates that the samples of working and nonworking women are quite different (recall that nonworkers have less experience).

Exercise 2: Estimating the Hours Worked Equation Using Procedure I

GOALS: The purpose of this exercise is to introduce students to a common, but unfortunately inappropriate procedure for estimating the hours worked equation.

TASKS: Estimate by OLS an hours worked equation using the entire sample of observations and the predicted wages for nonworkers, setting the hours worked for nonworkers equal to zero. This is often called a truncated normal regression equation. The implied responses to changes in the wage rate and in property income are computed, both in level and in elasticity form.

(a) Using all 753 observations and OLS estimation procedures, the equation you obtain should look like this (absolute t-stats in parentheses):

$$WHRS = 1383.1 - 497.75*KL6 - 79.16*K618 - 20.31*WA + 43.66*WE$$
$$(4.82) \quad (7.78) \quad (3.17) \quad (4.48) \quad (2.83)$$

$$+ 111.08*LWW1 - 0.01*PRIN \quad R^2 = 0.122469$$
$$(1.94) \quad (3.88) \quad SER = 819.494$$

The low R^2 value is not surprising, given the large number of observations massed at the WHRS = 0 point.

(b) The uncompensated elasticity of hours worked with respect to wages is 0.074, and that with respect to property income is -0.007. The effect of a $1 increase in the wage rate is to increase hours worked by about 24.7 hours, and the effect of a $1000 increase in property income is to decrease hours worked by 10.5 hours. The wage effect is on the low side when compared to entries in Table 11.2, as is the income effect; but the range of values is so large in Table 11.2 that these numbers fall within the scope of those presented there.

(c) As discussed in the text, Procedure I involves a model misspecification in that it is assumed that this equation holds for all values of LWW1, not just for those values in excess of the reservation wage.

Exercise 3: Comparing OLS, Probit and Logit Estimates of the Labor Force Participation Decision

GOALS: The goal of this exercise is to give students "hands-on" experience in implementing relatively simple limited dependent variable estimation techniques by computing and then comparing OLS, probit and logit estimates of a typical labor force participation equation.

TASKS: Estimate a linear probability model by OLS, and check on whether fitted values are outside 0-1 interval. Then estimate an LFP equation using the logit procedure, and compare estimates to OLS using Amemiya's approximation procedure. Also estimate the same equation using the probit procedure, and compare with OLS estimates again. Evaluate the effect of a change in an explanatory variable on the probability of participating in the labor force. Comment on the appropriateness of the above procedures.

(a) Using all 753 observations and OLS estimation procedures, the linear probability model I obtained looked like this (absolute t-stats in parentheses):

$$LFP = 0.692 + 0.093*LWW1 - 0.291*KL6 - 0.008*K618 - 0.012*WA + 0.042*WE$$
$$\quad\;\; (4.26) \quad\; (2.92) \qquad\;\; (8.14) \qquad\quad (0.60) \qquad\quad (4.55) \qquad\quad (4.87)$$

$$\quad - 0.003*UN - 0.004*CIT - 0.000007*PRIN$$
$$\qquad (0.64) \qquad\;\; (0.12) \qquad\quad\; (4.40)$$

having an R^2 of 0.157 and a standard error of the regression (SER) equal to 0.458. Nine observations have fitted values greater than one, ranging from 1.01031 to 1.16957, and seven have fitted values that are negative, ranging from -0.44766 to -0.00063. How one interprets probabilities that are negative or greater than one is of course problematic!

(b) Based on the entire sample of 753 observations and using the logit estimation procedure, the results I obtained after four iterations to convergence were as follows (absolute t-statistics are in parentheses):

$$LFP = 0.951 + 0.464*LWW1 - 1.47*KL6 - 0.051*K618 - 0.058*WA + 0.212*WE$$
$$\quad\;\; (1.18) \quad\;\; (2.95) \quad\quad\; (7.40) \quad\quad\;\; (0.75) \quad\quad\quad (4.51) \quad\quad\;\; (4.81)$$

$$\quad - 0.019*UN + 0.013*CIT - 0.000035*PRIN$$
$$\quad\;\;\; (0.70) \quad\quad\; (0.17) \quad\quad\quad\; (4.36)$$

where the percent of observations predicted correctly (based on fitted probabilities being less or greater than 0.5) was 0.677291, and the sample maximized log-likelihood was -449.476. The Amemiya approximation works quite well for most slope coefficients (except for the sign change involving that on CIT), but the ratio appears to be closer to 0.20 than 0.25; the intercept approximation is also satisfactory.

(c) Based on the entire sample of 753 observations and using the probit estimation procedure, the results I obtained after four iterations to convergence were as follows (absolute t-statistics are in parentheses):

$$LFP = 0.568 + 0.282*LWW1 - 0.881*KL6 - 0.030*K618 - 0.035*WA + 0.128*WE$$
$$\quad\;\; (1.18) \quad\;\; (3.04) \quad\quad\;\; (7.68) \quad\quad\;\; (0.73) \quad\quad\quad (4.55) \quad\quad\;\; (4.92)$$

$$\quad - 0.011*UN + 0.010*CIT - 0.000021*PRIN$$
$$\quad\;\;\; (0.69) \quad\quad\; (0.09) \quad\quad\quad\; (4.51)$$

where the percent of observations predicted correctly (based on fitted probabilities being less or greater than 0.5) was 0.675963, and the sample maximized log-likelihood was -449.397, slightly larger than for the logit.

(d) With the logit model, multiply the relevant coefficient times (0.568*0.432) = 0.245; in the case of LWW1, for example, multiply 0.464 by 0.245, obtaining a derivative of 0.114. For the probit model, simply multiply the coefficient times 0.393; for LWW1, for example, the effect of a change is 0.393*0.282 = 0.111, and when P = 0.9 and f(P) = 0.175, this effect is much smaller, which is intuitively plausible. Notice how similar are the values of these estimated derivatives for the probit and logit models.

(e) The ratio of probit to logit parameter estimates ranges from 0.582 to 0.608 (except for the imprecisely estimated CIT coefficient, where the ratio is 0.846), indicating that the ratio is approximately halfway between the 0.5513 value and the 0.625 approximation suggested by Amemiya.

(f) See the text discussion for details.

Exercise 4: Relating the Tobit and Conditional OLS Estimates

GOALS: The purpose of this exercise is to have students gain "hands-on" experience in implementing empirically and in interpreting the Tobin estimation procedure.

TASKS: Restricting the sample to working women, estimate a conditional OLS model of labor supply (Procedure II). Compute robust standard errors, and evaluate the Goldberger-Greene approximation. Estimate a Tobit model, and decompose the effort of a change in a regressor into its two components.

(a) There's a potential source of confusion here. In the exercise, the text states the various regressors that should be used, and then asks the student to compare results obtained by Mroz and reproduced in Eq. (11.49); however, Mroz employs PRIN as a regressor, and it is inadvertently omitted in the Exercise 4(a) discussion! Based on observations 1 through 428, the OLS conditional model of labor supply (with PRIN omitted) that you obtain should look like this, with absolute values of t-statistics in parentheses:

WHRS = 2153.1 - 339.72*KL6 - 119.41*K618 - 8.62*WA - 20.17*WE - 20.40*LWW
       (6.36)   (3.40)   (3.90)   (1.57)   (1.17)   (0.38)

with an R^2 of 0.06397 and a SER of 755.473. However, when PRIN is added as a regressor, as in Mroz's Eq. (11.49), you instead obtain the following:

WHRS = 2114.7 - 342.50*KL6 - 115.02*K618 - 7.73*WA - 14.45*WE
       (6.22)   (3.42)   (3.73)   (1.40)   (0.80)

       - 17.41*LWW - 0.0042*PRIN
         (0.32)   (1.16)

which has an R^2 of 0.06696 and a SER of 755.161. Based on White's

heteroskedasticity-consistent standard errors, the t-statistics of the seven

coefficients above are, respectively, 6.09, -2.62, -3.93, -1.33, -0.800,

-0.216 and -1.33.   The parameter estimates match those reported by Mroz and

reproduced in Eq. (11.49); note that Mroz must have divided PRIN by 1000, for

his coefficient estimate is 1000 times that on PRIN above.

(b) Dividing these conditional OLS estimates by 0.568 yields the

Goldberger-Greene consistent estimates of the labor supply parameters; these

are, respectively, 3723, -602.99, -202.5, -13.61, -25.44 , -30.65 and -0.0084.

Obviously, since the OLS standard errors are inconsistent, one cannot say

anything about the statistical significance of these transformed parameters.

(c) Using all 753 observations and the Tobit maximum likelihood

estimation procedure, I obtained the following results (convergence was

achieved after five iterations, and the sample log-likelihood was -3891.12):

WHRS = 1172.1 - 1045.1*KL6 - 100.35*K618 - 36.51*WA + 104.90*WE
     (2.45)   (8.36)   (2.37)   (4.78)   (4.08)

   + 199.37*LWW1 - 0.022*PRIN
     (2.25)   (4.54)

where numbers in parentheses are ratios of estimated coefficients to their

asymptotic standard errors, and the estimate of σ was 1258.6 (26.65). These

Tobit estimates do not correspond particularly well with the Goldberger-Greene

transformed OLS approximation; in fact, some even change sign, and become

significant.

(d) To do this calculation, it is useful to note that $X\hat{\beta}$ evaluated at

the sample mean of the X's is 1163.3, and that given the values of F(z), f(z)

and z, A = 0.400. The second term on the right-hand side of Eq. (11.35) is

equal to $0.635*\beta_k$, whereas the first term equals $0.227*\beta_k$. Hence a very small

change (say, a 0.01 increase) in LWW1 increases hours worked by

0.01*199.37*0.862 = 1.718 hours, and of this change, 40% is from those already working, while 60% is from new entrants into the labor force.

(e) Results obtained here may depend on the software you are using. I used PC-TSP in this exercise, and it yielded results almost precisely numerically equivalent to the OLS estimates.

(f) See the text for further discussion of this issue.

Exercise 5: Identifying Parameters in a Reduced Form Estimation

GOALS: The purpose of this exercise is to have students work through issues of identification of structural parameters when the reduced form Procedure IV is implemented empirically. Separate over-, just- and under-identified models are considered.

TASKS: Estimate a wage determination equation by OLS, and retrieve parameter estimates. Specify three alternative structural reservation wage equations, and write out their reduced forms using a transform of Heckman's proportionality relation. Estimate the just-identified model by indirect least squares, and verify a numerical equivalence by estimating a transformed model by OLS. Then demonstrate the parameter restriction implicit in the over-identified model, estimate this model, and test for its empirical validity. Comment on why the fit is the same in a just- and under-identified model. Comment on the appropriateness of this reduced form procedure.

(a) Students might express some confusion here, for the regressors in (11.60) are not quite the same as those used in Exercise 1, part (d). Here I'll report results consistent with the set of regressors specified in this exercise (analogous results can be obtained using the other equation). Using OLS on the first 428 observations, I obtained the following equation, where absolute values of t-statistics are in parentheses:

LWW = -1.6398 + 0.0605*WA - 0.0007*WA2 + 0.1074*WE + 0.0616*CIT + 0.0171*AX2
      (1.656)   (1.312)   (1.361)   (7.466)   (0.896)   (3.704)

with an R^2 of 0.153952, a SSR of 188.946 and an ln L of -432.326.

(b) This is relatively straightforward.

(c) Estimates of the a_0 through a_8 parameters (absolute values of t-statistics in parentheses) for the just-identified model are, respectively, -1.6808 (5.25), 0.0464 (3.088), -0.0004 (2.47), 0.0954 (18.510), 0.0633 (2.800), 0.1615 (5.986), 0.0159 (1.700), 0.00000133 (1.32) and 0.0046 (1.36); the estimate of D is 2663.9 (11.969), the R^2 is 0.265991, the SER is 751.000 and the sample ln L is -6049.35. These a-estimates suggest that the log of the reservation wage increases with WA and decreases with WA2, and that it increases with WE, CIT, KL6, K618, PRIN and UN; the results on KL6, K618 and PRIN are all consistent with a priori expectations. I obtained the same results when the data were transformed, but notice that since the resulting standard errors do not take account of the uncertainty of the estimated g parameters from (a), they are likely to understate the variance and overstate statistical significance.

(d) With over-identification, there is a restriction involving the d, g_4 and g_5 parameters. When the over-identified model is estimated with the over-identifying restriction imposed, the ln L falls to -6053.10, the SER increases to 754.242, and the R^2 drops to 0.258644. The likelihood ratio test statistic is 7.50, which is greater than the χ^2 critical value at usual significance levels. Hence the null hypothesis for the empirical validity of the over-identifying restriction is rejected. However, even with this restriction imposed, the parameter estimates are plausible.

(e) The R^2 would be the same as that for the just-identified model, for with that model no restrictions are imposed, and the under-identified model is observationally equivalent to the just-identified model.

(f) See the text for a discussion of this issue.

Exercise 6: Implementing the Heckit Generalized Tobit Estimator

GOALS: The purpose of this exercise is to have students gain "hands-on" experience with Heckman's multistage Procedure VIII, often called the Heckit generalized Tobit estimator. Students will also compare the Heckit sample selectivity procedure to an OLS-based method due to Olsen.

TASKS: Estimate a probit model of labor force participation (LFP), retrieve the inverse Mills ratio, and do this also for a model with the AX and AX2 experience variables included. Compare OLS and sample selectivity-adjusted estimates of a wage determination equation, with and without the experience variables included, and compute robust standard errors. Then do instrumental variable (2SLS) estimation of the hours worked equation, comparing results with and without sample selectivity adjustments, and with and without the experience variables. As an alternative to the inverse Mills ratio, consider an OLS-based procedure by Olsen. Comment on the empirical significance of sample selectivity, and how this sensitivity depends on whether experience variables are viewed as being exogenous. Conclude by outlining how this estimation procedure generalizes the traditional Tobit estimation method.

(a) The probit estimates I obtained with and without the AX, AX2 variables included are as follows:

VARIABLE	AX, AX2 EXCLUDED PARAMETER	t-STAT	AX, AX2 INCLUDED PARAMETER	t-STAT
C	-14.066	0.8799	-10.125	-0.6124
KL6	-0.85795	-7.2192	-0.85047	-6.8959
K618	-0.60310E-01	-1.3735	0.23610E-01	0.4971
WA	0.75210	0.9770	0.49386	0.6132
WE	1.0991	0.5716	0.96221	0.4806
WA2	-0.15185E-01	-1.0434	-0.11555E-01	-0.7502
WE2	-0.63659E-01	-0.6024	-0.72327E-01	-0.6484
WAWE	-0.15456E-01	-0.3460	-0.55927E-02	-0.1206
WA3	0.10698E-03	1.0586	0.94934E-04	0.8790

WE3	0.12697E-02	0.5406	0.15105E-02	0.6069
WA2WE	-0.20976E-05	-0.0056	-0.12003E-03	-0.3021
WAWE2	0.66869E-03	0.7634	0.67196E-03	0.7355
WFED	-0.12513E-01	-0.7136	-0.42132E-02	-0.2287
WMED	0.26455E-02	0.1432	0.10323E-01	0.5336
UN	-0.10297E-01	-0.6394	-0.14943E-01	-0.8748
CIT	0.41442E-01	0.3818	0.23171E-01	0.2010
PRIN	-0.22003E-04	-4.6161	-0.12931E-04	-2.5720
AX			0.12414	6.4070
AX2			-0.19205E-02	-3.0570

Note that most of the coefficients are statistically insignificant, and that only KL6, PRIN, AX and AX2 have substantial t-statistics. Although LWW is excluded, in a sense this probit equation can be envisaged as a reduced form equation, and in that sense the wage rate is included implicitly.

(b) Results from the four OLS regressions are presented below, with and without allowing for sample selectivity (denoted SS if sample selectivity is incorporated), and with and without the AX and AX2 variables included as regressors. The t-statistics are heteroskedasticity-robust.

VARIABLE	no SS,AX AX2 PARAM	t-stat	AX,AX2, no SS PARAM	t-stat	SS, no AX AX2 PARAM	t-stat	SS, AX, AX2 PARAM	t-stat
C	2.6682	0.314	4.3794	0.540	-3.2485	-0.303	2.9744	0.326
KL6	-0.1266	-1.155	-0.1055	-1.017	-0.4323	-1.371	-0.2062	-0.990
K618	-0.0464	-1.568	-0.0171	-0.556	-0.0686	-1.825	-0.0147	-0.470
WA	0.1113	0.258	0.0216	0.052	0.4063	0.739	0.0817	0.176
WE	-0.8515	-0.757	-0.9660	-0.891	-0.4739	-0.400	-0.8606	-0.775
WA2	-0.0060	-0.655	-0.0048	-0.527	-0.0118	-1.032	-0.0061	-0.600
WE2	0.0120	0.181	0.0142	0.217	-0.0055	-0.081	0.0079	0.118
WAWE	0.0302	1.279	0.0332	1.488	0.0230	0.932	0.0320	1.431
WA3	0.0000	0.502	0.0000	0.400	0.0001	0.883	0.0000	0.485
WE3	0.0018	1.182	0.0019	1.245	0.0021	1.351	0.0020	1.292
WA2WE	0.0001	0.375	0.0001	0.375	0.0001	0.492	0.0001	0.352
WAWE2	-0.0015	-2.988	-0.0016	-3.303	-0.0013	-2.331	-0.0016	-3.043
WMED	-0.0090	-0.739	-0.0105	-0.878	-0.0074	-0.600	-0.0091	-0.736
WFED	-0.0168	-1.547	-0.1297	-1.220	-0.0211	-1.744	-0.0134	-1.256
UN	-0.0015	-0.165	-0.0027	-0.297	-0.0053	-0.536	-0.0042	-0.445
CIT	0.0790	1.184	0.0699	1.048	0.0925	1.335	0.0722	1.081
PRIN	0.0000	0.661	0.0000	1.613	-0.0000	-0.659	0.0000	0.703
AX			0.0398	2.494			0.0547	1.584
AX2			-0.0007	-1.583			-0.0009	-1.445
INVR1					0.6290	0.957		
INVR2							0.2274	0.433
SSR	183.744		176.432		183.452		176.303	
R2	0.17724		0.20999		0.17855		0.21056	

In interpreting these results, note that the experience variables tend to be more significant if sample selectivity issues are ignored, but that in both cases the t-statistic on the INVR inverse Mills ratio variable is statistically insignificant.

(c) Results from the four 2SLS (or INST) regressions are presented below, with and without allowing for sample selectivity (denoted SS if sample selectivity is incorporated), and with and without the AX and AX2 variables included as regressors. The t-statistics are computed as ratios of the coefficient estimate to the heteroskedasticity-robust standard error.

VARIABLE	no SS,AX AX2 PARAM	t-stat	SS, no AX AX2 PARAM	t-stat	AX, AX2 no SS PARAM	t-stat	SS, AX, AX2 PARAM	t-stat
C	2127.5	6.046	2319.4	5.332	2073.8	5.812	2358.2	5.368
KL6	-337.18	-2.565	-183.80	-0.670	-303.05	-2.420	-123.83	-0.523
K618	-112.29	-3.694	-105.48	-3.321	-71.522	-2.283	-78.395	-2.508
WA	-7.8534	-1.351	-2.5680	-0.259	-19.495	-3.262	-9.2636	-0.752
WE	-21.034	-0.698	-49.070	-1.013	-27.570	-0.959	-54.177	-1.278
LWW	45.740	0.207	64.430	0.299	47.873	0.223	50.750	0.237
PRIN	-0.0044	-1.360	-0.0010	-0.175	0.0002	0.051	0.0026	0.628
AX					45.056	2.561	19.312	0.647
AX2					-0.4779	-1.079	-0.0632	-0.110
INVR1			-294.08	-0.680				
INVR2							-388.03	-1.024
E'HH'E	727270		730792		696992		681997	
R^2	0.064018		0.063018		0.133309		0.134915	

These results match those obtained by Mroz, reproduced in Eqs. (11.51)-(11.53) in the text.

(d) Notice that the experience variables are statistically significant only when sample selectivity is not taken into account. Moreover, as Mroz argued, the uncompensated wage effect and the income effect are very small in this preferred model—very much like results obtained for married men.

(e) To conserve on space, I will not report the entire set of results when the two sample selectivity runs are re-done using the Olsen procedure.

With AX and AX2 excluded, the t-statistic on the sample selectivity correction variable is -1.3635, whereas when AX and AX2 are included, it changes to -1.5524; however, the t-statistics on AX and AX2 are 3.337 and -1.507, respectively. Hence results differ somewhat when the Olsen procedure is used in place of the Heckman inverse Mills ratio.

(f) See the text for further discussion of this issue.

Exercise 7: Incorporating Income Taxes into a Model of Labor Supply

GOALS: The purpose of this exercise is to have students construct empirical counterparts to the theoretical notions of virtual income and after-tax marginal wage rates that are consistent with a linearized budget constraint specification, to involve them in estimating a labor supply equation with tax variables included using the Heckit generalized Tobit procedure that accounts for sample selectivity, to test for alternative behavioral responses to tax variables, and to compare results with those reported by Mroz.

TASKS: Create several tax-related variables, estimate a probit LFP equation, and retrieve the inverse Mills ratio. Estimate a sample selectivity-adjusted hours worked equation with tax variables included. Test whether women optimally take taxes into account when making labor supply decisions, and/or whether they entirely ignore income taxes.

(a) Generating these variables is a straightforward procedure. The sample means of VPRIN, LTAX and LTWW over all 753 observations are, respectively, 7250.30092, -1.17292 and -0.07580.

(b) The probit parameter estimates and t-statistics from this estimation are presented in Exercise 6(a) above, in the column marked "AX, AX2 Excluded."

(c) The 2SLS model I obtained when taxes were included was as follows, where the t-statistics are computed as the ratio of the absolute value of the coefficient estimate to the heteroskedasticity-robust standard error:

LFP = 3037.9 + 155.94*LTWW + 508.15*LTAX - 279.16*KL6 - 6.74*K618
      (1.59)   (0.58)   (0.42)   (1.33)   (0.10)

     - 9.19*WA - 8.19*WE - 0.10*PRIN + 0.16*VPRIN - 227.52*INVR
       (1.02)   (0.16)   (2.11)   (2.05)   (0.79)

with an R^2 of 0.23863, an E'HH'E of 982178 and a SER of 764.899. Although the sign of the wage coefficient is positive, its standard error is very large; also, it is not clear how to interpret the changed signs on the PRIN and VPRIN coefficients, each of which is statistically significant. When the hypothesis that women optimally take taxes into account is tested by estimating a model with the LTAX and PRIN variables excluded, the E'HH'E increases by about 25% to 1235670; although in the presence of the Heckman inverse Mills ratio sample selectivity adjustment context this test criterion is not strictly appropriate, the change is very large, and it would not be surprising if this null hypothesis were decisively rejected. When the null hypothesis is instead that women entirely ignore taxes when making their labor supply decisions (this is done by deleting the VPRIN variable, and replacing the LTWW and LTAX variables with a variable called ROSEN, defined as ROSEN = LTAX - LTWW), similar results are obtained, although the apparent rejection is not nearly as decisive.

(d) This portion of the exercise is very open-ended, and so I will not present specific results here.

Exercise 8: Specifying and Estimating an Extended Tobit Model

GOALS: The purpose of this exercise is to have students write out the likelihood function of a multi-equation Tobit model, estimate it, interpret its assumptions, and compare its implicit assumptions to those made in the Heckit generalized Tobit procedure.

TASKS: Specify an extended Tobit simultaneous equations model, and write out the likelihood function for the entire sample. Estimate this two-equation model by maximum likelihood, and then re-do this with the experience variable excluded from the wage rate equation. Impose the appropriate cross-equation constraints. Interpret this model in terms of its assumption concerning the continuity of the hours worked relationship.

(a) This part is quite straightforward.

(b) The likelihood is very similar to that in Eq. (11.47).

(c,d) For this part of the exercise, you will need to have access to statistical software that lets you write out the likelihood function explicitly. Not all computer software programs do this (it is relatively straightforward in TSP, PC-TSP and in GAUSS). You should be able to replicate the qualitative results reported by Mroz.

(e) Although computationally somewhat complex, in fact this specification is somewhat restrictive in that it assumes the hours worked relationship is continuous. For example, if there are fixed costs in labor supply, as has been discussed by John Cogan, then this continuity assumption would be violated, and in such cases the Heckit multistage generalized Tobit procedure may be preferable.

FINAL COMMENTS:

The data in the subdirectory CHAP11.DAT in the data diskette can be used for numerous other exercises. For example, although data on the husband's hours of work and wage data are provided in the MROZ data file, we have made no use of that data in the exercises of this chapter. Such data could be useful in, for example, a model of family labor supply. In brief, the data in the MROZ file can be used in numerous other useful and stimulating exercises.

The Mroz data from the 1975 Panel Study of Income Dynamics in the U.S. is unfortunately a dated one. In many countries, governmental departments have carried out occasional population surveys in which data on most of the variables in the 1975 PSID data set are collected (often, however, the experience variables are unavailable). If you are interested in obtaining updated data, check through the most recent articles in the references at the end of Chapter 11; a number of these studies use data from countries other than the U.S.